TEAR DOWN
THIS WALL

TEAR DOWN THIS WALL

The Reagan Revolution—A *National Review* History

Compiled by the Editors of
National Review

A NATIONAL REVIEW BOOK

continuum
NEW YORK • LONDON

2004

The Continuum International Publishing Group Inc
15 East 26 Street, New York, NY 10010

The Continuum International Publishing Group Ltd
The Tower Building, 11 York Road, London SE1 7NX

Introduction and compilation Copyright © 2004 by
The Continuum International Publishing Group Inc

Printed in the United States of America

Library of Congress Cataloging-in-Publication Data

Tear down this wall : the Reagan revolution — a National Review history /
compiled by the editors of National Review.
p.   cm.
"A National Review book."
ISBN 0-8264-1695-0 (pbk. : alk. paper)
1. Reagan, Ronald—Political and social views.   2. Reagan,
Ronald—influence.   3. United States—Politics and government—1981–1989.
4. Conservatism—United States—History—20th century.   I. Reagan, Ronald.
II. National Review Books.
E877.T43   2004
352.23′8′097309048—dc22
2004018742

Contents

Introduction
by Rich Lowry

National Review always had a special relationship with Ronald Reagan. We looked at him—as we put it on one of our covers—as "Our Man." Reagan came directly out of the conservative movement that *NR* crucially formed, and we shared the same ideals and aspirations. Without that movement there wouldn't have been a Reagan presidency, so there was truth to the lighthearted matchbook cover that *NR* produced so many years ago with a picture of Reagan together with the legend I GOT MY JOB THROUGH NATIONAL REVIEW.

Reagan called *National Review* his "favorite magazine." Not only, he said at a *NR* dinner in Washington in 1983, "because it's fought the good fight so long and so well, although that would be reason enough. It's splendidly written, brilliantly edited, and a pleasure to read." That compliment alone was enough to make us chant, "Four more years!" Reagan understood the importance of ideas, and the intellectual spadework necessary to support them, to politics.

None of this, however, is to underestimate the contribution of Reagan the man. No victory is inevitable, and conservatism wouldn't have achieved all it did in the late 20th century if it hadn't been for this singular man, his vision, his faith, his optimism, his determination. He saw through many of our ideas to reality, with his political skill and horse sense. He won the Cold War and reinvigorated the American economy, two historic achievements that spread the benefits of liberty to millions and reinforced the bedrock of American greatness.

His legacies will live on for decades, including the creation of a new generation of conservatives invigorated by his ideas and committed to fighting for them. I remember first becoming seriously aware of politics around 1984. I would watch Reagan, drawn to his strength, humor, and patriotism, and say to myself, "What he believes, I believe too." What Reagan believed in, most fundamentally, was America, a nation conceived in liberty and in faith in God. He saw it through a dark hour, and every patriot is in his debt.

Honoring that debt begins with memory, one of the purposes of this very volume.

Acknowledgments

National Review has always been more than merely a magazine. For the hundreds of thousands of people who have subscribed to or read it since its founding in 1955, it has also been a cause.

Causes are by nature associated with individuals, and the two people to whom the cause of *National Review* have been linked—inextricably—over the years are, of course, its founder, William F. Buckley Jr., and the man most universally revered by conservatives: Ronald Wilson Reagan.

Legend has it that Mr. Reagan began subscribing to *National Review* soon after its launch, in the late 1950s. What isn't legend is the fact that *NR* played an important role in helping him formulate his own political beliefs. No wonder it was his favorite magazine—as he himself admitted when President.

The dots are easily connected. *National Review* was the flag around which conservatives rallied. From such, a conservative political movement was formed. Still young, it seemed to have met an early demise—to the delight of liberal pundits—with Barry Goldwater's defeat in the 1964 presidential election. But in the movement's ashes, many embers still burned. So it was that in two short years Mr. Reagan, derided as a mere actor and shill for General Electric, had unseated California's incumbent governor, Pat Brown. A decade later, though defeated by Gerald Ford in a close-fought Republican primary, "The Gipper" had become the right's ranking, and beloved, political champion. Within four years, he was President.

It may seem brazen to claim that without *National Review*, there would be no President Reagan. But false humility being sinful, we will stand by that claim.

It should come as no surprise then that, at the passing of this good and true friend, his favorite magazine, which has reported on and about him since the early 1960s, and even published some articles by him in that time, would assemble some of the best works from our archives on or by Ronald Wilson Reagan, and have them republished in this collection, so as to bring to the public some sense of what he, as a man of many aspects—the Goldwater advocate, the gubernatorial candidate, the governor, the national contender, the man of destiny, the President, the tax-cutter, the man who willed the fall of the Berlin Wall, the elder statesman—has meant to conservatism for four decades, and what his accomplishments still mean to the world. No institution is in a better position to do such.

Thanks here go to Rich Lowry, *National Review*'s editor, for his Introduction, to Elizabeth Capano and Tim Wolff for their proofreading efforts, to Ed Capano for approving and overseeing this project, to my good friend at Continuum,

Evander Lomke, with whom it is a joy to work, and especially to Russell Jenkins, the manager of our book-publishing efforts, who did much of the hard labor that goes with assembling a limited collection out of so much good available material (kudos also to Research Director John Virtes for his assistance on this matter).

Ronald Reagan is so large a figure that no collection can capture all of him. But we are confident that this book will show him in his essence, from the point of view of those who knew him best, and who cherish him now the most, as we always have.

Jack Fowler
Associate Publisher
National Review

Ronald Reagan's Most Important Speeches

"Rendezvous with Destiny"

EDITOR'S NOTE: *This is the text of the televised speech Mr. Reagan gave on October 24, 1964, on behalf of the Goldwater campaign. Popular reaction to Reagan was so positive that this speech is widely considered to have launched his political career.*

Thank you very much. Thank you and good evening. The sponsor has been identified, but unlike most television programs, the performer hasn't been provided with a script. As a matter of fact, I have been permitted to choose my own ideas regarding the choice that we face in the next few weeks.

I have spent most of my life as a Democrat. I recently have seen fit to follow another course. I believe that the issues confronting us cross party lines. Now, one side in this campaign has been telling us that the issues of this election are the maintenance of peace and prosperity. The line has been used "We've never had it so good."

But I have an uncomfortable feeling that this prosperity isn't something on which we can base our hopes for the future. No nation in history has ever survived a tax burden that reached a third of its national income. Today, 37 cents of every dollar earned in this country is the tax collector's share, and yet our government continues to spend $17 million a day more than the government takes in. We haven't balanced our budget 28 out of the last 34 years. We have raised our debt limit three times in the last twelve months, and now our national debt is one and a half times bigger than all the combined debts of all the nations in the world. We have $15 billion in gold in our treasury—we don't own an ounce. Foreign dollar claims are $27.3 billion, and we have just had announced that the dollar of 1939 will now purchase 45 cents in its total value.

As for the peace that we would preserve, I wonder who among us would like to approach the wife or mother whose husband or son has died in South Vietnam and ask them if they think this is a peace that should be maintained indefinitely. Do they mean peace, or do they mean we just want to be left in peace? There can be no real peace while one American is dying some place in the world for the rest of us. We are at war with the most dangerous enemy that has ever faced mankind in his long climb from the swamp to the stars, and it has been said if we lose that war, and in doing so lose this way of freedom of ours, history will record with the greatest astonishment that those who had the most to lose did the least to prevent its happening. Well, I think it's time we ask ourselves if we still know the freedoms that were intended for us by the Founding Fathers.

Not too long ago two friends of mine were talking to a Cuban refugee, a businessman who had escaped from Castro, and in the midst of his story one of my friends turned to the other and said, "We don't know how lucky we are." And the Cuban stopped and said, "How lucky you are! I had someplace to escape to." In that sentence he told us the entire story. If we lose freedom here, there is no place to escape to. This is the last stand on Earth. And this idea that government is beholden to the people, that it has no other source of power except to sovereign people, is still the newest and most unique idea in all the long history of man's relation to man. This is the issue of this election. Whether we believe in our capacity for self-government or whether we abandon the American revolution and confess that a little intellectual elite in a far-distant capital can plan our lives for us better than we can plan them ourselves.

You and I are told increasingly that we have to choose between a left or right, but I would like to suggest that there is no such thing as a left or right. There is only an up or down—up to man's age-old dream, the ultimate in individual freedom consistent with law and order—or down to the ant heap totalitarianism, and regardless of their sincerity, their humanitarian motives, those who would trade our freedom for security have embarked on this downward course.

In this vote-harvesting time, they use terms like the "Great Society," or as we were told a few days ago by the President, we must accept a "greater government activity in the affairs of the people." But they have been a little more explicit in the past and among themselves—and all of the things that I now will quote have appeared in print. These are not Republican accusations. For example, they have voices that say "the Cold War will end through acceptance of a not undemocratic socialism." Another voice says that the profit motive has become outmoded, it must be replaced by the incentives of the welfare state; or our traditional system of individual freedom is incapable of solving the complex problems of the 20th century. Senator Fullbright has said at Stanford University that the Constitution is outmoded. He referred to the president as our moral teacher and our leader, and he said he is hobbled in his task by the restrictions in power imposed on him by this antiquated document. He must be freed so that he can do for us what he knows is best. And Senator Clark of Pennsylvania, another articulate spokesman, defines liberalism as "meeting the material needs of the masses through the full power of centralized government." Well, I for one resent it when a representative of the people refers to you and me—the free men and women of this country—as "the masses." This is a term we haven't applied to ourselves in America. But beyond that, "the full power of centralized government"—this was the very thing the Founding Fathers sought to minimize. They knew that governments don't control things. A government can't control the economy without controlling people. And they know when a government sets out to do that, it must use force and coercion to achieve its purpose. They also knew, those Founding Fathers, that outside of its legitimate functions, government does nothing as well or as economically as the private sector of the economy.

Now, we have no better example of this than the government's involvement in the farm economy over the last 30 years. Since 1955, the cost of this program has nearly doubled. One-fourth of farming in America is responsible for 85 per cent of the farm surplus. Three-fourths of farming is out on the free market and has known a 21 per cent increase in the per capita consumption of all its produce. You see, that one-fourth of farming is regulated and controlled by the federal government. In the last three years we have spent $43 in a feed-grain program for every bushel of corn we don't grow.

Senator Humphrey last week charged that Barry Goldwater as President would seek to eliminate farmers. He should do his homework a little better, because he will find out that we have had a decline of 5 million in the farm population under these government programs. He will also find that the Democratic administration has sought to get from Congress an extension of the farm program to include that three-fourths that is now free. He will find that they have also asked for the right to imprison farmers who wouldn't keep books as prescribed by the federal government. The Secretary of Agriculture asked for the right to seize farms through condemnation and resell them to other individuals. And contained in that same program was a provision that would have allowed the federal government to remove 2 million farmers from the soil.

At the same time, there has been an increase in the Department of Agriculture employees. There is now one for every 30 farms in the United States, and still they can't tell us how 66 shiploads of grain headed for Austria disappeared without a trace and Billie Sol Estes never left shore.

Every responsible farmer and farm organization has repeatedly asked the government to free the farm economy, but who are farmers to know what is best for them? The wheat farmers voted against a wheat program. The government passed it anyway. Now the price of bread goes up; the price of wheat to the farmer goes down.

Meanwhile, back in the city, under urban renewal the assault on freedom carries on. Private property rights are so diluted that public interest is almost anything that a few government planners decide it should be. In a program that takes for the needy and gives to the greedy, we see such spectacles as in Cleveland, Ohio, a million-and-a-half-dollar building completed only three years ago must be destroyed to make way for what government officials call a "more compatible use of the land." The President tells us he is now going to start building public housing units in the thousands where heretofore we have only built them in the hundreds.

But FHA and the Veterans Administration tell us that they have 120,000 housing units they've taken back through mortgage foreclosures. For three decades, we have sought to solve the problems of unemployment through government planning, and the more the plans fail, the more the planners plan. The latest is the Area Redevelopment Agency. They have just declared Rice County, Kansas, a depressed area. Rice County, Kansas, has two hundred oil wells, and the 14,000 people there have over $30 million on deposit in personal savings in their banks. When the government tells you you're depressed, lie down and be depressed.

We have so many people who can't see a fat man standing beside a thin one without coming to the conclusion that the fat man got that way by taking advantage of the thin one. So they are going to solve all the problems of human misery through government and government planning. Well, now, if government planning and welfare had the answer and they've had almost 30 years of it, shouldn't we expect government to almost read the score to us once in a while? Shouldn't they be telling us about the decline each year in the number of people needing help? The reduction in the need for public housing?

But the reverse is true. Each year the need grows greater, the program grows greater. We were told four years ago that 17 million people went to bed hungry each night. Well, that was probably true. They were all on a diet. But now we are told that 9.3 million families in this country are poverty-stricken on the basis of earning less than $3,000 a year. Welfare spending is 10 times greater than in the dark depths of the Depression. We are spending $45 billion on welfare. Now do a little arithmetic, and you will find that if we divided the $45 billion up equally among those 9 million poor families, we would be able to give each family $4,600 a year, and this added to their present income should eliminate poverty! Direct aid to the poor, however, is running only about $600 per family. It would seem that someplace there must be some overhead.

So now we declare "war on poverty," or "you, too, can be a Bobby Baker!" Now, do they honestly expect us to believe that if we add $1 billion to the $45 million we are spending . . . one more program to the 30-odd we have—and remember, this new program doesn't replace any, it just duplicates existing programs—do they believe that poverty is suddenly going to disappear by magic? Well, in all fairness I should explain that there is one part of the new program that isn't duplicated. This is the youth feature. We are now going to solve the dropout problem, juvenile delinquency, by reinstituting something like the old CCC camps, and we are going to put our young people in camps, but again we do some arithmetic, and we find that we are going to spend each year just on room and board for each young person that we help $4,700 a year! We can send them to Harvard for $2,700! Don't get me wrong. I'm not suggesting that Harvard is the answer to juvenile delinquency.

But seriously, what are we doing to those we seek to help? Not too long ago, a judge called me here in Los Angeles. He told me of a young woman who had come before him for a divorce. She had six children, was pregnant with her seventh. Under his questioning, she revealed her husband was a laborer earning $250 a month. She wanted a divorce so that she could get an $80 raise. She is eligible for $330 a month in the Aid to Dependent Children Program. She got the idea from two women in her neighborhood who had already done that very thing.

Yet anytime you and I question the schemes of the do-gooders, we are denounced as being against their humanitarian goals. They say we are always "against" things, never "for" anything. Well, the trouble with our liberal friends is not that they are ignorant, but that they know so much that isn't so. We are for a provision that destitution should not follow unemployment by reason of old age, and to that end we have accepted Social Security as a step toward meeting the problem.

But we are against those entrusted with this program when they practice deception regarding its fiscal shortcomings, when they charge that any criticism of the program means that we want to end payments to those who depend on them for livelihood. They have called it insurance to us in a hundred million pieces of literature. But then they appeared before the Supreme Court and they testified that it was a welfare program. They only use the term "insurance" to sell it to the people. And they said Social Security dues are a tax for the general use of the government, and the government has used that tax. There is no fund, because Robert Byers, the actuarial head, appeared before a congressional committee and admitted that Social Security as of this moment is $298 billion in the hole. But he said there should be no cause for worry because as long as they have the power to tax, they could always take away from the people whatever they needed to bail them out of trouble! And they are doing just that.

A young man, 21 years of age, working at an average salary . . . his Social Security contribution would, in the open market, buy him an insurance policy that would guarantee $220 a month at age 65. The government promises $127. He could live it up until he is 31 and then take out a policy that would pay more than Social Security. Now, are we so lacking in business sense that we can't put this program on a sound basis so that people who do require those payments will find that they can get them when they are due . . . that the cupboard isn't bare? Barry Goldwater thinks we can.

At the same time, can't we introduce voluntary features that would permit a citizen who can do better on his own to be excused upon presentation of evidence that he had made provisions for the non-earning years? Should we allow a widow with children to work, and not lose the benefits supposedly paid for by her deceased husband? Shouldn't you and I be allowed to declare who our beneficiaries will be under these programs, which we cannot do? I think we are for telling our senior citizens that no one in this country should be denied medical care because of a lack of funds. But I think we are against forcing all citizens, regardless of need, into a compulsory government program, especially when we have such examples, as announced last week, when France admitted that their Medicare program was now bankrupt. They've come to the end of the road.

In addition, was Barry Goldwater so irresponsible when he suggested that our government give up its program of deliberate planned inflation so that when you do get your Social Security pension, a dollar will buy a dollar's worth, and not 45 cents' worth?

I think we are for an international organization, where the nations of the world can seek peace. But I think we are against subordinating American interests to an organization that has become so structurally unsound that today you can muster a two-thirds vote on the floor of the General Assembly among the nations that represent less than 10 per cent of the world's population. I think we are against the hypocrisy of assailing our allies because here and there they cling to a colony, while we engage in a conspiracy of silence and never open our mouths about the millions of people enslaved in Soviet colonies in the satellite nation.

I think we are for aiding our allies by sharing of our material blessings with those nations which share in our fundamental beliefs, but we are against doling out money government to government, creating bureaucracy, if not socialism, all over the world. We set out to help 19 countries. We are helping 107. We spent $146 billion. With that money, we bought a $2 million yacht for Haile Selassie. We bought dress suits for Greek undertakers, extra wives for Kenyan government officials. We bought a thousand TV sets for a place where they have no electricity. In the last six years, 52 nations have bought $7 billion worth of our gold, and all 52 are receiving foreign aid from this country.

No government ever voluntarily reduces itself in size. Government programs, once launched, never disappear. Actually, a government bureau is the nearest thing to eternal life we'll ever see on this Earth. Federal employees number 2.5 million, and federal, state, and local, one out of six of the nation's work force is employed by the government. These proliferating bureaus with their thousands of regulations have cost us many of our constitutional safeguards. How many of us realize that today federal agents can invade a man's property without a warrant? They can impose a fine without a formal hearing, let alone a trial by jury, and they can seize and sell his property in auction to enforce the payment of that fine. In Chico County, Arkansas, James Wier overplanted his rice allotment. The government obtained a $17,000 judgment, and a U.S. marshal sold his 950-acre farm at auction. The government said it was necessary as a warning to others to make the system work. Last February 19 at the University of Minnesota, Norman Thomas, six-time candidate for President on the Socialist Party ticket, said, "If Barry Goldwater became President, he would stop the advance of socialism in the United States." I think that's exactly what he will do.

As a former Democrat, I can tell you Norman Thomas isn't the only man who has drawn this parallel to socialism with the present administration. Back in 1936, Mr. Democrat himself, Al Smith, the great American, came before the American people and charged that the leadership of his party was taking the part of Jefferson, Jackson, and Cleveland down the road under the banners of Marx, Lenin, and Stalin. And he walked away from his party, and he never returned to the day he died, because to this day, the leadership of that party has been taking that party, that honorable party, down the road in the image of the labor socialist party of England. Now it doesn't require expropriation or confiscation of private property or business to impose socialism on a people. What does it mean whether you hold the deed or the title to your business or property if the government holds the power of life and death over that business or property? Such machinery already exists. The government can find some charge to bring against any concern it chooses to prosecute. Every businessman has his own tale of harassment. Somewhere a perversion has taken place. Our natural, inalienable rights are now considered to be a dispensation of government, and freedom has never been so fragile, so close to slipping from our grasp as it is at this moment. Our Democratic opponents seem unwilling to debate these issues. They want to make you and I believe that this is a contest between two men . . . that we are to choose just between two personalities.

Well, what of this man that they would destroy? And in destroying, they would destroy that which he represents, the ideas that you and I hold dear. Is he the brash and shallow and trigger-happy man they say he is? Well, I have been privileged to know him "when." I knew him long before he ever dreamed of trying for high office, and I can tell you personally I have never known a man in my life I believe so incapable of doing a dishonest or dishonorable thing.

This is a man who in his own business, before he entered politics, instituted a profit-sharing plan, before unions had ever thought of it. He put in health and medical insurance for all his employees. He took 50 per cent of the profits before taxes and set up a retirement program, a pension plan for all his employees. He sent checks for life to an employee who was ill and couldn't work. He provided nursing care for the children of mothers who work in the stores. When Mexico was ravaged by floods from the Rio Grande, he climbed in his airplane and flew medicine and supplies down there.

An ex-GI told me how he met him. It was the week before Christmas during the Korean War, and he was at the Los Angeles airport trying to get a ride home to Arizona for Christmas, and he said that there were a lot of servicemen there and no seats available on the planes. Then a voice came over the loudspeaker and said, "Any men in uniform wanting a ride to Arizona, go to runway such-and-such," and they went down there, and there was this fellow named Barry Goldwater sitting in his plane. Every day in the weeks before Christmas, all day long, he would load up the plane, fly to Arizona, fly them to their homes, then fly back over to get another load.

During the hectic split-second timing of a campaign, this is a man who took time out to sit beside an old friend who was dying of cancer. His campaign managers were understandably impatient, but he said, "There aren't many left who care what happens to her. I'd like her to know I care." This is a man who said to his 19-year-old son, "There is no foundation like the rock of honesty and fairness, and when you begin to build your life upon that rock, with the cement of the faith in God that you have, then you have a real start." This is not a man who could carelessly send other people's sons to war. And that is the issue of this campaign that makes all of the other problems I have discussed academic, unless we realize that we are in a war that must be won.

Those who would trade our freedom for the soup kitchen of the welfare state have told us that they have a utopian solution of peace without victory. They call their policy "accommodation." And they say if we only avoid any direct confrontation with the enemy, he will forget his evil ways and learn to love us. All who oppose them are indicted as warmongers. They say we offer simple answers to complex problems. Well, perhaps there is a simple answer—not an easy answer—but simple.

If you and I have the courage to tell our elected officials that we want our national policy based upon what we know in our hearts is morally right, we cannot buy our security, our freedom from the threat of the bomb by committing an immorality so great as saying to a billion now in slavery behind the Iron Curtain, "Give up your dreams of freedom because to save our own skin, we are willing to make a deal with your slave masters." Alexander Hamilton said, "A nation which can prefer disgrace to danger is prepared for a master, and deserves one." Let's set the record straight. There is no argument over the choice between peace and war, but there is only one guaranteed way you can have peace—and you can have it in the next second—surrender.

Admittedly there is a risk in any course we follow other than this, but every lesson in history tells us that the greater risk lies in appeasement, and this is the specter our well-meaning liberal friends refuse to face—that their policy of accommodation is appeasement, and it gives no choice between peace and war, only between fight and surrender. If we continue to accommodate, continue to back and retreat, eventually we have to face the final demand—the ultimatum. And what then? When Nikita Khrushchev has told his people he knows what our answer will be? He has told them that we are retreating under the pressure of the Cold War, and someday when the time comes to deliver the ultimatum, our surrender will be voluntary because by that time we will have weakened from within spiritually, morally, and economically. He believes this because from our side he has heard voices pleading for "peace at any price" or "better Red than dead," or as one commentator put it, he would rather "live on his knees than die on his feet." And therein lies the road to war, because those voices don't speak for the rest of us. You and I know and do not believe that life is so dear and peace so sweet as to be purchased at the price of chains and slavery. If nothing in life is worth dying for, when did this begin—just in the face of this enemy? Or should Moses have told the children of Israel to live in slavery under the pharaohs? Should Christ have refused the cross? Should the patriots at Concord Bridge have thrown down their guns and refused to fire the shot heard 'round the world? The martyrs of history were not fools, and our honored dead who gave their lives to stop the advance of the Nazis didn't die in vain. Where, then, is the road to peace? Well, it's a simple answer after all.

You and I have the courage to say to our enemies, "There is a price we will not pay." There is a point beyond which they must not advance. This is the meaning in the phrase of Barry Goldwater's "peace through strength." Winston Churchill said that "the destiny of man is not measured by material computation. When great forces are on the move in the world, we learn we are spirits—not animals." And he said, "There is something going on in time and space, and beyond time and space, which, whether we like it or not, spells duty."

You and I have a rendezvous with destiny. We will preserve for our children this, the last best hope of man on Earth, or we will sentence them to take the last step into a thousand years of darkness.

We will keep in mind and remember that Barry Goldwater has faith in us. He has faith that you and I have the ability and the dignity and the right to make our own decisions and determine our own destiny.

Thank you very much.

Remarks at the 1976 Republican National Convention

EDITOR'S NOTE: *This speech was delivered impromptu—on August 19, 1976, in Kansas City, Missouri—at the urging of President Gerald Ford, who had won the party's presidential nomination.*

Thank you very much. Mr. President, Mrs. Ford, Mr. Vice President, Mr. Vice President to be—(Applause and laughter)—the distinguished guests here, and you ladies and gentlemen: I am going to say fellow Republicans here, but also those who are watching from a distance, all of those millions of Democrats and Independents who I know are looking for a cause around which to rally and which I believe we can give them.

Mr. President, before you arrived tonight, these wonderful people here when we came in gave Nancy and myself a welcome. That, plus this, and plus your kindness and generosity in honoring us by bringing us down here will give us a memory that will live in our hearts forever.

Watching on television these last few nights, and I have seen you also with the warmth that you greeted Nancy, and you also filled my heart with joy when you did that.

May I just say some words? There are cynics who say that a party platform is something that no one bothers to read and it doesn't very often amount to much.

Whether it is different this time than it has ever been before, I believe the Republican Party has a platform that is a banner of bold, unmistakable colors, with no pastel shades.

We have just heard a call to arms based on that platform, and a call to us to really be successful in communicating and reveal to the American people the difference between this platform and the platform of the opposing party, which is nothing but a revamp and a reissue and a running of a late, late show of the thing that we have been hearing from them for the last 40 years.

If I could just take a moment; I had an assignment the other day. Someone asked me to write a letter for a time capsule that is going to be opened in Los Angeles a hundred years from now, on our Tricentennial.

It sounded like an easy assignment. They suggested I write something about the problems and the issues today. I set out to do so, riding down the coast in an automobile, looking at the blue Pacific out on one side and the Santa Ynez Mountains on the other, and I couldn't help but wonder if it was going to be that beautiful a hundred years from now as it was on that summer day.

Then as I tried to write—let your own minds turn to that task. You are going to write for people a hundred years from now, who know all about us. We know nothing about them. We don't know what kind of a world they will be living in.

And suddenly I thought to myself if I write of the problems, they will be the domestic problems the President spoke of here tonight; the challenges confronting us, the erosion of freedom that has taken place under Democratic rule in this country, the invasion of private rights, the controls and restrictions on the vitality of the great free economy that we enjoy. These are our challenges that we must meet.

And then again there is that challenge of which he spoke that we live in a world in which the great powers have poised and aimed at each other horrible missiles of destruction, nuclear weapons that can in a matter of minutes arrive at each other's country and destroy, virtually, the civilized world we live in.

And suddenly it dawned on me, those who would read this letter a hundred years from now will know whether those missiles were fired. They will know whether we met our challenge. Whether they have the freedoms that we have known up until now will depend on what we do here.

Will they look back with appreciation and say, "Thank God for those people in 1976 who headed off that loss of freedom, who kept us now 100 years later free, who kept our world from nuclear destruction"?

And if we failed, they probably won't get to read the letter at all because it spoke of individual freedom, and they won't be allowed to talk of that or read of it.

This is our challenge; and this is why here in this hall tonight, better than we have ever done before, we have got to quit talking to each other and about each other and go out and communicate to the world that we may be fewer in numbers than we have ever been, but we carry the message they are waiting for.

We must go forth from here united, determined that what a great general said a few years ago is true: There is no substitute for victory, Mr. President. (Applause)

Speech Announcing Presidential Candidacy

EDITOR'S NOTE: *This speech was delivered in New York City on November 13, 1979.*

Good evening. I am here tonight to announce my intention to seek the Republican nomination for President of the United States.

I'm sure that each of us has seen our country from a number of viewpoints depending on where we've lived and what we've done. For me it has been as a boy growing up in several small towns in Illinois. As a young man in Iowa trying to get a start in the years of the Great Depression and later in California for most of my adult life.

I've seen America from the stadium press box as a sportscaster, as an actor, officer of my labor union, soldier, officeholder and as both a Democrat and Republican. I've lived in America where those who often had too little to eat outnumbered those who had enough. There have been four wars in my lifetime and I've seen our country face financial ruin in the Depression. I have also seen the great strength of this nation as it pulled itself up from that ruin to become the dominant force in the world.

To me our country is a living, breathing presence, unimpressed by what others say is impossible, proud of its own success, generous, yes and naive, sometimes wrong, never mean and always impatient to provide a better life for its people in a framework of a basic fairness and freedom.

Someone once said that the difference between an American and any other kind of person is that an American lives in anticipation of the future because he knows it will be a great place. Other people fear the future as just a repetition of past failures. There's a lot of truth in that. If there is one thing we are sure of it is that history need not be relived; that nothing is impossible, and that man is capable of improving his circumstances beyond what we are told is fact.

There are those in our land today, however, who would have us believe that the United States, like other great civilizations of the past, has reached the zenith of its power; that we are weak and fearful, reduced to bickering with each other and no longer possessed of the will to cope with our problems.

Much of this talk has come from leaders who claim that our problems are too difficult to handle. We are supposed to meekly accept their failures as the most which humanly can be done. They tell us we must learn to live with less, and teach our children that their lives will be less full and prosperous than ours have been; that the America of the coming years will be a place where—because of our past excesses—it will be impossible to dream and make those dreams come true.

I don't believe that. And, I don't believe you do either. That is why I am seeking the presidency. I cannot and will not stand by and see this great country destroy itself. Our leaders attempt to blame their failures on circumstances beyond their control, on false estimates by unknown, unidentifiable experts who rewrite modern history in an attempt to convince us our high standard of living, the result of thrift and hard work, is somehow selfish extravagance which we must renounce as we join in sharing scarcity. I don't agree that our nation must resign itself to inevitable decline, yielding its proud position to other hands. I am totally unwilling to see this country fail in its obligation to itself and to the other free peoples of the world.

The crisis we face is not the result of any failure of the American spirit; it is failure of our leaders to establish rational goals and give our people something to order their lives by. If I am elected, I shall regard my election as proof that the people of the United States have decided to set a new agenda and have recognized that the human spirit thrives best when goals are set and progress can be measured in their achievement.

During the next year I shall discuss in detail a wide variety of problems which a new administration must address. Tonight I shall mention only a few.

No problem that we face today can compare with the need to restore the health of the American economy and the strength of the American dollar. Double-digit inflation has robbed you and your family of the ability to plan. It has destroyed the confidence to buy and it threatens the very structure of family life itself as more and more wives are forced to work in order to help meet the ever-increasing cost of living. At the same time, the lack of real growth in the economy has introduced the justifiable fear in the minds of working men and women who are already over-extended that soon there will be fewer jobs and no money to pay for even the necessities of life. And tragically as the cost of living keeps going up, the standard of living which has been our great pride keeps going down.

The people have not created this disaster in our economy; the federal govern-ment has. It has overspent, overestimated, and over-regulated. It has failed to deliver services within the revenues it should be allowed to raise from taxes. In the 34 years since the end of World War II, it has spent $448 billion more than it has collected in taxes—$448 billion of printing-press money, which has made every dollar you earn worth less and less. At the same time, the federal government has cynically told us that high taxes on business will in some way "solve" the problem and allow the average taxpayer to pay less. Well, business is not a taxpayer; it is a tax collector. Business has to pass its tax burden on to the customer as part of the cost of doing business. You and I pay taxes imposed on business every time we go to the store. Only people pay taxes and it is political demagoguery or economic illiteracy to try and tell us otherwise.

The key to restoring the health of the economy lies in cutting taxes. At the same time, we need to get the waste out of federal spending. This does not mean sacrific-ing essential services, nor do we need to destroy the system of benefits which flow to the poor, elderly, the sick and the handicapped. We have long since committed ourselves, as a people, to help those among us who cannot take care of themselves. But the federal government has proven to be the costliest and most inefficient pro-vider of such help we could possibly have.

We must put an end to the arrogance of a federal establishment which accepts no blame for our condition, cannot be relied upon to give us a fair estimate of our situation and utterly refuses to live within its means. I will not accept the supposed "wisdom" which has it that the federal bureaucracy has become so powerful that it can no longer be changed or controlled by any administration. As President I would use every power at my command to make the federal establishment respond to the will and the collective wishes of the people.

We must force the entire federal bureaucracy to live in the real world of reduced spending, streamlined function and accountability to the people it serves. We must review the function of the federal government to determine which of those are the proper province of levels of government closer to the people.

The 10th article of the Bill of Rights is explicit in pointing out that the federal government should do only those things specifically called for in the Constitution.

All others shall remain with the states or the people. We haven't been observing that 10th article of late. The federal government has taken on functions it was never intended to perform and which it does not perform well. There should be a planned, orderly transfer of such functions to states and communities and a transfer with them of the sources of taxation to pay for them.

The savings in administrative overhead would be considerable and certainly there would be increased efficiency and less bureaucracy.

By reducing federal tax rates where they discourage individual initiative—especially personal income tax rates—we can restore incentives, invite greater economic growth and at the same time help give us better government instead of bigger government. Proposals such as the Kemp-Roth bill would bring about this kind of realistic reductions in tax rates.

In short, a punitive tax system must be replaced by one that restores incentive for the worker and for industry; a system that rewards initiative and effort and encourages thrift.

All these things are possible; none of them will be easy. But the choice is clear. We can go on letting the country slip over the brink to financial ruin with the disaster that it means for the individual or we can find the will to work together to restore confidence in ourselves and to regain the confidence of the world. I have lived through one Depression. I carry with me the memory of a Christmas Eve when my brother and I and our parents exchanged our modest gifts—there was no lighted tree as there had been on Christmases past. I remember watching my father open what he thought was a greeting from his employer. We all watched and yes, we were hoping it was a bonus check. It was notice that he no longer had a job. And in those days the government ran the radio announcements telling workers not to leave home looking for jobs—there were no jobs. I'll carry with me always the memory of my father sitting there holding that envelope, unable to look at us. I cannot and will not stand by while inflation and joblessness destroy the dignity of our people.

Another serious problem which must be discussed tonight is our energy situation. Our country was built on cheap energy. Today, energy is not cheap and we face the prospect that some forms of energy may soon not be available at all.

Last summer, you probably spent hours sitting in gasoline lines. This winter, some will be without heat and everyone will be paying much more simply to keep home and family warm. If you ever had any doubt of the government's inability to provide for the needs of the people, just look at the utter fiasco we now call "the energy crisis." Not one straight answer nor any realistic hope of relief has come from the present administration in almost three years of federal treatment of the problem. As gas lines grew, the administration again panicked and now has proposed to put the country on a wartime footing; but for this "war" there is no victory in sight. And, as always, when the federal bureaucracy fails, all it can suggest is more of the same. This time it's another bureau to untangle the mess by the ones we already have.

But, this just won't work. Solving the energy crisis will not be easy, but it can be done. First we must decide that "less" is not enough. Next, we must remove government obstacles to energy production. And, we must make use of those technological advantages we still possess.

It is no program simply to say "use less energy." Of course waste must be eliminated and efficiently promoted, but for the government simply to tell people to conserve is not an energy policy. At best it means we will run out of energy a little more slowly. But a day will come when the lights will dim and the wheels of industry will turn more slowly and finally stop. As President I will not endorse any course which has this as its principal objective.

We need more energy and that means diversifying our sources of supply away from the OPEC countries. Yes, it means more efficient automobiles. But it also means more exploration and development of oil and natural gas here in our own country. The only way to free ourselves from the monopoly pricing power of OPEC is to be less dependent on outside sources of fuel.

The answer, obvious to anyone except those in the administration it seems, is more domestic production of oil and gas. We must also have wider use of nuclear power within strict safety rules, of course. There must be more spending by the energy industries on research and development of substitutes for fossil fuels.

In years to come solar energy may provide much of the answer but for the next two or three decades we must do such things as master the chemistry of coal. Putting the market system to work for these objectives is an essential first step for their achievement. Additional multi-billion-dollar federal bureaus and programs are not the answer.

In recent weeks there has been much talk about "excess" oil company profits. I don't believe we've been given all the information we need to make a judgment about this. We should have that information. Government exists to protect us from each other. It is not government's function to allocate fuel or impose unnecessary restrictions on the marketplace. It is government's function to determine whether we are being unfairly exploited and if so to take immediate and appropriate action. As President I would do exactly that.

On the foreign front, the decade of the 1980s will place severe pressures upon the United States and its allies. We can expect to be tested in ways calculated to try our patience, to confound our resolve and to erode our belief in ourselves. During a time when the Soviet Union may enjoy nuclear superiority over this country, we must never waiver in our commitment to our allies nor accept any negotiation which is not clearly in the national interest. We must judge carefully. Though we should leave no initiative untried in our pursuit of peace, we must be clear voiced in our resolve to resist any unpeaceful act wherever it may occur. Negotiation with the Soviet Union must never become appeasement.

For the most of the last 40 years, we have been preoccupied with the global struggle—the competition—with the Soviet Union and with our responsibilities to our allies. But too often in recent times we have just drifted along with events, responding as if we thought of ourselves as a nation in decline. To our allies we seem to appear to be a nation unable to make decisions in its own interests, let alone in the common interest. Since the Second World War we have spent large amounts of money and much of our time protecting and defending freedom all over the world. We must continue this, for if we do not accept the responsibilities of leadership, who will? And if no one will, how will we survive?

The 1970s have taught us the foolhardiness of not having a long-range diplomatic strategy of our own. The world has become a place where, in order to survive, our country needs more than just allies—it needs real friends. Yet, in recent times we often seem not to have recognized who our friends are. This must change. It is now time to take stock of our own house and to resupply its strength.

Part of that process involves taking stock of our relationship with Puerto Rico. I favor statehood for Puerto Rico and if the people of Puerto Rico vote for statehood in their coming referendum I would, as President, initiate the enabling legislation to make this a reality.

We live on a continent whose three countries possess the assets to make it the strongest, most prosperous and self-sufficient area on Earth. Within the borders of this North American continent are the food, resources, technology, and undeveloped territory which, properly managed, could dramatically improve the quality of life of all its inhabitants.

It is no accident that this unmatched potential for progress and prosperity exists in three countries with such long-standing heritages of free government. A developing closeness among Canada, Mexico, and the United States—a North American accord—would permit achievement of that potential in each country beyond that which I believe any of them—strong as they are—could accomplish in the absence of such cooperation. In fact, the key to our own future security may lie in both Mexico and Canada becoming much stronger countries than they are today.

No one can say at this point precisely what form future cooperation among our three countries will take. But if I am elected President, I would be willing to invite each of our neighbors to send a special representative to our government to sit in on high level planning sessions with us, as partners, mutually concerned about the future of our continent. First, I would immediately seek the views and ideas of Canadian and Mexican leaders on this issue, and work tirelessly with them to develop closer ties among our peoples. It is time we stopped thinking of our nearest neighbors as foreigners.

By developing methods of working closely together, we will lay the foundations for future cooperation on a broader and more significant scale. We will put to rest any doubts of those cynical enough to believe that the United States would seek to dominate any relationship among our three countries, or foolish enough to think that the governments and peoples of Canada and Mexico would ever permit such domination to occur. I for one, am confident that we can show the world by example that the nations of North America are ready, within the context of an unswerving commitment to freedom, to see new forms of accommodation to meet a changing world. A developing closeness between the United States, Canada, and Mexico would serve notice on friends and foe alike that we were prepared for a long haul, looking outward again and confident of our future; that together we are going to create jobs, to generate new fortunes of wealth for many and provide a legacy for the children of each of our countries. Two hundred years ago, we taught the world that a new form of government, created out of the genius of man to cope with his circumstances, could succeed in bringing a measure of quality to human life previously thought impossible.

Now let us work toward the goal of using the assets of this continent, its resources, technology, and foodstuffs in the most efficient ways possible for the common good of all its people. It may take the next 100 years but we can dare to dream that at some future date a map of the world might show the North American continent as one in which the people's commerce of its three strong countries flow more freely across their present borders than they do today.

In recent months leaders in our government have told us that, we, the people, have lost confidence in ourselves; that we must regain our spirit and our will to achieve our national goals. Well, it is true there is a lack of confidence, an unease with things the way they are. But the confidence we have lost is confidence in our government's policies. Our unease can almost be called bewilderment at how our defense strength has deteriorated. The great productivity of our industry is now surpassed by virtually all the major nations who compete with us for world markets. And, our currency is no longer the stable measure of value it once was.

But there remains the greatness of our people, our capacity for dreaming up fantastic deeds and bringing them off to the surprise of an unbelieving world. When Washington's men were freezing at Valley Forge, Tom Paine told his fellow Americans: "We have it in our power to begin the world over again." We still have that power.

We—today's living Americans—have in our lifetime fought harder, paid a higher price for freedom, and done more to advance the dignity of man than any people who have ever lived on this Earth. The citizens of this great nation want leadership—yes—but not a "man on a white horse" demanding obedience to his commands. They want someone who believes they can "begin the world over again." A leader who will unleash their great strength and remove the roadblocks government has put in their way. I want to do that more than anything I've ever wanted. And it's something that I believe with God's help I can do.

I believe this nation hungers for a spiritual revival; hungers to once again see honor placed above political expediency; to see government once again the protector of our liberties, not the distributor of gifts and privilege. Government should uphold and not undermine those institutions which are custodians of the very values upon which civilization is founded—religion, education and, above all, family. Government cannot be clergyman, teacher, and patriot. It is our servant, beholden to us.

We who are privileged to be Americans have had a rendezvous with destiny since the moment in 1630 when John Winthrop, standing on the deck of the tiny Arbella off the coast of Massachusetts, told the little band of Pilgrims, "We shall be a city upon a hill. The eyes of all people are upon us so that if we shall deal falsely with our God in this work we have undertaken and so cause Him to withdraw His present help from us, we shall be made a story and a byword throughout the world."

A troubled and afflicted mankind looks to us, pleading for us to keep our rendezvous with destiny; that we will uphold the principles of self-reliance, self-discipline, morality, and—above all—responsible liberty for every individual that we will become that shining city on a hill.

I believe that you and I together can keep this rendezvous with destiny.

Thank you and good night.

Speech Accepting the Republican Nomination for President

EDITOR'S NOTE: *This speech was delivered on July 17, 1980, at the Republican National Convention in Detroit, Michigan.*

Mr. Chairman, Mr. Vice President to be, this convention, my fellow citizens of this great nation:

With a deep awareness of the responsibility conferred by your trust, I accept your nomination for the presidency of the United States. I do so with deep gratitude, and I think also I might interject on behalf of all of us, our thanks to Detroit and the people of Michigan and to this city for the warm hospitality they have shown. And I thank you for your wholehearted response to my recommendation in regard to George Bush as a candidate for vice president.

I am very proud of our party tonight. This convention has shown to all America a party united, with positive programs for solving the nation's problems; a party ready to build a new consensus with all those across the land who share a community of values embodied in these words: family, work, neighborhood, peace, and freedom.

I know we have had a quarrel or two, but only as to the method of attaining a goal. There was no argument about the goal. As president, I will establish a liaison with the 50 governors to encourage them to eliminate, where it exists, discrimination against women. I will monitor federal laws to insure their implementation and to add statutes if they are needed.

More than anything else, I want my candidacy to unify our country; to renew the American spirit and sense of purpose. I want to carry our message to every American, regardless of party affiliation, who is a member of this community of shared values.

Never before in our history have Americans been called upon to face three grave threats to our very existence, any one of which could destroy us. We face a disintegrating economy, a weakened defense, and an energy policy based on the sharing of scarcity.

The major issue of this campaign is the direct political, personal, and moral responsibility of Democratic Party leadership—in the White House and in Congress—for this unprecedented calamity which has befallen us. They tell us they have done the most that humanly could be done. They say that the United States has had its day in the sun; that our nation has passed its zenith. They expect you to tell your children that the American people no longer have the will to cope with their problems; that the future will be one of sacrifice and few opportunities.

My fellow citizens, I utterly reject that view. The American people, the most generous on earth, who created the highest standard of living, are not going to accept the notion that we can only make a better world for others by moving backward ourselves. Those who believe we can have no business leading the nation.

I will not stand by and watch this great country destroy itself under mediocre leadership that drifts from one crisis to the next, eroding our national will and purpose. We have come together here because the American people deserve better from those to whom they entrust our nation's highest offices, and we stand united in our resolve to do something about it.

We need rebirth of the American tradition of leadership at every level of government and in private life as well. The United States of America is unique in world history because it has a genius for leaders—many leaders—on many levels. But, back in 1976, Mr. Carter said, "Trust me." And a lot of people did. Now, many of those people are out of work. Many have seen their savings eaten away by inflation. Many others on fixed incomes, especially the elderly, have watched helplessly as the cruel tax of inflation wasted away their purchasing power. And, today, a great many who trusted Mr. Carter wonder if we can survive the Carter policies of national defense.

"Trust me" government asks that we concentrate our hopes and dreams on one man; that we trust him to do what's best for us. My view of government places trust not in one person or one party, but in those values that transcend persons and parties. The trust is where it belongs—in the people. The responsibility to live up to that trust is where it belongs, in their elected leaders. That kind of relationship, between the people and their elected leaders, is a special kind of compact.

Three hundred and sixty years ago, in 1620, a group of families dared to cross a mighty ocean to build a future for themselves in a new world. When they arrived at Plymouth, Massachusetts, they formed what they called a "compact"; an agreement among themselves to build a community and abide by its laws.

The single act—the voluntary binding together of free people to live under the law—set the pattern for what was to come.

A century and a half later, the descendants of those people pledged their lives, their fortunes and their sacred honor to found this nation. Some forfeited their fortunes and their lives; none sacrificed honor.

Four score and seven years later, Abraham Lincoln called upon the people of all America to renew their dedication and their commitment to a government of, for, and by the people.

Isn't it once again time to renew our compact of freedom; to pledge to each other all that is best in our lives; all that gives meaning to them—for the sake of this, our beloved and blessed land?

Together, let us make this a new beginning. Let us make a commitment to care for the needy; to teach our children the values and the virtues handed down to us by our families; to have the courage to defend those values and the willingness to sacrifice for them.

Let us pledge to restore, in our time, the American spirit of voluntary service, of cooperation, of private and community initiative; a spirit that flows like a deep and mighty river through the history of our nation.

As your nominee, I pledge to restore to the federal government the capacity to do the people's work without dominating their lives. I pledge to you a government that will not only work well, but wisely; its ability to act tempered by prudence and its willingness to do good balanced by the knowledge that government is never more dangerous than when our desire to have it help us blinds us to its great power to harm us.

The first Republican president once said, "While the people retain their virtue and their vigilance, no administration by any extreme of wickedness or folly can seriously injure the government in the short space of four years."

If Mr. Lincoln could see what's happened in these last three-and-a-half years, he might hedge a little on that statement. But, with the virtues that our legacy as a free people and with the vigilance that sustains liberty, we still have time to use our renewed compact to overcome the injuries that have been done to America these past three-and-a-half years.

First, we must overcome something the present administration has cooked up: a new and altogether indigestible economic stew, one part inflation, one part high unemployment, one part recession, one part runaway taxes, one part deficit spending, and seasoned by an energy crisis. It's an economic stew that has turned the national stomach.

Ours are not problems of abstract economic theory. Those are problems of flesh and blood; problems that cause pain and destroy the moral fiber of real people who should not suffer the further indignity of being told by the government that it is all somehow their fault. We do not have inflation because—as Mr. Carter says—we have lived too well.

The head of a government which has utterly refused to live within its means and which has, in the last few days, told us that this year's deficit will be $60 billion, dares to point the finger of blame at business and labor, both of which have been engaged in a losing struggle just trying to stay even.

High taxes, we are told, are somehow good for us, as if, when government spends our money it isn't inflationary, but when we spend it, it is.

Those who preside over the worst energy shortage in our history tell us to use less, so that we will run out of oil, gasoline, and natural gas a little more slowly. Conservation is desirable, of course, for we must not waste energy. But conservation is not the sole answer to our energy needs.

America must get to work producing more energy. The Republican program for solving economic problems is based on growth and productivity.

Large amounts of oil and natural gas lay beneath our land and off our shores, untouched because the present administration seems to believe the American people would rather see more regulation, taxes, and controls than more energy.

Coal offers great potential. So does nuclear energy produced under rigorous safety standards. It could supply electricity for thousands of industries and millions of jobs and homes. It must not be thwarted by a tiny minority opposed to economic growth which often finds friendly ears in regulatory agencies for its obstructionist campaigns.

Make no mistake. We will not permit the safety of our people or our environment heritage to be jeopardized, but we are going to reaffirm that the economic prosperity of our people is a fundamental part of our environment.

Our problems are both acute and chronic, yet all we hear from those in positions of leadership are the same tired proposals for more government tinkering, more meddling and more control—all of which led us to this state in the first place.

Can anyone look at the record of this administration and say, "Well done?" Can anyone compare the state of our economy when the Carter Administration took office with where we are today and say, "Keep up the good work?" Can anyone look at our reduced standing in the world today and say, "Let's have four more years of this?"

I believe the American people are going to answer these questions the first week of November and their answer will be, "No—we've had enough." And then it will be up to us—beginning next January twentieth—to offer an administration and congressional leadership of competence and more than a little courage.

We must have the clarity of vision to see the difference between what is essential and what is merely desirable, and then the courage to bring our government back under control and make it acceptable to the people.

It is essential that we maintain both the forward momentum of economic growth and the strength of the safety net beneath those in society who need help. We also believe it is essential that the integrity of all aspects of Social Security are preserved.

Beyond these essentials, I believe it is clear our federal government is overgrown and overweight. Indeed, it is time for our government to go on a diet. Therefore, my first act as chief executive will be to impose an immediate and thorough freeze on federal hiring. Then, we are going to enlist the very best minds from business, labor, and whatever quarter to conduct a detailed review of every department, bureau, and agency that lives by federal appropriations. We are also going to enlist the help and ideas of many dedicated and hard working government employees at all levels who want a more efficient government as much as the rest of us do. I know that many are demoralized by the confusion and waste they confront in their work as a result of failed and failing policies.

Our instructions to the groups we enlist will be simple and direct. We will remind them that government programs exist at the sufferance of the American taxpayer and are paid for with money earned by working men and women. Any program that represents a waste of their money—a theft from their pocketbooks—

must have that waste eliminated or the program must go—by executive order where possible; by congressional action where necessary. Everything that can be run more effectively by state and local government we shall turn over to state and local government, along with the funding sources to pay for it. We are going to put an end to the money merry-go-round where our money becomes Washington's money, to be spent by the states and cities exactly the way the federal bureaucrats tell them to.

I will not accept the excuse that the federal government has grown so big and powerful that it is beyond the control of any president, any administration or Congress. We are going to put an end to the notion that the American taxpayer exists to fund the federal government. The federal government exists to serve the American people. On January 20, we are going to re-establish that truth.

Also on that date we are going to initiate action to get substantial relief for our taxpaying citizens and action to put people back to work. None of this will be based on any new form of monetary tinkering or fiscal sleight-of-hand. We will simply apply to government the common sense we all use in our daily lives.

Work and family are at the center of our lives; the foundation of our dignity as a free people. When we deprive people of what they have earned, or take away their jobs, we destroy their dignity and undermine their families. We cannot support our families unless there are jobs; and we cannot have jobs unless people have both money to invest and the faith to invest it.

These are concepts that stem from an economic system that for more than 200 years has helped us master a continent, create a previously undreamed of prosperity for our people, and has fed millions of others around the globe. That system will continue to serve us in the future if our government will stop ignoring the basic values on which it was built and stop betraying the trust and good will of the American workers who keep it going.

The American people are carrying the heaviest peacetime tax burden in our nation's history—and it will grow even heavier, under present law, next January. We are taxing ourselves into economic exhaustion and stagnation, crushing our ability and incentive to save, invest, and produce.

This must stop. We must halt this fiscal self-destruction and restore sanity to our economic system.

I have long advocated a 30 per cent reduction in income tax rates over a period of three years. This phased tax reduction would begin with a 10 per cent "down payment" tax cut in 1981, which the Republicans in Congress and I have already proposed.

A phased reduction of tax rates would go a long way toward easing the heavy burden on the American people. But, we should not stop here.

Within the context of economic conditions and appropriate budget priorities during each fiscal year of my presidency, I would strive to go further. This would include improvement in business depreciation taxes so we can stimulate investment in order to get plants and equipment replaced, put more Americans back to work, and put our nation back on the road to being competitive in world commerce. We will also work to reduce the cost of government as a percentage of our gross national product.

The first task of national leadership is to set honest and realistic priorities in our policies and our budget and I pledge that my administration will do that.

When I talk of tax cuts, I am reminded that every major tax cut in this century has strengthened the economy, generated renewed productivity, and ended up yielding new revenues for the government by creating new investment, new jobs, and more commerce among our people.

The present administration has been forced by us Republicans to play follow-the-leader with regard to a tax cut. But in this election year, we must take with the proverbial "grain of salt" any tax cut proposed by those who have given us the greatest tax increase in our history. When those in leadership give us tax increases and tell us we must also do with less, have they thought about those who have always had less—especially the minorities? This is like telling them that just as they step on the first rung of the ladder of opportunity, the ladder is being pulled out from under them. That may be the Democratic leadership's message to the minorities, but it won't be ours. Our message will be: we have to move ahead, but we're not going to leave anyone behind. Thanks to the economic policies of the Democratic Party, millions of Americans find themselves out of work. Millions more have never even had a fair chance to learn new skills, hold a decent job, or secure for themselves and their families a share in the prosperity of this nation.

It is time to put America back to work; to make our cities and towns resound with the confident voices of men and women of all races, nationalities, and faiths bringing home to their families a decent paycheck they can cash for honest money.

For those without skills, we'll find a way to help them get skills.

For those without job opportunities, we'll stimulate new opportunities, particularly in the inner cities where they live.

For those who have abandoned hope, we'll restore hope and we'll welcome them into a great national crusade to make America great again!

When we move from domestic affairs and cast our eyes abroad, we see an equally sorry chapter on the record of the present administration.

- A Soviet combat brigade trains in Cuba, just 90 miles from our shores
- A Soviet army of invasion occupies Afghanistan, further threatening our vital interests in the Middle East
- America's defense strength is at its lowest ebb in a generation, while the Soviet Union is vastly outspending us in both strategic and conventional arms
- Our European allies, looking nervously at the growing menace from the East, turn to us for leadership and fail to find it
- And, incredibly, more than 50 of our fellow Americans have been held captive for over eight months by a dictatorial foreign power that holds us up to ridicule before the world

Adversaries large and small test our will and seek to confound our resolve, but we are given weakness when we need strength; vacillation when the times demand firmness.

The Carter Administration lives in the world of make-believe; every day, drawing up a response to that day's problems, troubles, regardless of what happened yesterday and what will happen tomorrow.

The rest of us, however, live in the real world. It is here that disasters are overtaking our nation without any real response from Washington.

This is make-believe, self-deceit, and—above all—transparent hypocrisy.

For example, Mr. Carter says he supports the volunteer army, but he lets military pay and benefits slip so low that many of our enlisted personnel are actually eligible for food stamps. Re-enlistment rates drop and, just recently, after he fought all week against a proposal to increase the pay of our men and women in uniform, he helicoptered to our carrier, the *U.S.S. Nimitz*, which was returning from long months of duty. He told the crew that he advocated better pay for them and their comrades! Where does he really stand, now that he's back on shore?

I'll tell you where I stand. I do not favor a peacetime draft or registration, but I do favor pay and benefit levels that will attract and keep highly motivated men and women in our volunteer forces and an active reserve trained and ready for an instant call in case of an emergency.

There may be a sailor at the helm of the ship of state, but the ship has no rudder. Critical decisions are made at times almost in comic fashion, but who can laugh? Who was not embarrassed when the administration handed a major propaganda victory in the United Nations to the enemies of Israel, our staunch Middle East ally for three decades, and then claims that the American vote was a "mistake," the result of a "failure of communication" between the president, his secretary of state, and his U.N. ambassador?

Who does not feel a growing sense of unease as our allies, facing repeated instances of an amateurish and confused administration, reluctantly conclude that America is unwilling or unable to fulfill its obligations as the leader of the free world?

Who does not feel rising alarm when the question in any discussion of foreign policy is no longer, "Should we do something?", but "Do we have the capacity to do anything?"

The administration which has brought us to this state is seeking your endorsement for four more years of weakness, indecision, mediocrity, and incompetence. No American should vote until he or she has asked, is the United States stronger and more respected now than it was three-and-a-half years ago? Is the world today a safer place in which to live?

It is the responsibility of the President of the United States, in working for peace, to insure that the safety of our people cannot successfully be threatened by a hostile foreign power. As president, fulfilling that responsibility will be my number one priority.

We are not a warlike people. Quite the opposite. We always seek to live in peace. We resort to force infrequently and with great reluctance—and only after we have determined that it is absolutely necessary. We are awed—and rightly so—by the forces of destruction at loose in the world in this nuclear era. But neither can we be naive or foolish. Four times in my lifetime America has gone to war, bleeding the lives of its young men into the sands of beachheads, the fields of Europe, and the jungles and rice paddies of Asia. We know only too well that war comes not when the forces of freedom are strong, but when they are weak. It is then that tyrants are tempted.

We simply cannot learn these lessons the hard way again without risking our destruction.

Of all the objectives we seek, first and foremost is the establishment of lasting world peace. We must always stand ready to negotiate in good faith, ready to pursue any reasonable avenue that holds forth the promise of lessening tensions and furthering the prospects of peace. But let our friends and those who may wish us ill take note: the United States has an obligation to its citizens and to the people of the world never to let those who would destroy freedom dictate the future course of human life on this planet. I would regard my election as proof that we have renewed our resolve to preserve world peace and freedom. This nation will once again be strong enough to do that.

This evening marks the last step—save one—of a campaign that has taken Nancy and me from one end of this great land to the other, over many months and thousands of miles. There are those who question the way we choose a president; who say that our process imposes difficult and exhausting burdens on those who seek the office. I have not found it so.

It is impossible to capture in words the splendor of this vast continent which God has granted as our portion of this creation. There are no words to express the extraordinary strength and character of this breed of people we call Americans.

Everywhere we have met thousands of Democrats, Independents, and Republicans from all economic conditions and walks of life bound together in that community of shared values of family, work, neighborhood, peace, and freedom. They are concerned, yes, but they are not frightened. They are disturbed, but not dismayed. They are the kind of men and women Tom Paine had in mind when he wrote—during the darkest days of the American Revolution—"We have it in our power to begin the world over again."

Nearly 150 years after Tom Paine wrote those words, an American president told the generation of the Great Depression that it had a "rendezvous with destiny." I believe that this generation of Americans today has a rendezvous with destiny.

Tonight, let us dedicate ourselves to renewing the American compact. I ask you not simply to "Trust me," but to trust your values—our values—and to hold me responsible for living up to them. I ask you to trust that American spirit which knows no ethnic, religious, social, political, regional, or economic boundaries; the spirit that burned with zeal in the hearts of millions of immigrants from every corner of the Earth who came here in search of freedom.

Some say that spirit no longer exists. But I have seen it—I have felt it—all across the land; in the big cities, the small towns and in rural America. The American spirit is still there, ready to blaze into life if you and I are willing to do what has to be done; the practical, down-to-earth things that will stimulate our economy, increase productivity and put America back to work. The time is now to resolve that the basis of a firm and principled foreign policy is one that takes the world as it is and seeks to change it by leadership and example; not by harangue, harassment, or wishful thinking.

The time is now to say that while we shall seek new friendships and expand and improve others, we shall not do so by breaking our word or casting aside old friends and allies.

And, the time is now to redeem promises once made to the American people by another candidate, in another time and another place. He said, "For three long years I have been going up and down this country preaching that government—federal, state, and local—costs too much. I shall not stop that preaching. As an immediate program of action, we must abolish useless offices. We must eliminate unnecessary functions of government . . . we must consolidate subdivisions of government and, like the private citizen, give up luxuries which we can no longer afford.

"I propose to you, my friends, and through you that government of all kinds, big and little be made solvent and that the example be set by the President of the United States and his Cabinet."

So said Franklin Delano Roosevelt in his acceptance speech to the Democratic National Convention in July 1932.

The time is now, my fellow Americans, to recapture our destiny, to take it into our own hands. But, to do this will take many of us, working together. I ask you tonight to volunteer your help in this cause so we can carry our message throughout the land.

Yes, isn't now the time that we, the people, carried out these unkept promises? Let us pledge to each other and to all America on this July day 48 years later, we intend to do just that.

I have thought of something that is not part of my speech and I'm worried over whether I should do it.

Can we doubt that only a Divine Providence placed this land, this island of freedom, here as a refuge for all those people in the world who yearn to breathe freely: Jews and Christians enduring persecution behind the Iron Curtain, the boat people of Southeast Asia, of Cuba and Haiti, the victims of drought and famine in Africa, the freedom fighters of Afghanistan, and our own countrymen held in savage captivity?

I'll confess that I've been a little afraid to suggest what I'm going to suggest—I'm more afraid not to—that we begin our crusade joined together in a moment of silent prayer. God bless America.

First Inaugural Address

EDITOR'S NOTE: *This speech was delivered on January 20, 1981, at the U.S. Capitol.*

Senator Hatfield, Mr. Chief Justice, Mr. President, Vice President Bush, Vice President Mondale, Senator Baker, Speaker O'Neill, Reverend Moomaw, and my fellow citizens.

To a few of us here today this is a solemn and most momentous occasion, and yet in the history of our nation it is a commonplace occurrence. The orderly transfer of authority as called for in the Constitution routinely takes place, as it has for almost two centuries, and few of us stop to think how unique we really are. In the eyes of many in the world, this every-four-year ceremony we accept as normal is nothing less than a miracle.

Mr. President, I want our fellow citizens to know how much you did to carry on this tradition. By your gracious cooperation in the transition process, you have shown a watching world that we are a united people pledged to maintaining a political system which guarantees individual liberty to a greater degree than any other, and I thank you and your people for all your help in maintaining the continuity which is the bulwark of our republic. The business of our nation goes forward. These United States are confronted with an economic affliction of great proportions. We suffer from the longest and one of the worst sustained inflations in our national history. It distorts our economic decisions, penalizes thrift, and crushes the struggling young and the fixed-income elderly alike. It threatens to shatter the lives of millions of our people.

Idle industries have cast workers into unemployment, human misery, and personal indignity. Those who do work are denied a fair return for their labor by a tax system which penalizes successful achievement and keeps us from maintaining full productivity.

But great as our tax burden is, it has not kept pace with public spending. For decades we have piled deficit upon deficit, mortgaging our future and our children's future for the temporary convenience of the present. To continue this long trend is to guarantee tremendous social, cultural, political, and economic upheavals.

You and I, as individuals, can, by borrowing, live beyond our means, but for only a limited period of time. Why, then, should we think that collectively, as a nation, we're not bound by that same limitation? We must act today in order to preserve tomorrow. And let there be no misunderstanding: We are going to begin to act, beginning today.

The economic ills we suffer have come upon us over several decades. They will not go away in days, weeks, or months, but they will go away. They will go away because we as Americans have the capacity now, as we've had in the past, to do whatever needs to be done to preserve this last and greatest bastion of freedom.

In this present crisis, government is not the solution to our problem; government is the problem. From time to time we've been tempted to believe that society has become too complex to be managed by self-rule, that government by an elite group is superior to government for, by, and of the people. Well, if no one among us is capable of governing himself, then who among us has the capacity to govern someone else? All of us together, in and out of government, must bear the burden. The solutions we seek must be equitable, with no one group singled out to pay a higher price.

We hear much of special interest groups. Well, our concern must be for a special interest group that has been too long neglected. It knows no sectional boundaries or ethnic and racial divisions, and it crosses political party lines. It is made up of men and women who raise our food, patrol our streets, man our mines and factories, teach our children, keep our homes, and heal us when we're sick—professionals, industrialists, shopkeepers, clerks, cabbies, and truck drivers. They are, in short, "we the people," this breed called Americans.

Well, this administration's objective will be a healthy, vigorous, growing economy that provides equal opportunities for all Americans, with no barriers born of bigotry or discrimination. Putting America back to work means putting all Americans back to work. Ending inflation means freeing all Americans from the terror of runaway living costs. All must share in the productive work of this "new beginning," and all must share in the bounty of a revived economy. With the idealism and fair play which are the core of our system and our strength, we can have a strong and prosperous America, at peace with itself and the world.

So, as we begin, let us take inventory. We are a nation that has a government—not the other way around. And this makes us special among the nations of the Earth. Our government has no power except that granted it by the people. It is time to check and reverse the growth of government, which shows signs of having grown beyond the consent of the governed.

It is my intention to curb the size and influence of the federal establishment and to demand recognition of the distinction between the powers granted to the federal government and those reserved to the states or to the people. All of us need to be reminded that the federal government did not create the states; the states created the federal government.

Now, so there will be no misunderstanding, it's not my intention to do away with government. It is rather to make it work—work with us, not over us; to stand by our side, not ride on our back. Government can and must provide opportunity, not smother it; foster productivity, not stifle it.

If we look to the answer as to why for so many years we achieved so much, prospered as no other people on earth, it was because here in this land we unleashed the energy and individual genius of man to a greater extent than has ever been done before. Freedom and the dignity of the individual have been more available and assured here than in any other place on earth. The price for this freedom at times has been high, but we have never been unwilling to pay the price.

It is no coincidence that our present troubles parallel and are proportionate to the intervention and intrusion in our lives that result from unnecessary and excessive growth of government. It is time for us to realize that we're too great a nation to limit ourselves to small dreams. We're not, as some would have us believe, doomed to an inevitable decline. I do not believe in a fate that will fall on us no matter what we do. I do believe in a fate that will fall on us if we do nothing. So, with all the creative energy at our command, let us begin an era of national renewal. Let us renew our determination, our courage, and our strength. And let us renew our faith and our hope.

We have every right to dream heroic dreams. Those who say that we're in a time when there are no heroes, they just don't know where to look. You can see heroes every day going in and out of factory gates. Others, a handful in number, produce enough food to feed all of us and then the world beyond. You meet heroes across a counter, and they're on both sides of that counter. There are entrepreneurs with faith in themselves and faith in an idea who create new jobs, new wealth and opportunity. They're individuals and families whose taxes support the government and whose voluntary gifts support church, charity, culture, art, and education. Their patriotism is quiet, but deep. Their values sustain our national life.

Now, I have used the words "they" and "their" in speaking of these heroes. I could say "you" and "your," because I'm addressing the heroes of whom I speak— you, the citizens of this blessed land. Your dreams, your hopes, your goals are going to be the dreams, the hopes, and the goals of this administration, so help me God.

We shall reflect the compassion that is so much a part of your makeup. How can we love our country and not love our countrymen; and loving them, reach out a hand when they fall, heal them when they're sick, and provide opportunity to make them self-sufficient so they will be equal in fact and not just in theory?

Can we solve the problems confronting us? Well, the answer is an unequivocal and emphatic "yes." To paraphrase Winston Churchill, I did not take the oath I've just taken with the intention of presiding over the dissolution of the world's strongest economy.

In the days ahead I will propose removing the roadblocks that have slowed our economy and reduced productivity. Steps will be taken aimed at restoring the balance between the various levels of government. Progress may be slow, measured in inches and feet, not miles, but we will progress. It is time to reawaken this industrial giant, to get government back within its means, and to lighten our punitive tax burden. And these will be our first priorities, and on these principles there will be no compromise.

On the eve of our struggle for independence a man who might have been one of the greatest among the Founding Fathers, Dr. Joseph Warren, president of the Massachusetts Congress, said to his fellow Americans, "Our country is in danger, but not to be despaired of . . . On you depend the fortunes of America. You are to decide the important questions upon which rests the happiness and the liberty of millions yet unborn. Act worthy of yourselves." Well, I believe we, the Americans of today, are ready to act worthy of ourselves, ready to do what must be done to ensure happiness and liberty for ourselves, our children, and our children's children. And as we renew ourselves here in our own land, we will be seen as having greater strength throughout the world. We will again be the exemplar of freedom and a beacon of hope for those who do not now have freedom.

To those neighbors and allies who share our freedom, we will strengthen our historic ties and assure them of our support and firm commitment. We will match loyalty with loyalty. We will strive for mutually beneficial relations. We will not use our friendship to impose on their sovereignty, for our own sovereignty is not for sale. As for the enemies of freedom, those who are potential adversaries, they will be reminded that peace is the highest aspiration of the American people. We will negotiate for it, sacrifice for it; we will not surrender for it, now or ever.

Our forbearance should never be misunderstood. Our reluctance for conflict should not be misjudged as a failure of will. When action is required to preserve our national security, we will act. We will maintain sufficient strength to prevail if need be, knowing that if we do so we have the best chance of never having to use that strength. Above all, we must realize that no arsenal or no weapon in the arsenals of the world is so formidable as the will and moral courage of free men and women. It is a weapon our adversaries in today's world do not have. It is a weapon that we as Americans do have. Let that be understood by those who practice terrorism and prey upon their neighbors. I'm told that tens of thousands of prayer meetings are being held on this day, and for that I'm deeply grateful. We are a nation under God, and I believe God intended for us to be free. It would be fitting and good, I think, if on each Inaugural Day in future years it should be declared a day of prayer.

This is the first time in our history that this ceremony has been held, as you've been told, on the West Front of the Capitol. Standing here, one faces a magnificent vista, opening up on the city's special beauty and history. At the end of this open mall are those shrines to the giants on whose shoulders we stand.

Directly in front of me, the monument to a monumental man, George Washington, father of our country. A man of humility who came to greatness reluctantly. He led Americans out of revolutionary victory into infant nationhood. Off to one side, the stately memorial to Thomas Jefferson. The Declaration of Independence flames with his eloquence. And then, beyond the Reflecting Pool, the dignified columns of the Lincoln Memorial. Whoever would understand in his heart the meaning of America will find it in the life of Abraham Lincoln.

Beyond those monuments to heroism is the Potomac River, and on the far shore the sloping hills of Arlington National Cemetery, with its row upon row of simple white markers bearing crosses or Stars of David. They add up to only a tiny fraction of the price that has been paid for our freedom. Each one of those markers is a monument to the kind of hero I spoke of earlier. Their lives ended in places called Belleau Wood, the Argonne, Omaha Beach, Salerno, and halfway around the world on Guadalcanal, Tarawa, Pork Chop Hill, the Chosin Reservoir, and in a hundred rice paddies and jungles of a place called Vietnam.

Under one such marker lies a young man, Martin Treptow, who left his job in a small town barbershop in 1917 to go to France with the famed Rainbow Division. There, on the western front, he was killed trying to carry a message between battalions under heavy artillery fire.

We're told that on his body was found a diary. On the flyleaf under the heading "My Pledge," he had written these words: "America must win this war. Therefore I will work, I will save, I will sacrifice, I will endure, I will fight cheerfully and do my utmost, as if the issue of the whole struggle depended on me alone."

The crisis we are facing today does not require of us the kind of sacrifice that Martin Treptow and so many thousands of others were called upon to make. It does require, however, our best effort and our willingness to believe in ourselves and to believe in our capacity to perform great deeds, to believe that together with God's help we can and will resolve the problems which now confront us.

And after all, why shouldn't we believe that? We are Americans.

God bless you, and thank you.

Remarks to the National Association of Evangelicals

EDITOR'S NOTE: *This speech was delivered on March 8, 1983, in Orlando, Florida. It is known as the "Evil Empire" speech.*

Thank you. Thank you very much. Thank you very much. Thank you very much. Thank you very much.

And, Reverend Clergy all, Senator Hawkins, distinguished members of the Florida congressional delegation, and all of you: I can't tell you how you have warmed my heart with your welcome. I'm delighted to be here today.

Those of you in the National Association of Evangelicals are known for your spiritual and humanitarian work. And I would be especially remiss if I didn't discharge right now one personal debt of gratitude. Thank you for your prayers. Nancy and I have felt their presence many times in many ways. And believe me, for us they've made all the difference.

The other day in the East Room of the White House at a meeting there, someone asked me whether I was aware of all the people out there who were praying for the President. And I had to say, "Yes, I am. I've felt it. I believe in intercessionary prayer." But I couldn't help but say to that questioner after he'd asked the question that—or at least say to them that if sometimes when he was praying he got a busy signal, it was just me in there ahead of him. I think I understand how Abraham Lincoln felt when he said, "I have been driven many times to my knees by the overwhelming conviction that I had nowhere else to go." From the joy and the good feeling of this conference, I go to a political reception. Now, I don't know why, but that bit of scheduling reminds me of a story which I'll share with you.

An evangelical minister and a politician arrived at Heaven's gate one day together. And St. Peter, after doing all the necessary formalities, took them in hand to show them where their quarters would be. And he took them to a small, single room with a bed, a chair, and a table and said this was for the clergyman. And the politician was a little worried about what might be in store for him. And he couldn't believe it then when St. Peter stopped in front of a beautiful mansion with lovely grounds, many servants, and told him that these would be his quarters.

And he couldn't help but ask, he said, "But wait, how—there's something wrong—how do I get this mansion while that good and holy man only gets a single room?" And St. Peter said, "You have to understand how things are up here. We've got thousands and thousands of clergy. You're the first politician who ever made it."

But I don't want to contribute to a stereotype. So I tell you there are a great many God-fearing, dedicated, noble men and women in public life, present company included. And yes, we need your help to keep us ever-mindful of the ideas and the principles that brought us into the public arena in the first place. The basis of those ideals and principles is a commitment to freedom and personal liberty that itself is grounded in the much deeper realization that freedom prospers only where the blessings of God are avidly sought and humbly accepted.

The American experiment in democracy rests on this insight. Its discovery was the great triumph of our Founding Fathers, voiced by William Penn when he said: "If we will not be governed by God, we must be governed by tyrants." Explaining the inalienable rights of men, Jefferson said, "The God who gave us life, gave us liberty at the same time." And it was George Washington who said that "of all the dispositions and habits which lead to political prosperity, religion and morality are indispensable supports."

And finally, that shrewdest of all observers of American democracy, Alexis de Tocqueville, put it eloquently after he had gone on a search for the secret of America's greatness and genius—and he said: "Not until I went into the churches of America and heard her pulpits aflame with righteousness did I understand the greatness and the genius of America. America is good. And if America ever ceases to be good, America will cease to be great."

Well, I'm pleased to be here today with you who are keeping America great by keeping her good. Only through your work and prayers and those of millions of others can we hope to survive this perilous century and keep alive this experiment in liberty, this last, best hope of man.

I want you to know that this administration is motivated by a political philosophy that sees the greatness of America in you, her people, and in your families, churches, neighborhoods, communities: the institutions that foster and nourish values like concern for others and respect for the rule of law under God.

Now, I don't have to tell you that this puts us in opposition to, or at least out of step with, a—a prevailing attitude of many who have turned to a modern-day secularism, discarding the tried and time-tested values upon which our very civilization is based. No matter how well intentioned, their value system is radically different from that of most Americans. And while they proclaim that they're freeing us from superstitions of the past, they've taken upon themselves the job of superintending us by government rule and regulation. Sometimes their voices are louder than ours, but they are not yet a majority.

An example of that vocal superiority is evident in a controversy now going on in Washington. And since I'm involved I've been waiting to hear from the parents of young America. How far are they willing to go in giving to government their prerogatives as parents?

Let me state the case as briefly and simply as I can. An organization of citizens, sincerely motivated, deeply concerned about the increase in illegitimate births and abortions involving girls well below the age of consent, some time ago established a nationwide network of clinics to offer help to these girls and, hopefully, alleviate this situation. Now, again, let me say, I do not fault their intent. However, in their well-intentioned effort, these clinics decided to provide advice and birth control drugs and devices to underage girls without the knowledge of their parents.

For some years now, the federal government has helped with funds to subsidize these clinics. In providing for this, the Congress decreed that every effort would be made to maximize parental participation. Nevertheless, the drugs and devices are prescribed without getting parental consent or giving notification after they've done so. Girls termed "sexually active"—and that has replaced the word "promiscuous"—are given this help in order to prevent illegitimate birth or abortion.

Well, we have ordered clinics receiving federal funds to notify the parents such help has been given. One of the nation's leading newspapers has created the term "squeal rule" in editorializing against us for doing this, and we're being criticized for violating the privacy of young people. A judge has recently granted an injunction against an enforcement of our rule. I've watched TV panel shows discuss this issue, seen columnists pontificating on our error, but no one seems to mention morality as playing a part in the subject of sex.

Is all of Judeo-Christian tradition wrong? Are we to believe that something so sacred can be looked upon as a purely physical thing with no potential for emotional and psychological harm? And isn't it the parents' right to give counsel and advice to keep their children from making mistakes that may affect their entire lives?

Many of us in government would like to know what parents think about this intrusion in their family by government. We're going to fight in the courts. The right of parents and the rights of family take precedence over those of Washington-based bureaucrats and social engineers.

But the fight against parental notification is really only one example of many attempts to water down traditional values and even abrogate the original terms of American democracy. Freedom prospers when religion is vibrant and the rule of law under God is acknowledged. When our Founding Fathers passed the First Amendment, they sought to protect churches from government interference. They never intended to construct a wall of hostility between government and the concept of religious belief itself.

The evidence of this permeates our history and our government. The Declaration of Independence mentions the Supreme Being no less than four times. IN GOD WE TRUST is engraved on our coinage. The Supreme Court opens its proceedings with a religious invocation. And the members of Congress open their sessions with a prayer. I just happen to believe the schoolchildren of the United States are entitled to the same privileges as Supreme Court justices and congressmen.

Last year, I sent the Congress a constitutional amendment to restore prayer to public schools. Already this session, there's growing bipartisan support for the amendment, and I am calling on the Congress to act speedily to pass it and to let our children pray.

Perhaps some of you read recently about the Lubbock school case, where a judge actually ruled that it was unconstitutional for a school district to give equal treatment to religious and nonreligious student groups, even when the group meetings were being held during the students' own time. The First Amendment never intended to require government to discriminate against religious speech.

Senators Denton and Hatfield have proposed legislation in the Congress on the whole question of prohibiting discrimination against religious forms of student speech. Such legislation could go far to restore freedom of religious speech for public school students. And I hope the Congress considers these bills quickly. And with your help, I think it's possible we could also get the constitutional amendment through the Congress this year.

More than a decade ago, a Supreme Court decision literally wiped off the books of fifty states statutes protecting the rights of unborn children. Abortion on demand now takes the lives of up to one and a half million unborn children a year. Human life legislation ending this tragedy will someday pass the Congress, and you and I must never rest until it does. Unless and until it can be proven that the unborn child is not a living entity, then its right to life, liberty, and the pursuit of happiness must be protected.

You may remember that when abortion on demand began, many, and indeed, I'm sure many of you, warned that the practice would lead to a decline in respect for human life, that the philosophical premises used to justify abortion on demand would ultimately be used to justify other attacks on the sacredness of human life—infanticide or mercy killing. Tragically enough, those warnings proved all too true. Only last year a court permitted the death by starvation of a handicapped infant.

I have directed the Health and Human Services Department to make clear to every health care facility in the United States that the Rehabilitation Act of 1973 protects all handicapped persons against discrimination based on handicaps, including infants. And we have taken the further step of requiring that each and every recipient of federal funds who provides health care services to infants must post and keep posted in a conspicuous place a notice stating that "discriminatory failure to feed and care for handicapped infants in this facility is prohibited by federal law." It also lists a twenty-four-hour toll-free number so that nurses and others may report violations in time to save the infant's life.

In addition, recent legislation introduced in the Congress by Representative Henry Hyde of Illinois not only increases restrictions on publicly financed abortions, it also addresses this whole problem of infanticide. I urge the Congress to begin hearings and to adopt legislation that will protect the right of life to all children, including the disabled or handicapped.

Now, I'm sure that you must get discouraged at times, but there you've done better than you know, perhaps. There's a great spiritual awakening in America, a renewal of the traditional values that have been the bedrock of America's goodness and greatness.

One recent survey by a Washington-based research council concluded that Americans were far more religious than the people of other nations; 95 per cent of those surveyed expressed a belief in God and a huge majority believed the Ten Commandments had real meaning in their lives. And another study has found that an overwhelming majority of Americans disapprove of adultery, teenage sex, pornography, abortion, and hard drugs. And this same study showed a deep reverence for the importance of family ties and religious belief.

I think the items that we've discussed here today must be a key part of the nation's political agenda. For the first time the Congress is openly and seriously debating and dealing with the prayer and abortion issues and that's enormous progress right there. I repeat: America is in the midst of a spiritual awakening and a moral renewal. And with your biblical keynote, I say today, "Yes, let justice roll on like a river, righteousness like a never-failing stream."

Now, obviously, much of this new political and social consensus I've talked about is based on a positive view of American history, one that takes pride in our country's accomplishments and record. But we must never forget that no government schemes are going to perfect man. We know that living in this world means dealing with what philosophers would call the phenomenology of evil or, as theologians would put it, the doctrine of sin.

There is sin and evil in the world, and we're enjoined by Scripture and the Lord Jesus to oppose it with all our might. Our nation, too, has a legacy of evil with which it must deal. The glory of this land has been its capacity for transcending the moral evils of our past. For example, the long struggle of minority citizens for equal rights, once a source of disunity and civil war is now a point of pride for all Americans. We must never go back. There is no room for racism, anti-Semitism, or other forms of ethnic and racial hatred in this country.

I know that you've been horrified, as have I, by the resurgence of some hate groups preaching bigotry and prejudice. Use the mighty voice of your pulpits and the powerful standing of your churches to denounce and isolate these hate groups in our midst. The commandment given us is clear and simple: "Thou shalt love thy neighbor as thyself."

But whatever sad episodes exist in our past, any objective observer must hold a positive view of American history, a history that has been the story of hopes fulfilled and dreams made into reality. Especially in this century, America has kept alight the torch of freedom, but not just for ourselves but for millions of others around the world.

And this brings me to my final point today. During my first press conference as president, in answer to a direct question, I pointed out that, as good Marxist-Leninists, the Soviet leaders have openly and publicly declared that the only morality they recognize is that which will further their cause, which is world revolution. I think I should point out I was only quoting Lenin, their guiding spirit, who said in 1920 that they repudiate all morality that proceeds from supernatural ideas—that's their name for religion—or ideas that are outside class conceptions. Morality is entirely subordinate to the interests of class war. And everything is moral that is necessary for the annihilation of the old, exploiting social order and for uniting the proletariat.

Well, I think the refusal of many influential people to accept this elementary fact of Soviet doctrine illustrates a historical reluctance to see totalitarian powers for what they are. We saw this phenomenon in the 1930s. We see it too often today.

This doesn't mean we should isolate ourselves and refuse to seek an understanding with them. I intend to do everything I can to persuade them of our peaceful intent, to remind them that it was the West that refused to use its nuclear monopoly in the Forties and Fifties for territorial gain and which now proposes a 50 per cent cut in strategic ballistic missiles and the elimination of an entire class of land-based, intermediate-range nuclear missiles.

At the same time, however, they must be made to understand we will never compromise our principles and standards. We will never give away our freedom. We will never abandon our belief in God, and we will never stop searching for a genuine peace. But we can assure none of these things America stands for through the so-called nuclear freeze solutions proposed by some.

The truth is that a freeze now would be a very dangerous fraud, for that is merely the illusion of peace. The reality is that we must find peace through strength.

I would agree to a freeze if only we could freeze the Soviets' global desires. A freeze at current levels of weapons would remove any incentive for the Soviets to negotiate seriously in Geneva and virtually end our chances to achieve the major arms reductions which we have proposed. Instead, they would achieve their objectives through the freeze.

A freeze would reward the Soviet Union for its enormous and unparalleled military buildup. It would prevent the essential and long overdue modernization of United States and allied defenses and would leave our aging forces increasingly vulnerable. And an honest freeze would require extensive prior negotiations on the systems and numbers to be limited and on the measures to ensure effective verification and compliance. And the kind of a freeze that has been suggested would be virtually impossible to verify. Such a major effort would divert us completely from our current negotiations on achieving substantial reductions.

A number of years ago, I heard a young father, a very prominent young man in the entertainment world, addressing a tremendous gathering in California. It was during the time of the Cold War, and Communism and our own way of life were very much on people's minds. And he was speaking to that subject. And suddenly, though, I heard him saying, "I love my little girls more than anything." And I said to myself, "Oh, no, don't. You can't—don't say that." But I had underestimated him. He went on: "I would rather see my little girls die now, still believing in God, than have them grow up under Communism and one day die no longer believing in God."

There were thousands of young people in that audience. They came to their feet with shouts of joy. They had instantly recognized the profound truth in what he had said, with regard to the physical and the soul and what was truly important.

Yes, let us pray for the salvation of all of those who live in that totalitarian darkness. Pray they will discover the joy of knowing God. But until they do, let us be aware that while they preach the supremacy of the State, declare its omnipotence over individual man, and predict its eventual domination of all peoples on the earth, they are the focus of evil in the modern world.

It was C. S. Lewis who, in his unforgettable *Screw Tape Letters*, wrote: "The greatest evil is not done now in those sordid 'dens of crime' that Dickens loved to paint. It is not even done in concentration camps and labor camps. In those we see its final result. But it is conceived and ordered, moved, seconded, carried and minuted in clear, carpeted, warmed, and well-lighted offices by quiet men with white collars and cut fingernails and smooth-shaven cheeks who do not need to raise their voice."

Well, because these quiet men do not raise their voices; because they sometimes speak in soothing tones of brotherhood and peace; because, like other dictators before them, they're always making "their final territorial demand," some would have us accept them at their word and accommodate ourselves to their aggressive impulses. But if history teaches anything, it teaches that simpleminded appeasement or wishful thinking about our adversaries is folly. It means the betrayal of our past, the squandering of our freedom.

So, I urge you to speak out against those who would place the United States in a position of military and moral inferiority. You know, I've always believed that old Screw Tape reserved his best efforts for those of you in the Church. So, in your discussions of the nuclear freeze proposals, I urge you to beware the temptation of pride—the temptation of blithely declaring yourselves above it all and label both sides equally at fault; to ignore the facts of history and the aggressive impulses of an evil empire; to simply call the arms race a giant misunderstanding and thereby remove yourself from the struggle between right and wrong and good and evil.

I ask you to resist the attempts of those who would have you withhold your support for our efforts, this administration's efforts, to keep America strong and free, while we negotiate real and verifiable reductions in the world's nuclear arsenals and one day, with God's help, their total elimination.

While America's military strength is important, let me add here that I've always maintained that the struggle now going on for the world will never be decided by bombs or rockets, by armies or military might. The real crisis we face today is a spiritual one; at root, it is a test of moral will and faith.

Whittaker Chambers, the man whose own religious conversion made him a witness to one of the terrible traumas of our time, the Hiss-Chambers case, wrote that the crisis of the Western world exists to the degree in which the West is indifferent to God, the degree to which it collaborates in Communism's attempt to make man stand alone without God. And then he said, for Marxism-Leninism is actually the second-oldest faith, first proclaimed in the Garden of Eden with the words of temptation, "Ye shall be as gods."

The Western world can answer this challenge, he wrote, "but only provided that its faith in God and the freedom He enjoins is as great as Communism's faith in Man."

I believe we shall rise to the challenge. I believe that Communism is another sad, bizarre chapter in human history whose last pages even now are being written. I believe this because the source of our strength in the quest for human freedom is not material, but spiritual. And because it knows no limitation, it must terrify and ultimately triumph over those who would enslave their fellow man. For in the words of Isaiah: "He giveth power to the faint; and to them that have no might He increased strength. But they that wait upon the Lord shall renew their strength; they shall mount up with wings as eagles; they shall run, and not be weary."

Yes, change your world. One of our Founding Fathers, Thomas Paine, said, "We have it within our power to begin the world over again." We can do it, doing together what no one church could do by itself. God bless you and thank you very much.

Remarks Commemorating the Fortieth Anniversary of the Normandy Invasion

EDITOR'S NOTE: *This is the first of two D-Day speeches President Reagan made in Europe. It was given at Omaha Beach, in France, on June 6, 1984.*

Mr. President, distinguished guests, we stand today at a place of battle, one that 40 years ago saw and felt the worst of war. Men bled and died here for a few feet or inches of sand, as bullets and shellfire cut through their ranks. About them, General Omar Bradley later said, "Every man who set foot on Omaha Beach that day was a hero."

No speech can adequately portray their suffering, their sacrifice, their heroism. President Lincoln once reminded us that through their deeds, the dead of battle have spoken more eloquently for themselves than any of the living ever could. But we can only honor them by rededicating ourselves to the cause for which they gave a last full measure of devotion.

Today we do rededicate ourselves to that cause. And at this place of honor, we're humbled by the realization of how much so many gave to the cause of freedom and to their fellow man.

Some who survived the battle of June 6, 1944, are here today. Others who hoped to return never did.

"Someday, Lis, I'll go back," said Private First Class Peter Robert Zanatta, of the 37th Engineer Combat Battalion, and first assault wave to hit Omaha Beach. "I'll go back, and I'll see it all again. I'll see the beach, the barricades, and the graves."

Those words of Private Zanatta come to us from his daughter, Lisa Zanatta Henn, in a heartrending story about the event her father spoke of so often. "In his words, the Normandy invasion would change his life forever," she said. She tells some of his stories of World War II but says of her father, "the story to end all stories was D-Day."

"He made me feel the fear of being on that boat waiting to land. I can smell the ocean and feel the seasickness. I can see the looks on his fellow soldiers' faces—the fear, the anguish, the uncertainty of what lay ahead. And when they landed, I can feel the strength and courage of the men who took those first steps through the tide to what must have surely looked like instant death."

Private Zanatta's daughter wrote to me: "I don't know how or why I can feel this emptiness, this fear, or this determination, but I do. Maybe it's the bond I had with my father. All I know is that it brings tears to my eyes to think about my father as a 20-year-old boy having to face that beach."

The anniversary of D-Day was always special for her family. And like all the families of those who went to war, she describes how she came to realize her own father's survival was a miracle: "So many men died. I know that my father watched many of his friends be killed. I know that he must have died inside a little each time. But his explanation to me was, 'You did what you had to do, and you kept on going.'"

When men like Private Zanatta and all our Allied forces stormed the beaches of Normandy 40 years ago they came not as conquerors, but as liberators. When these troops swept across the French countryside and into the forests of Belgium and Luxembourg they came not to take, but to return what had been wrongly seized. When our forces marched into Germany they came not to prey on a brave and defeated people, but to nurture the seeds of democracy among those who yearned to be free again.

We salute them today. But, Mr. President, we also salute those who, like yourself, were already engaging the enemy inside your beloved country—the French Resistance. Your valiant struggle for France did so much to cripple the enemy and spur the advance of the armies of liberation. The French Forces of the Interior will forever personify courage and national spirit. They will be a timeless inspiration to all who are free and to all who would be free.

Today, in their memory, and for all who fought here, we celebrate the triumph of democracy. We reaffirm the unity of democratic peoples who fought a war and then joined with the vanquished in a firm resolve to keep the peace.

From a terrible war we learned that unity made us invincible; now, in peace, that same unity makes us secure. We sought to bring all freedom-loving nations together in a community dedicated to the defense and preservation of our sacred values. Our alliance, forged in the crucible of war, tempered and shaped by the realities of the postwar world, has succeeded. In Europe, the threat has been contained, the peace has been kept.

Today the living here assembled—officials, veterans, citizens—are a tribute to what was achieved here 40 years ago. This land is secure. We are free. These things are worth fighting and dying for.

Lisa Zanatta Henn began her story by quoting her father, who promised that he would return to Normandy. She ended with a promise to her father, who died eight years ago of cancer: "I'm going there, Dad, and I'll see the beaches and the barricades and the monuments. I'll see the graves, and I'll put flowers there just like you wanted to do. I'll feel all the things you made me feel through your stories and your eyes. I'll never forget what you went through, Dad, nor will I let anyone else forget. And, Dad, I'll always be proud."

Through the words of his loving daughter, who is here with us today, a D-Day veteran has shown us the meaning of this day far better than any President can. It is enough for us to say about Private Zanatta and all the men of honor and courage who fought beside him four decades ago: We will always remember. We will always be proud. We will always be prepared, so we may always be free. Thank you.

Remarks at the *U.S. Ranger Monument* Commemorating the Normandy Invasion Anniversary

EDITOR'S NOTE: *This speech was delivered at Pointe du Hoc, France on June 6, 1984.*

We're here to mark that day in history when the Allied armies joined in battle to reclaim this continent to liberty. For four long years, much of Europe had been under a terrible shadow. Free nations had fallen, Jews cried out in the camps, millions cried out for liberation. Europe was enslaved, and the world prayed for its rescue. Here in Normandy the rescue began. Here the Allies stood and fought against tyranny in a giant undertaking unparalleled in human history.

We stand on a lonely, windswept point on the northern shore of France. The air is soft, but 40 years ago at this moment, the air was dense with smoke and the cries of men, and the air was filled with the crack of rifle fire and the roar of cannon. At dawn, on the morning of the sixth of June, 1944, 225 Rangers jumped off the British landing craft and ran to the bottom of these cliffs. Their mission was one of the most difficult and daring of the invasion: to climb these sheer and desolate cliffs and take out the enemy guns. The Allies had been told that some of the mightiest of these guns were here and they would be trained on the beaches to stop the Allied advance.

The Rangers looked up and saw the enemy soldiers—the edge of the cliffs shooting down at them with machine guns and throwing grenades. And the American Rangers began to climb. They shot rope ladders over the face of these cliffs and began to pull themselves up. When one Ranger fell, another would take his place. When one rope was cut, a Ranger would grab another and begin his climb again. They climbed, shot back, and held their footing. Soon, one by one, the Rangers pulled themselves over the top, and in seizing the firm land at the top of these cliffs, they began to seize back the continent of Europe. Two hundred and twenty-five came here. After two days of fighting, only 90 could still bear arms.

Behind me is a memorial that symbolizes the Ranger daggers that were thrust into the top of these cliffs. And before me are the men who put them there.

These are the boys of Pointe du Hoc. These are the men who took the cliffs. These are the champions who helped free a continent. These are the heroes who helped end a war.

Gentlemen, I look at you and I think of the words of Stephen Spender's poem. You are men who in your "lives fought for life . . . and left the vivid air signed with your honor."

I think I know what you may be thinking right now—thinking, "We were just part of a bigger effort; everyone was brave that day." Well, everyone was. Do you remember the story of Bill Millin of the 51st Highlanders? Forty years ago today, British troops were pinned down near a bridge, waiting desperately for help. Suddenly, they heard the sound of bagpipes, and some thought they were dreaming. Well, they weren't. They looked up and saw Bill Millin with his bagpipes, leading the reinforcements and ignoring the smack of the bullets into the ground around him.

Lord Lovat was with him—Lord Lovat of Scotland, who calmly announced when he got to the bridge, "Sorry I'm a few minutes late," as if he'd been delayed by a traffic jam, when in truth he'd just come from the bloody fighting on Sword Beach, which he and his men had just taken.

There was the impossible valor of the Poles who threw themselves between the enemy and the rest of Europe as the invasion took hold, and the unsurpassed courage of the Canadians who had already seen the horrors of war on this coast. They knew what awaited them there, but they would not be deterred. And once they hit Juno Beach, they never looked back.

All of these men were part of a roll call of honor with names that spoke of a pride as bright as the colors they bore: the Royal Winnipeg Rifles, Poland's 24th Lancers, the Royal Scots Fusiliers, the Screaming Eagles, the Yeomen of England's armored divisions, the forces of Free France, the Coast Guard's "Matchbox Fleet" and you, the American Rangers.

Forty summers have passed since the battle that you fought here. You were young the day you took these cliffs; some of you were hardly more than boys, with the deepest joys of life before you. Yet, you risked everything here. Why? Why did you do it? What impelled you to put aside the instinct for self-preservation and risk your lives to take these cliffs? What inspired all the men of the armies that met here? We look at you, and somehow we know the answer. It was faith and belief; it was loyalty and love.

The men of Normandy had faith that what they were doing was right, faith that they fought for all humanity, faith that a just God would grant them mercy on this beachhead or on the next. It was the deep knowledge—and pray God we have not lost it—that there is a profound, moral difference between the use of force for liberation and the use of force for conquest. You were here to liberate, not to conquer, and so you and those others did not doubt your cause. And you were right not to doubt.

You all knew that some things are worth dying for. One's country is worth dying for, and democracy is worth dying for, because it's the most deeply honorable form of government ever devised by man. All of you loved liberty. All of you were willing to fight tyranny, and you knew the people of your countries were behind you.

The Americans who fought here that morning knew word of the invasion was spreading through the darkness back home. They thought—or felt in their hearts, though they couldn't know in fact, that in Georgia they were filling the churches at four A.M., in Kansas they were kneeling on their porches and praying, and in Philadelphia they were ringing the Liberty Bell.

Something else helped the men of D-Day: their rock-hard belief that Providence would have a great hand in the events that would unfold here; that God was an ally in this great cause. And so, the night before the invasion, when Colonel Wolverton asked his parachute troops to kneel with him in prayer he told them: Do not bow your heads, but look up so you can see God and ask His blessing in what we're about to do. Also that night, General Matthew Ridgway on his cot, listening in the darkness for the promise God made to Joshua: "I will not fail thee nor forsake thee."

These are the things that impelled them; these are the things that shaped the unity of the Allies.

When the war was over, there were lives to be rebuilt and governments to be returned to the people. There were nations to be reborn. Above all, there was a new peace to be assured. These were huge and daunting tasks. But the Allies summoned strength from the faith, belief, loyalty, and love of those who fell here. They rebuilt a new Europe together.

There was first a great reconciliation among those who had been enemies, all of whom had suffered so greatly. The United States did its part, creating the Marshall Plan to help rebuild our allies and our former enemies. The Marshall Plan led to the Atlantic alliance—a great alliance that serves to this day as our shield for freedom, for prosperity, and for peace.

In spite of our great efforts and successes, not all that followed the end of the war was happy or planned. Some liberated countries were lost. The great sadness of this loss echoes down to our own time in the streets of Warsaw, Prague, and East Berlin. Soviet troops that came to the center of this continent did not leave when peace came. They're still there, uninvited, unwanted, unyielding, almost 40 years after the war. Because of this, Allied forces still stand on this continent. Today, as 40 years ago, our armies are here for only one purpose—to protect and defend democracy. The only territories we hold are memorials like this one and graveyards where our heroes rest.

We in America have learned bitter lessons from two World Wars: It is better to be here ready to protect the peace than to take blind shelter across the sea, rushing to respond only after freedom is lost. We've learned that isolationism never was and never will be an acceptable response to tyrannical governments with an expansionist intent.

But we try always to be prepared for peace; prepared to deter aggression; prepared to negotiate the reduction of arms; and, yes, prepared to reach out again in the spirit of reconciliation. In truth, there is no reconciliation we would welcome more than a reconciliation with the Soviet Union, so, together, we can lessen the risks of war, now and forever.

It's fitting to remember here the great losses also suffered by the Russian people during World War II: 20 million perished, a terrible price that testifies to all the world the necessity of ending war. I tell you from my heart that we in the United

States do not want war. We want to wipe from the face of the Earth the terrible weapons that man now has in his hands. And I tell you, we are ready to seize that beachhead. We look for some sign from the Soviet Union that they are willing to move forward, that they share our desire and love for peace, and that they will give up the ways of conquest. There must be a changing there that will allow us to turn our hope into action.

We will pray forever that some day that changing will come. But for now, particularly today, it is good and fitting to renew our commitment to each other, to our freedom, to the alliance that protects it.

We are bound today by what bound us 40 years ago, the same loyalties, traditions, and beliefs. We're bound by reality. The strength of America's allies is vital to the United States, and the American security guarantee is essential to the continued freedom of Europe's democracies. We were with you then; we are with you now. Your hopes are our hopes, and your destiny is our destiny.

Here, in this place where the West held together, let us make a vow to our dead. Let us show them by our actions that we understand what they died for. Let our actions say to them the words for which Matthew Ridgway listened: "I will not fail thee nor forsake thee."

Strengthened by their courage, heartened by their valor, and borne by their memory, let us continue to stand for the ideals for which they lived and died.

Thank you very much, and God bless you all.

Second Inaugural Address

EDITOR'S NOTE: *This speech was delivered on January 21, 1985, at the U.S. Capitol.*

Senator Mathias, Chief Justice Burger, Vice President Bush, Speaker O'Neill, Senator Dole, Reverend Clergy, and members of my family and friends and my fellow citizens:

This day has been made brighter with the presence here of one who, for a time, has been absent. Senator John Stennis, God bless you and welcome back. There is, however, one who is not with us today. Representative Gillis Long of Louisiana left us last night. And I wonder if we could all join in a moment of silent prayer.

[The President resumed speaking after a moment of silence.] Amen.

There are no words adequate to express my thanks for the great honor that you've bestowed on me. I'll do my utmost to be deserving of your trust. This is, as Senator Mathias told us, the fiftieth time that we, the people, have celebrated this historic occasion. When the first President, George Washington, placed his hand upon the Bible, he stood less than a single day's journey by horseback from raw, untamed wilderness. There were 4 million Americans in a union of 13 states. Today, we are 60 times as many in a union of 50 states. We've lighted the world with our inventions, gone to the aid of mankind wherever in the world there was a cry for help, journeyed to the Moon and safely returned. So much has changed, and yet we stand together as we did two centuries ago.

When I took this oath four years ago, I did so in a time of economic stress. Voices were raised saying that we had to look to our past for the greatness and glory. But we, the present-day Americans, are not given to looking backward. In this blessed land, there is always a better tomorrow. Four years ago, I spoke to you of a New Beginning, and we have accomplished that. But in another sense, our New Beginning is a continuation of that beginning created two centuries ago when, for the first time in history, government, the people said, was not our master, it is our servant; its only power that which we the people allow it to have.

That system has never failed us, but for a time we failed the system. We asked things of government that government was not equipped to give. We yielded authority to the national government that properly belonged to states or to local governments or to the people themselves. We allowed taxes and inflation to rob us of our earnings and savings and watched the great industrial machine that had made us the most productive people on Earth slow down and the number of unemployed increase.

By 1980 we knew it was time to renew our faith, to strive with all our strength toward the ultimate in individual freedom, consistent with an orderly society.

We believed then and now: There are no limits to growth and human progress when men and women are free to follow their dreams. And we were right to believe that. Tax rates have been reduced, inflation cut dramatically, and more people are employed than ever before in our history.

We are creating a nation once again vibrant, robust, and alive. But there are many mountains yet to climb. We will not rest until every American enjoys the fullness of freedom, dignity, and opportunity as our birthright. It is our birthright as citizens of this great Republic.

And if we meet this challenge, these will be years when Americans have restored their confidence and tradition of progress; when our values of faith, family, work, and neighborhood were restated for a modern age; when our economy was finally freed from government's grip; when we made sincere efforts at meaningful arms reductions and by rebuilding our defenses, our economy, and developing new technologies, helped preserve peace in a troubled world; when America courageously supported the struggle for individual liberty, self-government, and free enterprise throughout the world and turned the tide of history away from totalitarian darkness and into the warm sunlight of human freedom.

My fellow citizens, our nation is poised for greatness. We must do what we know is right, and do it with all our might. Let history say of us: "These were golden years—when the American Revolution was reborn, when freedom gained new life, and America reached for her best."

Our two-party system has solved us—served us, I should say, well over the years, but never better than in those times of great challenge when we came together not as Democrats or Republicans, but as Americans united in a common cause.

Two of our Founding Fathers, a Boston lawyer named Adams and a Virginia planter named Jefferson, members of that remarkable group who met in Independence Hall and dared to think they could start the world over again, left us an important lesson. They had become, in the years then in government, bitter political rivals in the Presidential election of 1800. Then, years later, when both were retired and age had softened their anger, they began to speak to each other again through letters. A bond was reestablished between those two who had helped create this government of ours.

In 1826, the fiftieth anniversary of the Declaration of Independence, they both died. They died on the same day, within a few hours of each other, and that day was the Fourth of July.

In one of those letters exchanged in the sunset of their lives, Jefferson wrote: "It carries me back to the times when, beset with difficulties and dangers, we were fellow laborers in the same cause, struggling for what is most valuable to man, his right of self-government. Laboring always at the same oar, with some wave ever ahead threatening to overwhelm us, and yet passing harmless . . . we rode through the storm with heart and hand." Well, with heart and hand let us stand as one today—one people under God, determined that our future shall be worthy of our past. As we do, we must not repeat the well-intentioned errors of our past. We must never again abuse the trust of working men and women by sending their earnings on a futile chase after the spiraling demands of a bloated federal establishment. You elected us in 1980 to end this prescription for disaster, and I don't believe you re-elected us in 1984 to reverse course.

At the heart of our efforts is one idea vindicated by 25 straight months of economic growth: Freedom and incentives unleash the drive and entrepreneurial genius that are the core of human progress. We have begun to increase the rewards for work, savings, and investment; reduce the increase in the cost and size of government and its interference in people's lives. We must simplify our tax system, make it more fair and bring the rates down for all who work and earn. We must think anew and move with a new boldness, so every American who seeks work can find work, so the least among us shall have an equal chance to achieve the greatest things—to be heroes who heal our sick, feed the hungry, protect peace among nations, and leave this world a better place.

The time has come for a new American emancipation—a great national drive to tear down economic barriers and liberate the spirit of enterprise in the most distressed areas of our country. My friends, together we can do this, and do it we must, so help me God.

From new freedom will spring new opportunities for growth, a more productive, fulfilled, and united people, and a stronger America—an America that will lead the technological revolution and also open its mind and heart and soul to the treasures of literature, music, and poetry, and the values of faith, courage, and love.

A dynamic economy, with more citizens working and paying taxes, will be our strongest tool to bring down budget deficits. But an almost unbroken 50 years of deficit spending has finally brought us to a time of reckoning. We've come to a turning point, a moment for hard decisions. I have asked the Cabinet and my staff a question and now I put the same question to all of you. If not us, who? And if not now, when? It must be done by all of us going forward with a program aimed at reaching a balanced budget. We can then begin reducing the national debt.

I will shortly submit a budget to the Congress aimed at freezing government program spending for the next year. Beyond this, we must take further steps to permanently control government's power to tax and spend. We must act now to protect future generations from government's desire to spend its citizens' money and tax them into servitude when the bills come due. Let us make it unconstitutional for the federal government to spend more than the federal government takes in.

We have already started returning to the people and to state and local governments responsibilities better handled by them. Now, there is a place for the federal government in matters of social compassion. But our fundamental goals must be to reduce dependency and upgrade the dignity of those who are infirm or disadvantaged. And here, a growing economy and support from family and community offer our best chance for a society where compassion is a way of life, where the old and infirm are cared for, the young and, yes, the unborn protected, and the unfortunate looked after and made self-sufficient.

Now, there is another area where the federal government can play a part. As an older American, I remember a time when people of different race, creed, or ethnic origin in our land found hatred and prejudice installed in social custom and, yes, in law. There's no story more heartening in our history than the progress that we've made toward the brotherhood of man that God intended for us. Let us resolve there will be no turning back or hesitation on the road to an America rich in dignity and abundant with opportunity for all our citizens.

Let us resolve that we, the people, will build an American opportunity society in which all of us—white and black, rich and poor, young and old—will go forward together, arm in arm. Again, let us remember that though our heritage is one of blood lines from every corner of the Earth, we are all Americans, pledged to carry on this last, best hope of man on Earth.

I've spoken of our domestic goals and the limitations we should put on our national government. Now let me turn to a task that is the primary responsibility of national government—the safety and security of our people.

Today, we utter no prayer more fervently than the ancient prayer for peace on Earth. Yet history has shown that peace does not come, nor will our freedom be preserved, by good will alone. There are those in the world who scorn our vision of human dignity and freedom. One nation, the Soviet Union, has conducted the greatest military buildup in the history of man, building arsenals of awesome offensive weapons.

We've made progress in restoring our defense capability. But much remains to be done. There must be no wavering by us, nor any doubts by others, that America will meet her responsibilities to remain free, secure, and at peace. There is only one way safely and legitimately to reduce the cost of national security, and that is to reduce the need for it. And this we're trying to do in negotiations with the Soviet Union. We're not just discussing limits on a further increase of nuclear weapons; we seek, instead, to reduce their number. We seek the total elimination one day of nuclear weapons from the face of the Earth.

Now, for decades, we and the Soviets have lived under the threat of mutual assured destruction—if either resorted to the use of nuclear weapons, the other could retaliate and destroy the one who had started it. Is there either logic or morality in believing that if one side threatens to kill tens of millions of our people our only recourse is to threaten killing tens of millions of theirs?

I have approved a research program to find, if we can, a security shield that will destroy nuclear missiles before they reach their target. It wouldn't kill people; it would destroy weapons. It wouldn't militarize space; it would help demilitarize the arsenals of Earth. It would render nuclear weapons obsolete. We will meet with the Soviets, hoping that we can agree on a way to rid the world of the threat of nuclear destruction. We strive for peace and security, heartened by the changes all around us. Since the turn of the century, the number of democracies in the world has grown fourfold. Human freedom is on the march, and nowhere more so than in our own hemisphere. Freedom is one of the deepest and noblest aspirations of the human spirit. People, worldwide, hunger for the right of self-determination, for those inalienable rights that make for human dignity and progress.

America must remain freedom's staunchest friend, for freedom is our best ally and it is the world's only hope to conquer poverty and preserve peace. Every blow we inflict against poverty will be a blow against its dark allies of oppression and war. Every victory for human freedom will be a victory for world peace.

So, we go forward today, a nation still mighty in its youth and powerful in its purpose. With our alliances strengthened, with our economy leading the world to a new age of economic expansion, we look to a future rich in possibilities. And all of this is because we worked and acted together, not as members of political parties but as Americans.

My friends, we live in a world that's lit by lightning. So much is changing and will change, but so much endures and transcends time.

History is a ribbon, always unfurling. History is a journey. And as we continue our journey, we think of those who traveled before us. We stand again at the steps of this symbol of our democracy—well, we would have been standing at the steps if it hadn't gotten so cold. [Laughter] Now we're standing inside this symbol of our democracy, and we see and hear again the echoes of our past: A general falls to his knees in the hard snow of Valley Forge; a lonely President paces the darkened halls and ponders his struggle to preserve the Union; the men of the Alamo call out encouragement to each other; a settler pushes west and sings a song, and the song echoes out forever and fills the unknowing air. It is the American sound. It is hopeful, big-hearted, idealistic, daring, decent, and fair. That's our heritage, that's our song. We sing it still. For all our problems, our differences, we are together as of old. We raise our voices to the God who is the author of this most tender music. And may He continue to hold us close as we fill the world with our sound—in unity, affection, and love—one people under God, dedicated to the dream of freedom that He has placed in the human heart, called upon now to pass that dream on to a waiting and hopeful world.

God bless you, and God bless America.

Address to the Nation on the *Challenger* Disaster

EDITOR'S NOTE: *This speech was delivered from the Oval Office on January 28, 1986.*

Ladies and gentlemen, I'd planned to speak to you tonight to report on the state of the union, but the events of earlier today have led me to change those plans. Today is a day for mourning and remembering. Nancy and I are pained to the core by the tragedy of the shuttle *Challenger*. We know we share this pain with all of the people of our country. This is truly a national loss.

Nineteen years ago, almost to the day, we lost three astronauts in a terrible accident on the ground. But we've never lost an astronaut in flight; we've never had a tragedy like this. And perhaps we've forgotten the courage it took for the crew of the shuttle; but they, the *Challenger* Seven, were aware of the dangers, but overcame them and did their jobs brilliantly. We mourn seven heroes: Michael Smith, Dick Scobee, Judith Resnik, Ronald McNair, Ellison Onizuka, Gregory Jarvis, and Christa McAuliffe. We mourn their loss as a nation together.

For the families of the seven, we cannot bear, as you do, the full impact of this tragedy. But we feel the loss, and we're thinking about you so very much. Your loved ones were daring and brave, and they had that special grace, that special spirit that says, "Give me a challenge and I'll meet it with joy." They had a hunger to explore the universe and discover its truths. They wished to serve, and they did. They served all of us.

We've grown used to wonders in this century. It's hard to dazzle us. But for twenty-five years the United States space program has been doing just that. We've grown used to the idea of space, and perhaps we forget that we've only just begun. We're still pioneers. They, the members of the *Challenger* crew, were pioneers.

And I want to say something to the school children of America who were watching the live coverage of the shuttle's takeoff. I know it is hard to understand, but sometimes painful things like this happen. It's all part of the process of exploration and discovery. It's all part of taking a chance and expanding man's horizons. The future doesn't belong to the fainthearted; it belongs to the brave. The *Challenger* crew was pulling us into the future, and we'll continue to follow them.

I've always had great faith in and respect for our space program, and what happened today does nothing to diminish it. We don't hide our space program. We don't keep secrets and cover things up. We do it all up front and in public. That's the way freedom is, and we wouldn't change it for a minute. We'll continue our quest in space. There will be more shuttle flights and more shuttle crews and yes, more volunteers, more civilians, more teachers in space. Nothing ends here; our hopes and our journeys continue.

I want to add that I wish I could talk to every man and woman who works for NASA or who worked on this mission and tell them: "Your dedication and professionalism have moved and impressed us for decades. And we know of your anguish. We share it."

There's a coincidence today. On this day 390 years ago, the great explorer Sir Francis Drake died aboard ship off the coast of Panama. In his lifetime the great frontiers were the oceans, and a historian later said, "He lived by the sea, died on it, and was buried in it." Well, today we can say of the *Challenger* crew: Their dedication was, like Drake's, complete.

The crew of the space shuttle *Challenger* honored us by the manner in which they lived their lives. We will never forget them, nor the last time we saw them, this morning, as they prepared for their journey and waved good-bye and "slipped the surly bonds of earth" to "touch the face of God."

Address at the Brandenburg Gate

EDITOR'S NOTE: *This speech was delivered in West Berlin, in the former West Germany, on June 12, 1987. It is best known as the "Berlin Wall" speech.*

Chancellor Kohl, Governing Mayor Diepgen, ladies and gentlemen: Twenty-four years ago, President John F. Kennedy visited Berlin, speaking to the people of this city and the world at the City Hall. Well, since then two other presidents have come, each in his turn, to Berlin. And today I, myself, make my second visit to your city.

We come to Berlin, we American presidents, because it's our duty to speak, in this place, of freedom. But I must confess, we're drawn here by other things as well: by the feeling of history in this city, more than 500 years older than our own nation; by the beauty of the Grunewald and the Tiergarten; most of all, by your courage and determination. Perhaps the composer Paul Lincke understood something about American presidents. You see, like so many presidents before me, I come here today because wherever I go, whatever I do: *Ich hab noch einen Koffer in Berlin.* [I still have a suitcase in Berlin.]

Our gathering today is being broadcast throughout Western Europe and North America. I understand that it is being seen and heard as well in the East. To those listening throughout Eastern Europe, a special word: Although I cannot be with you, I address my remarks to you just as surely as to those standing here before me. For I join you, as I join your fellow countrymen in the West, in this firm, this unalterable belief: *Es gibt nur ein Berlin.* [There is only one Berlin.]

Behind me stands a wall that encircles the free sectors of this city, part of a vast system of barriers that divides the entire continent of Europe. From the Baltic, south, those barriers cut across Germany in a gash of barbed wire, concrete, dog runs, and guard towers. Farther south, there may be no visible, no obvious wall.

But there remain armed guards and checkpoints all the same—still a restriction on the right to travel, still an instrument to impose upon ordinary men and women the will of a totalitarian state. Yet it is here in Berlin where the wall emerges most clearly; here, cutting across your city, where the news photo and the television screen have imprinted this brutal division of a continent upon the mind of the world. Standing before the Brandenburg Gate, every man is a German, separated from his fellow men. Every man is a Berliner, forced to look upon a scar.

President von Weizsacker has said, "The German question is open as long as the Brandenburg Gate is closed." Today I say: As long as the gate is closed, as long as this scar of a wall is permitted to stand, it is not the German question alone that remains open, but the question of freedom for all mankind. Yet I do not come here to lament. For I find in Berlin a message of hope, even in the shadow of this wall, a message of triumph.

In this season of spring in 1945, the people of Berlin emerged from their air-raid shelters to find devastation. Thousands of miles away, the people of the United States reached out to help. And in 1947 Secretary of State—as you've been told—George Marshall announced the creation of what would become known as the Marshall Plan. Speaking precisely 40 years ago this month, he said: "Our policy is directed not against any country or doctrine, but against hunger, poverty, desperation, and chaos."

In the Reichstag a few moments ago, I saw a display commemorating this fortieth anniversary of the Marshall Plan. I was struck by the sign on a burnt-out, gutted structure that was being rebuilt. I understand that Berliners of my own generation can remember seeing signs like it dotted throughout the western sectors of the city. The sign read simply: "The Marshall Plan is helping here to strengthen the free world." A strong, free world in the West, that dream became real. Japan rose from ruin to become an economic giant. Italy, France, Belgium—virtually every nation in Western Europe saw political and economic rebirth; the European Community was founded.

In West Germany and here in Berlin, there took place an economic miracle, the *Wirtschaftswunder*. Adenauer, Erhard, Reuter, and other leaders understood the practical importance of liberty—that just as truth can flourish only when the journalist is given freedom of speech, so prosperity can come about only when the farmer and businessman enjoy economic freedom. The German leaders reduced tariffs, expanded free trade, lowered taxes. From 1950 to 1960 alone, the standard of living in West Germany and Berlin doubled.

Where four decades ago there was rubble, today in West Berlin there is the greatest industrial output of any city in Germany—busy office blocks, fine homes and apartments, proud avenues, and the spreading lawns of parkland. Where a city's culture seemed to have been destroyed, today there are two great universities, orchestras and an opera, countless theaters, and museums. Where there was want, today there's abundance—food, clothing, automobiles—the wonderful goods of the Ku'damm. From devastation, from utter ruin, you Berliners have, in freedom, rebuilt a city that once again ranks as one of the greatest on earth. The Soviets may have had other plans. But my friends, there were a few things the Soviets didn't count on—*Berliner Herz, Berliner Humor, ja, und Berliner Schnauze.* [Berliner heart, Berliner humor, yes, and a Berliner Schnauze.]

In the 1950s, Khrushchev predicted: "We will bury you." But in the West today, we see a free world that has achieved a level of prosperity and well-being unprecedented in all human history. In the Communist world, we see failure, technological backwardness, declining standards of health, even want of the most basic kind—too little food. Even today, the Soviet Union still cannot feed itself. After these four decades, then, there stands before the entire world one great and inescapable conclusion: Freedom leads to prosperity. Freedom replaces the ancient hatreds among the nations with comity and peace. Freedom is the victor.

And now the Soviets themselves may, in a limited way, be coming to understand the importance of freedom. We hear much from Moscow about a new policy of reform and openness. Some political prisoners have been released. Certain foreign news broadcasts are no longer being jammed. Some economic enterprises have been permitted to operate with greater freedom from state control.

Are these the beginnings of profound changes in the Soviet state? Or are they token gestures, intended to raise false hopes in the West, or to strengthen the Soviet system without changing it? We welcome change and openness; for we believe that freedom and security go together, that the advance of human liberty can only strengthen the cause of world peace. There is one sign the Soviets can make that would be unmistakable, that would advance dramatically the cause of freedom and peace.

General Secretary Gorbachev, if you seek peace, if you seek prosperity for the Soviet Union and Eastern Europe, if you seek liberalization: Come here to this gate! Mr. Gorbachev, open this gate! Mr. Gorbachev, tear down this wall!

I understand the fear of war and the pain of division that afflict this continent—and I pledge to you my country's efforts to help overcome these burdens. To be sure, we in the West must resist Soviet expansion. So we must maintain defenses of unassailable strength. Yet we seek peace; so we must strive to reduce arms on both sides.

Beginning ten years ago, the Soviets challenged the Western alliance with a grave new threat, hundreds of new and more deadly SS-20 nuclear missiles, capable of striking every capital in Europe. The Western alliance responded by committing itself to a counter-deployment unless the Soviets agreed to negotiate a better solution; namely, the elimination of such weapons on both sides. For many months, the Soviets refused to bargain in earnestness. As the alliance, in turn, prepared to go forward with its counter-deployment, there were difficult days—days of protests like those during my 1982 visit to this city—and the Soviets later walked away from the table.

But through it all, the alliance held firm. And I invite those who protested then—I invite those who protest today—to mark this fact: Because we remained strong, the Soviets came back to the table. And because we remained strong, today we have within reach the possibility, not merely of limiting the growth of arms, but of eliminating, for the first time, an entire class of nuclear weapons from the face of the earth.

As I speak, NATO ministers are meeting in Iceland to review the progress of our proposals for eliminating these weapons. At the talks in Geneva, we have also proposed deep cuts in strategic offensive weapons. And the Western allies have likewise made far-reaching proposals to reduce the danger of conventional war and to place a total ban on chemical weapons.

While we pursue these arms reductions, I pledge to you that we will maintain the capacity to deter Soviet aggression at any level at which it might occur. And in cooperation with many of our allies, the United States is pursuing the Strategic Defense Initiative—research to base deterrence not on the threat of offensive retaliation, but on defenses that truly defend; on systems, in short, that will not target populations, but shield them. By these means we seek to increase the safety of Europe and all the world. But we must remember a crucial fact: East and West do not mistrust each other because we are armed; we are armed because we mistrust each other. And our differences are not about weapons but about liberty. When President Kennedy spoke at the City Hall those twenty-four years ago, freedom was encircled, Berlin was under siege. And today, despite all the pressures upon this city, Berlin stands secure in its liberty. And freedom itself is transforming the globe.

In the Philippines, in South and Central America, democracy has been given a rebirth. Throughout the Pacific, free markets are working miracle after miracle of economic growth. In the industrialized nations, a technological revolution is taking place—a revolution marked by rapid, dramatic advances in computers and telecommunications.

In Europe, only one nation and those it controls refuse to join the community of freedom. Yet in this age of redoubled economic growth, of information and innovation, the Soviet Union faces a choice: It must make fundamental changes, or it will become obsolete.

Today thus represents a moment of hope. We in the West stand ready to cooperate with the East to promote true openness, to break down barriers that separate people, to create a safe, freer world. And surely there is no better place than Berlin, the meeting place of East and West, to make a start. Free people of Berlin: Today, as in the past, the United States stands for the strict observance and full implementation of all parts of the Four Power Agreement of 1971. Let us use this occasion, the 750th anniversary of this city, to usher in a new era, to seek a still fuller, richer life for the Berlin of the future. Together, let us maintain and develop the ties between the Federal Republic and the Western sectors of Berlin, which is permitted by the 1971 agreement.

And I invite Mr. Gorbachev: Let us work to bring the Eastern and Western parts of the city closer together, so that all the inhabitants of all Berlin can enjoy the benefits that come with life in one of the great cities of the world.

To open Berlin still further to all Europe, East and West, let us expand the vital air access to this city, finding ways of making commercial air service to Berlin more convenient, more comfortable, and more economical. We look to the day when West Berlin can become one of the chief aviation hubs in all central Europe.

With our French and British partners, the United States is prepared to help bring international meetings to Berlin. It would be only fitting for Berlin to serve as the site of United Nations meetings, or world conferences on human rights and arms control or other issues that call for international cooperation.

There is no better way to establish hope for the future than to enlighten young minds, and we would be honored to sponsor summer youth exchanges, cultural events, and other programs for young Berliners from the East. Our French and British friends, I'm certain, will do the same. And it's my hope that an authority can be found in East Berlin to sponsor visits from young people of the Western sectors.

One final proposal, one close to my heart. Sport represents a source of enjoyment and ennoblement, and you may have noted that the Republic of Korea—South Korea—has offered to permit certain events of the 1988 Olympics to take place in the North. International sports competitions of all kinds could take place in both parts of this city. And what better way to demonstrate to the world the openness of this city than to offer in some future year to hold the Olympic games here in Berlin, East and West? In these four decades, as I have said, you Berliners have built a great city. You've done so in spite of threats—the Soviet attempts to impose the East-mark, the blockade. Today the city thrives in spite of the challenges implicit in the very presence of this wall. What keeps you here? Certainly there's a great deal to be said for your fortitude, for your defiant courage. But I believe there's something deeper, something that involves Berlin's whole look and feel and way of life—not mere sentiment. No one could live long in Berlin without being completely disabused of illusions. Something instead, that has seen the difficulties of life in Berlin but chose to accept them, that continues to build this good and proud city in contrast to a surrounding totalitarian presence that refuses to release human energies or aspirations. Something that speaks with a powerful voice of affirmation; that says yes to this city, yes to the future, yes to freedom. In a word, I would submit that what keeps you in Berlin is love—love both profound and abiding.

Perhaps this gets to the root of the matter, to the most fundamental distinction of all between East and West. The totalitarian world produces backwardness because it does such violence to the spirit, thwarting the human impulse to create, to enjoy, to worship. The totalitarian world finds even symbols of love and of worship an affront. Years ago, before the East Germans began rebuilding their churches, they erected a secular structure: the television tower at Alexanderplatz. Virtually ever since, the authorities have been working to correct what they view as the tower's one major flaw, treating the glass sphere at the top with paints and chemicals of every kind. Yet even today when the sun strikes that sphere—that sphere that towers over all Berlin—the light makes the sign of the cross. There in Berlin, like the city itself, symbols of love, symbols of worship, cannot be suppressed.

As I looked out a moment ago from the Reichstag, that embodiment of German unity, I noticed words crudely spray-painted upon the wall, perhaps by a young

Berliner: THIS WALL WILL FALL. BELIEFS BECOME REALITY. Yes, across Europe, this wall will fall. For it cannot withstand faith; it cannot withstand truth. The wall cannot withstand freedom.

And I would like, before I close, to say one word. I have read, and I have been questioned since I've been here about certain demonstrations against my coming. And I would like to say just one thing, and to those who demonstrate so. I wonder if they have ever asked themselves that if they should have the kind of government they apparently seek, no one would ever be able to do what they're doing again.

Thank you and God bless you all.

Farewell Address

EDITOR'S NOTE: *This speech was delivered from the Oval Office on January 11, 1989.*

This is the thirty-fourth time I'll speak to you from the Oval Office and the last. We've been together eight years now, and soon it'll be time for me to go. But before I do, I wanted to share some thoughts, some of which I've been saving for a long time.

It's been the honor of my life to be your president. So many of you have written the past few weeks to say thanks, but I could say as much to you. Nancy and I are grateful for the opportunity you gave us to serve.

One of the things about the presidency is that you're always somewhat apart. You spend a lot of time going by too fast in a car someone else is driving, and seeing the people through tinted glass—the parents holding up a child, and the wave you saw too late and couldn't return. And so many times I wanted to stop and reach out from behind the glass, and connect. Well, maybe I can do a little of that tonight.

People ask how I feel about leaving. And the fact is, "parting is such sweet sorrow." The sweet part is California, and the ranch and freedom. The sorrow—the goodbyes, of course, and leaving this beautiful place.

You know, down the hall and up the stairs from this office is the part of the White House where the president and his family live. There are a few favorite windows I have up there that I like to stand and look out of early in the morning. The view is over the grounds here to the Washington Monument, and then the Mall and the Jefferson Memorial. But on mornings when the humidity is low, you can see past the Jefferson to the river, the Potomac, and the Virginia shore. Someone said that's the view Lincoln had when he saw the smoke rising from the Battle of Bull Run. I see more prosaic things: the grass on the banks, the morning traffic as people make their way to work, now and then a sailboat on the river.

I've been thinking a bit at that window. I've been reflecting on what the past eight years have meant and mean. And the image that comes to mind like a refrain is a nautical one—a small story about a big ship, a refugee, and a sailor. It was back in the early '80s, at the height of the boat people. And the sailor was hard at work on the carrier *Midway*, which was patrolling the South China Sea. The sailor, like most American servicemen, was young, smart, and fiercely observant. The crew spied on the horizon a leaky little boat and crammed inside were refugees from Indochina hoping to get to America. The *Midway* sent a small launch to bring them to the ship and safety. As the refugees made their way through the choppy seas, one spied the sailor on deck and stood up and called out to him. He yelled, "Hello, American sailor. Hello, freedom man."

A small moment with a big meaning, a moment the sailor, who wrote it in a letter, couldn't get out of his mind. And when I saw it, neither could I. Because that's what it was to be an American in the 1980s. We stood, again, for freedom. I know we always have, but in the past few years the world again, and in a way, we ourselves, rediscovered it.

It's been quite a journey this decade, and we held together through some stormy seas. And at the end, together, we are reaching our destination.

The fact is, from Grenada to the Washington and Moscow summits, from the recession of '81 to '82, to the expansion that began in late '82 and continues to this day, we've made a difference. The way I see it, there were two great triumphs, two things that I'm proudest of. One is the economic recovery, in which the people of America created—and filled—19 million new jobs. The other is the recovery of our morale. America is respected again in the world and looked to for leadership.

Something that happened to me a few years ago reflects some of this. It was back in 1981, and I was attending my first big economic summit, which was held that year in Canada. The meeting place rotates among the member countries. The opening meeting was a formal dinner for the heads of government of the seven industrialized nations. Now, I sat there like the new kid in school and listened, and it was all François this and Helmut that. They dropped titles and spoke to one another on a first-name basis. Well, at one point I sort of leaned in and said, "My name's Ron." Well, in that same year, we began the actions we felt would ignite an economic comeback—cut taxes and regulation, started to cut spending. And soon the recovery began.

Two years later another economic summit, with pretty much the same cast. At the big opening meeting we all got together, and all of a sudden, just for a moment, I saw that everyone was just sitting there looking at me. And one of them broke the silence. "Tell us about the American miracle," he said.

Well, back in 1980, when I was running for president, it was all so different. Some pundits said our programs would result in catastrophe. Our views on foreign affairs would cause war. Our plans for the economy would cause inflation to soar and bring about economic collapse. I even remember one highly respected economist saying, back in 1982, that "the engines of economic growth have shut down here, and they're likely to stay that way for years to come." Well, he and the other opinion leaders were wrong. The fact is, what they called "radical" was really "right." What they called "dangerous" was just "desperately needed."

And in all of that time I won a nickname, "The Great Communicator." But I never thought it was my style or the words I used that made a difference: It was the content. I wasn't a great communicator, but I communicated great things, and they didn't spring full bloom from my brow, they came from the heart of a great nation—from our experience, our wisdom, and our belief in principles that have guided us for two centuries. They called it the Reagan Revolution. Well, I'll accept that, but for me it always seemed more like the great rediscovery, a rediscovery of our values and our common sense.

Common sense told us that when you put a big tax on something, the people will produce less of it. So, we cut the people's tax rates, and the people produced more than ever before. The economy bloomed like a plant that had been cut back and could now grow quicker and stronger. Our economic program brought about the longest peacetime expansion in our history: Real family income up, the poverty rate down, entrepreneurship booming, and an explosion in research and new technology. We're exporting more than ever because American industry became more competitive and at the same time, we summoned the national will to knock down protectionist walls abroad instead of erecting them at home. Common sense also told us that to preserve the peace, we'd have to become strong again after years of weakness and confusion. So, we rebuilt our defenses, and this New Year we toasted the new peacefulness around the globe. Not only have the superpowers actually begun to reduce their stockpiles of nuclear weapons—and hope for even more progress is bright—but the regional conflicts that rack the globe are also beginning to cease. The Persian Gulf is no longer a war zone. The Soviets are leaving Afghanistan. The Vietnamese are preparing to pull out of Cambodia, and an American-mediated accord will soon send 50,000 Cuban troops home from Angola.

The lesson of all this was, of course, that because we're a great nation, our challenges seem complex. It will always be this way. But as long as we remember our first principles and believe in ourselves, the future will always be ours. And something else we learned: Once you begin a great movement, there's no telling where it will end. We meant to change a nation, and instead, we changed a world.

Countries across the globe are turning to free markets and free speech and turning away from ideologies of the past. For them, the great rediscovery of the 1980s has been that, lo and behold, the moral way of government is the practical way of government: Democracy, the profoundly good, is also the profoundly productive.

When you've got to the point when you can celebrate the anniversaries of your thirty-ninth birthday, you can sit back sometimes, review your life, and see it flowing before you. For me there was a fork in the river, and it was right in the middle of my life. I never meant to go into politics. It wasn't my intention when I was young. But I was raised to believe you had to pay your way for the blessings bestowed on you. I was happy with my career in the entertainment world, but I ultimately went into politics because I wanted to protect something precious.

Ours was the first revolution in the history of mankind that truly reversed the course of government, and with three little words: "We the people." "We the people" tell the government what to do, it doesn't tell us. "We the people" are the driver, the government is the car. And we decide where it should go, by what route, and how fast. Almost all the world's constitutions are documents in which governments tell the people what their privileges are. Our Constitution is a document in which "We the people" tell the government what it is allowed to do. "We the people" are free. This belief has been the underlying basis for everything I've tried to do these past eight years.

But back in the 1960s, when I began, it seemed to me that we'd begun reversing the order of things—that through more and more rules and regulations and confiscatory taxes, the government was taking more of our money, more of our options, and more of our freedom. I went into politics in part to put up my hand and say, "Stop." I was a citizen politician, and it seemed the right thing for a citizen to do.

I think we have stopped a lot of what needed stopping. And I hope we have once again reminded people that man is not free unless government is limited. There's a clear cause and effect here that is as neat and predictable as a law of physics: As government expands, liberty contracts.

Nothing is less free than pure Communism, and yet we have, the past few years, forged a satisfying new closeness with the Soviet Union. I've been asked if this isn't a gamble, and my answer is no because we're basing our actions not on words but deeds. The detente of the 1970s was based not on actions but promises. They'd promise to treat their own people and the people of the world better. But the gulag was still the gulag, and the state was still expansionist, and they still waged proxy wars in Africa, Asia, and Latin America.

Well, this time, so far, it's different. President Gorbachev has brought about some internal democratic reforms and begun the withdrawal from Afghanistan. He has also freed prisoners whose names I've given him every time we've met.

But life has a way of reminding you of big things through small incidents. Once, during the heady days of the Moscow summit, Nancy and I decided to break off from the entourage one afternoon to visit the shops on Arbat Street—that's a little street just off Moscow's main shopping area. Even though our visit was a surprise, every Russian there immediately recognized us and called out our names and reached for our hands. We were just about swept away by the warmth. You could almost feel the possibilities in all that joy. But within seconds, a KGB detail pushed their way toward us and began pushing and shoving the people in the crowd. It was an interesting moment. It reminded me that while the man on the street in the Soviet Union yearns for peace, the government is Communist. And those who run it are Communists, and that means we and they view such issues as freedom and human rights very differently.

We must keep up our guard, but we must also continue to work together to lessen and eliminate tension and mistrust. My view is that President Gorbachev is different from previous Soviet leaders. I think he knows some of the things wrong with his society and is trying to fix them. We wish him well. And we'll continue to work to make sure that the Soviet Union that eventually emerges from this process is a less threatening one. What it all boils down to is this. I want the new closeness to continue. And it will, as long as we make it clear that we will continue to act in a certain way as long as they continue to act in a helpful manner. If and when they don't, at first pull your punches. If they persist, pull the plug. It's still trust but verify. It's still play, but cut the cards. It's still watch closely. And don't be afraid to see what you see.

I've been asked if I have any regrets. Well, I do. The deficit is one. I've been talking a great deal about that lately, but tonight isn't for arguments. And I'm going to hold my tongue. But an observation: I've had my share of victories in the Congress, but what few people noticed is that I never won anything you didn't win for me. They never saw my troops, they never saw Reagan's regiments, the American people. You won every battle with every call you made and letter you wrote demanding action. Well, action is still needed. If we're to finish the job, Reagan's regiments will have to become the Bush brigades. Soon he'll be the chief, and he'll need you every bit as much as I did. Finally, there is a great tradition of warnings in presidential farewells, and I've got one that's been on my mind for some time. But oddly enough it starts with one of the things I'm proudest of in the past eight years: the resurgence of national pride that I called the new patriotism. This national feeling is good, but it won't count for much, and it won't last unless it's grounded in thoughtfulness and knowledge.

An informed patriotism is what we want. And are we doing a good enough job teaching our children what America is and what she represents in the long history of the world? Those of us who are over 35 or so years of age grew up in a different America. We were taught, very directly, what it means to be an American. And we absorbed, almost in the air, a love of country and an appreciation of its institutions. If you didn't get these things from your family, you got them from the neighborhood, from the father down the street who fought in Korea or the family who lost someone at Anzio. Or you could get a sense of patriotism from school. And if all else failed, you could get a sense of patriotism from popular culture. The movies celebrated democratic values and implicitly reinforced the idea that America was special. TV was like that, too, through the mid–Sixties.

But now, we're about to enter the '90s, and some things have changed. Younger parents aren't sure that an unambivalent appreciation of America is the right thing to teach modern children. And as for those who create the popular culture, well-grounded patriotism is no longer the style. Our spirit is back, but we haven't reinstitutionalized it. We've got to do a better job of getting across that America is freedom—freedom of speech, freedom of religion, freedom of enterprise. And freedom is special and rare. It's fragile; it needs protection.

So, we've got to teach history based not on what's in fashion but what's important: Why the Pilgrims came here, who Jimmy Doolittle was, and what those 30 seconds over Tokyo meant. You know, four years ago on the fortieth anniversary of D-Day, I read a letter from a young woman writing of her late father, who'd fought on Omaha Beach. Her name was Lisa Zanatta Henn, and she said, "We will always remember, we will never forget what the boys of Normandy did." Well, let's help her keep her word. If we forget what we did, we won't know who we are. I'm warning of an eradication of the American memory that could result, ultimately, in an erosion of the American spirit. Let's start with some basics: More attention to American history and a greater emphasis on civic ritual. And let me offer lesson

No. 1 about America: All great change in America begins at the dinner table. So, tomorrow night in the kitchen I hope the talking begins. And children, if your parents haven't been teaching you what it means to be an American, let 'em know and nail 'em on it. That would be a very American thing to do.

And that's about all I have to say tonight. Except for one thng. The past few days when I've been at that window upstairs, I've thought a bit of the "shining city upon a hill." The phrase comes from John Winthrop, who wrote it to describe the America he imagined. What he imagined was important because he was an early Pilgrim, an early freedom man. He journeyed here on what today we'd call a little wooden boat; and like the other Pilgrims, he was looking for a home that would be free.

I've spoken of the shining city all my political life, but I don't know if I ever quite communicated what I saw when I said it. But in my mind it was a tall proud city built on rocks stronger than oceans, wind-swept, God-blessed, and teeming with people of all kinds living in harmony and peace, a city with free ports that hummed with commerce and creativity, and if there had to be city walls, the walls had doors and the doors were open to anyone with the will and the heart to get here. That's how I saw it and see it still.

And how stands the city on this winter night? More prosperous, more secure, and happier than it was eight years ago. But more than that; after 200 years, two centuries, she still stands strong and true on the granite ridge, and her glow has held steady no matter what storm. And she's still a beacon, still a magnet for all who must have freedom, for all the pilgrims from all the lost places who are hurtling through the darkness, toward home.

We've done our part. And as I walk off into the city streets, a final word to the men and women of the Reagan Revolution, the men and women across America who for eight years did the work that brought America back. My friends: We did it. We weren't just marking time. We made a difference. We made the city stronger. We made the city freer, and we left her in good hands. All in all, not bad, not bad at all.

And so, good-bye, God bless you, and God bless the United States of America.

Ronald Reagan's *National Review* Writings and Speeches

The Republican Party and the Conservative Movement

EDITOR'S NOTE: *This article appeared in the December 1, 1964, issue of* National Review.

B y now a new cliché has been added to the time-worn lit, but I know of no other way of comment on the election than to open with the by now familiar—"Well, it's over and we lost."

Yes, we did; we lost a battle in the continuing war for freedom, but our position is not untenable. First of all, there are 26 million of us and we can't be explained away as diehard party faithfuls. We cross party lines in our dedication to a philosophy.

There are no plans for retreating from our present positions, but we can't advance without reinforcements. Are reinforcements available? The answer is an unhesitating—"Yes!" They are to be found in the millions of so-called Republican defectors—those people who didn't really want LBJ, but who were scared of what they thought we represented. Read that sentence very carefully because in my opinion it tells the story. All of the landslide majority did not vote against the conservative philosophy; they voted against a false image our Liberal opponents successfully mounted. Indeed it was a double false image. Not only did they portray us as advancing a kind of radical departure from the status quo, but they took for themselves a costume of comfortable conservatism. Read again their campaign fiction and you will find their normal flamboyant Liberalism hidden under the protective coloration of "the great society," or as Hubert Horatio Humphrey (who can't ask what time it is without conducting a filibuster) put it: "We don't want a planned society—we want society planning."

Unfortunately, human nature resists change and goes over backward to avoid radical change. It's a head shaker, I know, but the whole Liberal apparatus which can be quoted ad infinitum on "the wave of the future, the need for new approaches to old problems, adopt new rules for complex new problems, forget the Constitution," was able to campaign in a last-year's model, singing, "The old songs—the old songs are good enough for me."

Very shortly, though, they'll bring the show into town for a four-year run, complete with a new score—words and music by Reuther, Joseph Rauh, and the "Great Society Chorale." Time then for the music critics—that's us. We must dwell unceasingly on the change of tune. Our job beginning now is not so much to sell conservatism as to prove that our conservatism is in truth what a lot of people thought they were voting for when they fell for the cornpone come-on.

In short—time now for the soft sell to prove our radicalism was an optical illusion. We represent the forgotten American—that simple soul who goes to work, bucks for a raise, takes out insurance, pays for his kids' schooling, contributes to his church and charity and knows there just "ain't no such thing as free lunch."

I'll add a postscript—I don't think we should turn the high command over to leaders who were traitors during the battle just ended.

Reflections on the Failure of Proposition #1: On Spending and the Nature of Government

EDITOR'S NOTE: *This article appeared in the December 7, 1973, issue of* National Review.

The November election results demonstrate once again that the people of America are firmly opposed to the philosophy of bigger and bigger government and higher and higher taxes. In Washington state, an unpopular legislative salary increase was overwhelmingly rescinded along with a proposed state income tax. New York rejected a $3.5 billion transportation bond issue by a 3 to 2 margin. Texas and Rhode Island turned down legislative salary issues, and Kentucky rejected a proposal for annual legislative sessions.

The widespread taxpayers' revolt also was evident in California where almost every local school and salary issue was soundly defeated. One county even voted to reduce the salaries of county supervisors by $2,000. These types of fiscal issues provide the only opportunity citizens have directly to influence government's fiscal policy, to protest their staggering tax burden. They made the most of the opportunity.

The only statewide issue on the ballot in California was Proposition #1, an initiative to reduce state income taxes by 7.5 per cent in 1974. It also offered an historic opportunity permanently to reduce taxes at the state level by placing a constitutional limit on the percentage of the people's income the state could take in taxes. Almost two million people voted for Proposition #1. Yet it failed by 54 per cent to 46 per cent in an election in which about 45 per cent of the state's eligible voters participated.

Why?

Why did a majority of those voting turn down a chance to vote themselves lower taxes and how, in view of the result, can I or anyone include California among those states where the people believe the total structure of government has grown too big and too costly?

The answer to this apparent contradiction can be found in the election returns and in the campaign of distortion and falsehood waged against Proposition #1 by a well-financed, well-organized opposition which desperately avoided debating the central issue: whether taxes are too high now and whether the tax burden should be reduced.

The almost two million citizens who voted Yes on Proposition #1 knew they were voting against higher taxes. Ironically a majority of those who voted No also believed they were voting against higher taxes. The last major public opinion survey on Proposition #1 (the Field poll) revealed that a majority was leaning toward a No vote. But it also disclosed that 69 per cent of those inclined to oppose Proposition #1 did so because they thought it would increase their tax burden.

Even though the measure was specifically designed to reduce state and local taxes and hold them down permanently, many voters were confused by the TV blitz and newspaper advertising campaign staged by the opposition.

In a way, the campaign strategy of the opposition paid the sincerest form of compliment to the goal of Proposition #1: lower taxes.

After repeatedly telling the people that the measure would limit government's ability to spend, that it would force government to hold down future budgets, after appealing to the fear of every possible special interest group, opponents finally keyed their campaign to the false claim that it would increase, not reduce, taxes. They dared no campaign against what they knew would be the ultimate impact of Proposition #1: a realistic and workable limit on the growth of government to keep taxes from going up faster than the incomes of the people who pay them.

The defeat of Proposition #1 can't be translated into a victory for advocates of higher taxes and unlimited government growth. It was a victory for political demagoguery; a triumph for the unsubstantiated charge that sounds convincing in a thirty-second television commercial but which does more to confuse than inform.

It is an axiom of politics that when people are confused about an issue, many will vote "No." They'll opt for the status quo, or not vote at all. On November 6, a sufficient number of California voters were confused enough about the impact of Proposition #1 to turn back possibly the most significant effort made in this century to bring government under some reasonable degree of financial restraint. Some of them voted No; others simply stayed home.

In California, this kind of cynicism could be justified. Too often in the past, the people have been promised tax relief or more efficient government, but only on condition that a particular measure be adopted or that government be given some new power or authority to change a previous budgetary restriction. Somehow the promises never materialize; the tax relief the people are told will be theirs is an illusion. Somehow, after the election, a great emergency is discovered, an unforeseen "need" that requires more revenue and more government, not less.

Since 1967

When I took office in 1967, we discovered that the promise of "no tax increases" could not be carried out. California was virtually insolvent, the precious administration having changed that state's system of budgetary bookkeeping in a way that allowed the spending of 15 months' revenue in twelve months' time, thus avoiding a major tax increase in election year 1966. The state government was spending $1 million a day more than it was collecting.

California, unlike the Federal Government, cannot print more money or pile up deficits. The governor is required to submit a balanced budget, and if any additional taxes are needed to balance revenues with spending, the constitution requires the governor to propose higher taxes.

So our first major lesson in government was painful: for the taxpayers and for us. We had to increase taxes by some $800 million to balance the unbalanced budget we inherited. At the time, I said we hoped this would be temporary, that when we had had time to institute reforms, to curb excessive spending, we would work to reduce the tax burden.

I believed that government could be run more economically using the same sound rules and principles that apply to the running of a business of even a household budget. The phrase "cut, squeeze, and trim" became the watchword of our administration and the result has confirmed my belief that the cost of government can be brought under control.

A task force of businessmen surveyed the state government and recommended almost two thousand steps to streamline it. Every reform, every challenge to the bureaucratic status quo brought screams of outrage, protests, and demonstrations. But contrary to the claims of the protesting groups, these economies did not curtail the state's ability to finance those programs which are properly government's responsibility. It made possible grater state support along with lower taxes.

In seven years we've managed to increase state support for public schools by 92 per cent, although enrollment this year is less than 6 per cent greater than it was in 1967. The state scholarship fund, which helps eligible young people attend college, totals more that $36 million this year, almost eight times higher than when we started.

California has pioneered the concept of treating the mentally ill with an expanded system of community mental health programs. When we started, the budget for community treatment was $18 million. This year it is more than $140 million and California's shift from the "warehousing of the mentally ill" in large state mental institutions has become a model for the nation.

No one objected to increased state support in these areas. But the economies that made them possible were vehemently opposed. When we sought to rebate budget surpluses, there were hysterical charges that fiscal chaos would result.

Before 1967, California homeowners were protesting an excessive property tax burden. But there could be no relief until economy and efficiency in government made relief possible. In 1968, we adopted a $750 homeowners' property tax exemption and this was raised to $1,750 last year (after a four year struggle), along with a revised school formula that rolled back local school tax rates and gave the schools the greatest single-year increase of state support in history. For most taxpayers, this has meant a saving of between $150 and $200 in their annual property tax bill.

We've tried to spread the benefit of more efficient government to all taxpayers. There have been tax credits for tenants (in lieu of property tax reductions); we've cut the business inventory tax in half and reduced bridge tolls eleven times.

Possibly our greatest success was in welfare reform. When I proposed this in 1971 the Democratic majority wouldn't even let me present the plan to a joint session. We were told there would be a $700 million budget deficit. There were dire predictions of fiscal chaos, charges that the state was simply shifting the burden to local government, and massive protests by welfare-rights groups that claimed the elimination of abuses and fraud in welfare would deprive the truly needy of help they should receive.

Welfare Reform

None of these things happened. When we started, California's welfare rolls were growing by forty thousand a month and costs were increasing three times as fast as the normal growth of state revenues (without increased taxes). At last count, there were 386,835 fewer people on welfare than when we began. We've managed to increase benefits for the truly needy by almost 30 per cent and provide cost of living adjustments for senior citizens and the disabled. Now the cost of welfare is between $1 and $2 billion less than the opponents of reform said it would be. These welfare reforms have since been adopted by a number of other states, and several of those capable and dedicated officials who helped achieve them have been recruited by the Nixon Administration to help reform welfare on a national basis.

There was no tax shift to local government. In the year after welfare reform, 42 of California's 58 counties reduced their basic tax rates. This year, 45 reduced their tax rates, most of them for the second year in a row. Instead of a $700 million budget deficit, we had an $800 million surplus this year. As opposed to 1967, we were collecting $1.5 million a day more than we needed and we wanted to return this to the people.

More than a year ago, while we were pushing property tax reform, I organized a task force to survey the entire structure of government, to discover how, without curtailing essential services, the tax burden could be permanently reduced. This task force included some of the nation's most distinguished economists; men like Milton Friedman of the University of Chicago, Peter Drucker of Claremont College, C. Lowell Harriss of Columbia University and the Tax Foundation, Roger Freeman of the Hoover Institution, and James Buchanan of Virginia Polytechnic Institute. Along with members of my own cabinet and staff, this task force worked for more than seven months. They discovered that taxes are the one exception to Newton's law of gravity. They always go up, in good times and bad, in periods of prosperity or recession.

In 1930, the total cost of government (federal, state, and local) was about 15 per cent of the personal income of the United States. This year, in California, the total cost of 44.7 per cent and a fraction less in the rest of the country. Of this total, the state was taking about 8.75 per cent. Along with a return of the $800 million surplus, we asked the task force to devise a way permanently to reduce this percentage, to provide lasting tax relief to the people of California. The result of their work was the tax initiative we offered November 6.

Because of inflation and population growth, we know government revenues must be permitted to expand to meet essential needs. Yet we were convinced that this could be done while gradually reducing the total tax burden. In the past twenty years in California, the cost of state government has been growing 10 per cent a year but the total income of the people has been going up only 7.7 per cent. The result has been periodic tax increases and a steady upward growth in the percentage of the people's income going for taxes.

Proposition #1 Goals

Proposition #1 was designed to bring government spending into balance with the growth of revenues. The key features were:

- An immediate 7.5 per cent state income tax reduction in 1974 income,
- The total and permanent elimination of the state income tax for all families earning $8,000 a year or less, and, most important,
- Adoption of a tax limit by imposing a ceiling on the growth of state revenues, which would slowly reduce the 8.75 per cent of personal income the state takes to a level of around 7 per cent over a period of 15 years.

Unless something is done to check government's unlimited power to tax, California's state budget will grow from this year's $9.3 billion to a staggering $47 billion by 1989.

Still opponents of our proposal charged we sought to impose a fiscal straitjacket on state government that would force massive cuts for education, for mental health, for almost every item in the budget—even though the budget could have doubled in ten years and tripled in 15 under Proposition #1, and funds for education, mental health, and all other essential programs could have grown at the same rate.

At the same time, California could have planned tax reduction on an orderly basis as a part of our budgeting process. In five years, we could have cut income taxes another 24 per cent or trimmed a penny from the sales tax; in ten years the income tax reduction could have been 60 per cent, or we could have cut two cents off the sales tax.

The legislature would have retained its full authority to revise the tax structure, to raise or lower specific taxes, to do anything it does now with one important exception: Any future tax increases above the limit would have to be ratified by the people. This provision, more than any other, generated the greatest alarm in the bureaucracy which knew full well that if the people ever get veto power on excessive spending, the days of spendthrift government are over.

One legislator complained to me that returning the $800 million surplus would be "an unnecessary expenditure of public funds." Another said Proposition #1 would restrict government's ability to redistribute the income of the people through taxes. That was one of the few completely accurate statements the opposition made during the campaign, but they didn't make it outside the legislative chambers.

Almost every group which derives status, income, and power from bigger government joined the ranks of the opposition, including the state teachers association, the state employees association, and welfare groups. Opponents said our tax reduction plan would favor the rich. The truth is: State income taxes would have been permanently eliminated for every family earning less than $8,000 a year. They said it contained no guaranteed tax reduction. Yet the constitutional amendment specifically said that every year for 15 years, the percentage of the people's income that state government could take in taxes must be reduced either through a rebate or reduced taxes. They said it would increase local taxes. The truth is Proposition #1 would have written into the constitution the same tax limits on local government contained in our 1972 property tax reform. This protection would be guaranteed, not simply by a law, but by constitutional language that only the people could change.

One of the most blatant falsehoods of the campaign was a statement that Proposition #1 would have authorized the legislature to permit the levying of local income taxes by any governmental unit "from counties to mosquito abatement districts." The truth is the legislature has that authority now and can do so by a simple majority vote. Proposition #1 would have made it harder; it would have required a two-thirds vote for any local income tax (something we haven't presently in California).

But truth is a fragile weapon in a heated campaign. It can be ignored or twisted and distorted until the average citizen, unfamiliar with government finance, finds himself totally confused. When we proposed the California revenue control and tax reduction program in February, we offered it along with a plan to return our $800 million surplus through another 20 per cent income tax rebate in 1973 and a six months' suspension of one penny of the state sales tax.

The legislative majority, controlled by those who would later lead the fight against Proposition #1, blocked the plan. It didn't get past the first committee, even though constitutional amendments are routinely offered each year and just as routinely put on the ballot. The legislators who fought Proposition #1 could not find time last spring to hold extensive public hearings on the measure. But in the final weeks of the campaign to put the initiative on the ballot, almost every major legislative committee held special hearings to generate publicity for attacks against it.

Because the legislature refused to vote on it, we were forced to gather more than half a million signatures to place it on the ballot. This consumed a great deal of time and part of the financial support we were able to muster in support of the plan.

Yet this part of the campaign made the whole effort worth while. Before the initiative qualified, the Democratic majority had refused to consider returning the $800 million surplus to the taxpayers. But once the people put it on the ballot, our opponents, anxious to make it as financially unattractive as possible, offered a compromise which would return the surplus by a one-time 20 to 35 per cent income tax rebate and suspension of a penny on the sales tax for six months.

Was it politically unwise to accept this? Should we have let the surplus pile up in the treasury and thus enhance the prospects of passing Proposition #1? We considered those arguments and rejected them because our purpose has always been to reduce taxes, not to play political games. The sales tax has gone down one cent for six months, the income tax is eliminated entirely for 1973 for those families earning $8,000 a year or less, and everyone else will receive a 1973 rebate of 20 to 35 per cent.

Qualifying Proposition #1 for the ballot accomplished part of our purpose by forcing the legislature to return the surplus. But the longer-term, permanent tax reduction remains an elusive goal. Naturally, I am disappointed.

It was, and is, a daring idea and I do not regret the exercise. It served a positive purpose. As a result of the battle waged in California, people all over America have been alerted to the staggering burden which taxes impose on our economy and on every family in this country.

The people did not reject the idea of reducing taxes or limiting the size and cost of government to a reasonable level. They endorsed lower taxes in elections through the country, including the confused vote on Proposition #1.

Perhaps we could and should have done more to draw the basic philosophical issues more clearly, to expose the distracting, irrelevant, and confusing play on human fears that was so effectively exploited by the opponents. We've learned again how powerful an array of forces there is at work in America to expand government, to maintain government's unlimited power to tax the people. These forces have seldom been defeated in the past forty years. Because they have prevailed, taxes now cost the typical family more than it spends for food, shelter, and clothing combined. A free economy cannot survive that kind of tax burden indefinitely.

More than a century ago, the French philosopher Frédéric Bastiat wrote: "The state, too, is subject to the Malthusian Law. It tends to expand in proportion to its means of existence and to live beyond its means, and these are, in the last analysis, nothing but the substance of the people. Woe to the people that cannot limit the sphere of action of the state: Freedom, private enterprise, wealth, happiness, independence, personal dignity, all vanish."

That is what will inevitably happen in America unless we act to curb the excessive spending of government. This cannot be done simply by changing the law. The national debt limit was supposed to check deficit financing. But it has been temporarily or permanently increased by changing the law two dozen times in the past twelve years alone.

Only the people, though a constitutional amendment or some other fail-safe method, can limit government's excesses. That's what we tried unsuccessfully to do with Proposition #1 at the state level.

The basic issue remains unchanged. The idea of lower taxes did not fail. There will be other elections, other days. We have suffered a setback. We have lost a battle, but this struggle will go on.

The people will find a way to bring big government under control, to put a reasonable limit on how much of their income government may take in taxes. This idea will become a reality. It must prevail because if it does not, the free society we have known for two hundred years, the ideal of a government by consent of the governed, will simply cease to exist.

Margaret Thatcher and the Revival of the West

EDITOR'S NOTE: *This article appeared in the May 19, 1989, issue of* National Review.

Some years ago, while I was still Governor of California, I was invited to address a large meeting of business leaders in London. Upon arrival I met another American and longtime friend, the late Justin Dart.

The British Conservative Party had just elected Margaret Thatcher Leader of the Party. She was the first woman to hold that position and, if the Conservative Party won an election, she would automatically become Prime Minister. That too would be a first.

Justin knew the Thatchers and arranged a meeting for me with the new Party Leader. I shall be forever grateful. We found there were great areas of agreement on the economy and government's proper role with regard to the private sector. That first meeting in her office lasted the better part of an hour and a half.

That evening I was the guest at a reception. One gentleman had learned of my morning visit and asked: "How did you like our Mrs. Thatcher?" I told him how greatly impressed I was and said, "I believe she'd make a magnificent Prime Minister." He replied, "Oh my dear fellow—a woman Prime Minister?" His tone suggested he believed the idea unthinkable. I couldn't resist reminding him that "England had a Queen named Victoria once who did rather well." He said, "By Jove, I'd forgotten all about that."

Well, Margaret Thatcher has now been Prime Minister of the United Kingdom for ten years. She is respected by all the Heads of State and Government who have had any contact with her. She has brought great improvement in England's economy and returned to private ownership businesses and industries that had been taken over by government. It is a remarkable achievement.

Looking back to the late 1970s, we recall it as a depressing period economically. In America there were gas lines, high inflation, rocketing interest rates, and some fellow talking about a "malaise." The "misery index" reached an all-time high. But the situation in Europe, particularly in Britain, was even worse than our own. What we called the misery index they called "the British disease": a combination of zero growth and high inflation, which in one year reached over 25 per cent. Still worse, after almost forty years of socialism, the habits of inefficiency on the factory floor and lack of enterprise in the executive suite had become deeply ingrained. The British spirit of enterprise, which had transformed half the world in Queen Victoria's day, seemed to have been put to sleep.

Margaret Thatcher changed all that. She demonstrated two great qualities. The first was that she had thought seriously about how to revive the British economy and entered office with a clear set of policies to do so. She brought down inflation by controlling the money supply, and she began removing the controls, subsidies, and regulations that kept business lazy. Her second great quality was the true grit of a true Brit (or perhaps I should say, or a true-blue Brit). We both realized that our policies wouldn't solve such deep-rooted problems overnight. The first effects, in the world recession of 1981–82, were painful. I remember meeting her in Washington at a time when people in both our countries were calling for a change of course. She never wavered. And she was proved right by events. Britain today is enjoying an unprecedented economic recovery—one as long as our own. British businesses, woken from the long sleep of socialism, are our feisty competitors in world markets. And, finally, Margaret Thatcher has begun to dismantle the undergirding of socialism itself by privatizing large nationalized industries like steel and airlines. Just as I would claim modestly that our tax cuts of 1981 have stimulated a wave of tax cutting around the world, so Margaret Thatcher's privatization program has been imitated as far afield as Turkey and New Zealand. We could do with a little more of it in the United States.

As a result, Margaret has brought about a resurgence of those things Great Britain always stood for. Never was this more evident than in her immediate response when Britain's sovereignty over the Falklands was challenged. We used our good offices to try to get a peaceful settlement on which all sides could agree. But it was always clear to me that if such a settlement wasn't available, then the British would fight. I knew Margaret's strength of determination by then; others maybe did not.

That determination was never more valuable than when NATO decided to install intermediate-range missiles in Western Europe to counter the Soviet SS-20s. I had offered the zero-zero option of withdrawing the missiles on both sides. Yet when the Soviets refused and walked out of the Geneva conference, it was *we* who were denounced as warmongers by the so-called peace movement. All over Europe the peace marchers demonstrated to prevent Western missiles from being installed for their defense, but they were silent about the Soviet missiles targeted against them! Again, in the face of these demonstrations, Margaret never wavered. Western Europe stood firm. We installed the missiles—and the Soviets, under the new leadership of Mikhail Gorbachev, returned to the bargaining table three years later to negotiate the INF Treaty withdrawing both sets of missiles. I believe that historians will see that as one of the great turning-points of the postwar world. It could not have been achieved without the endurance and courage of leaders like Margaret Thatcher. Once again the people of the "right little, tight little isle" are living those words: *"There'll always be an England / And England shall be free, / If England means as much to you / As England means to me."*

With all of her strength, Margaret Thatcher still is a lady. There is an attractive humanness to her. Our annual "Economic Summits" are meetings of the seven Heads of Government—the United Kingdom, Canada, France, Italy, West Germany, Japan, and the United States. The meetings rotate, with each member country hosting the Summit in turn. The Head of Government of the host country chairs the meeting.

A few years ago, when the Summit was in England with Margaret presiding, a Head of Government who is no longer holding office (and I won't name him) launched a veritable tirade at the chair. He claimed that the meeting was not being run in a democratic manner, that the chair was dictatorial, etc. He gave no illustrations or examples to support these charges. Margaret let him have his say and then continued with the business before the meeting. She remained cool and made no effort to respond to the charges.

When the meeting ended I caught up with Margaret. I told her what I thought of the charges he had made, that he was really out of line and had no business or right to do what he'd done. Her quiet response was. "Women know when men are being childish."

Now I find that I've been using Margaret's first name. I think I should explain that first names are the rule in our Economic Summits. It's amazing the difference it makes in sessions of this kind to be on a first-name basis rather than using formal titles. I have reason to believe this was brought about by Prime Minister Thatcher.

Personal relations matter more in international politics than the historians would have us believe. Of course, nations will follow their overriding interest on the great issues regardless, but there are many important occasions when the trust built up over several years of contacts makes a real difference to how things turn out. I found it personally advantageous to have a friend as well as an ally in Downing Street. Margaret was always frank and forthright in her dealings with us. Generally, she and I agreed with each other. I was grateful to have her moral and material backing when we decided that we would have to bomb terrorist targets in Libya in order to protect our forces in Europe and Americans around the world against state-sponsored terrorism. Whether we agreed or not, however, I knew that her advice came from someone who was a friend of the American people and who shared the same basic outlook. We place the same high value on freedom. We were fortunate in that, sharing the same outlook, we were elected at a time when opportunities were opening up for extending our own freedom to other countries—to many Third World countries, to Afghanistan, to Eastern Europe, to the Soviet Union itself.

When it was our turn to host the Summit, we decided to hold the meetings in Williamsburg, Virginia. This is a city that has been preserved as it was when Virginia was a British colony. It has become a historical showplace.

Customarily the Economic Summits open with an informal dinner for just the seven members plus the representative of the European Community. We held this dinner in what had been the British Governor General's home. Before general conversation started, I was going to address Margaret and say, "Margaret, if one of your predecessors had been a little more clever, you would have been the hostess at this meeting." Well, I started, "Margaret, if one of your predecessors had been a little more clever"—and that's as far as I got. She quietly interrupted me and said, "Yes, I know, I would have been hosting this gathering."

Margaret Thatcher—this great lady has not only served her country well, she has served the free world well. She is truly a great statesman. So much so that I'll correct what I just said: She is a great *stateswoman* holding her own among all the statesmen of the world.

"My Favorite Magazine"

EDITOR'S NOTE: *This speech was delivered at a* National Review *dinner at the Madison Hotel on February 21, 1983. Prior to the President's remarks, William F. Buckley Jr., the magazine's editor, had introduced the magazine's Washington editor, John McLaughlin, in Latin.*

I feel dutybound to prove that I, too, am a linguist with all of the languages that have been up here. So, in the language of my forefathers, "I'll have another drink of that fine Irish whiskey." [Laughter]

You know, there was a lot of talk when I first started to run for office about what was someone that had been in show business in Hollywood doing running for office. Well, you just saw a great example of how it pays off. [Laughter] In Hollywood on the set, the floor is laced with chalk marks so the actors will know where they're to arrive at and stand and so forth for various scenes. Well, you saw how effectively I've managed this up here. [Laughter]

Well, John McLaughlin, I thank you. He's your *NR*'s man in Washington. It's a pleasure to be here and see that you're looking so well. I can't tell you how happy I am to find out there really is life after death for former White House speechwriters. [Laughter]

Today we celebrate Washington's birthday, and I can't think of a more appropriate occasion to celebrate *National Review*'s heightened profile in the Nation's Capital; for if George Washington was the father of his country, *NR* has been the father of American conservative intellectual movement. And it's only fitting that at a time when conservative issues and philosophy are finally setting the terms of debate in the halls of government that *NR* has come to Washington in a big way.

I see a lot of friends in this room tonight, and I hope I'll have a chance to say a personal hello to many of you before I leave. But before I go any further, I just have to say a few words about three people who are very special to me and to *NR*.

Ladies first. There's a person here tonight who is respected and loved by everyone who's ever had any dealings with *National Review*. Her official title: managing editor. But I always think of Priscilla Buckley—and this is with all due respect to Marlon Brando—as the godmother of *National Review*. [Laughter] Priscilla, I hope we can count on you to keep the "East 35th Street irregulars" in fighting trim for many more years to come.

And then there's an old friend of mine, Bill Rusher. When he's not toying with the idea of a third party, he's always been tireless and a very valued support. [Laughter] I think that all of us who follow his column and who remember his many appearances on *The Advocates* appreciate how much the conservative cause owes to the energetic and articulate champion of the principles that we believe in so deeply. Bill, congratulations on your fine work as a conservative leader and your outstanding service as *NR*'s publisher.

Finally, I want to say just a word or two about your editor, Bill Buckley. And unlike Bill, I'll try to keep my words to single syllables, or at the worst, only two. [Laughter] You know, I've often thought when I've been faced with memorandums from deep in the bowels of the bureaucracy what I wouldn't give to have Bill as an interpreter. [Laughter]

You know, a fellow comes in, stands in front of your desk, hands you a memorandum, and he stays and waits there while you read it. And so you read: "Action-oriented orchestration, innovation, inputs generated by escalation of meaningful, indigenous decision-making dialog, focusing on multilinked problem complexes, can maximize the vital thrust toward nonalienated and viable urban infrastructure." [Laughter] I take a chance and say, "Let's try busing." [Laughter] And if he walks away, I know I guessed right. [Laughter]

But I think you know that *National Review* is my favorite magazine. I've even paid the ultimate compliment of commandeering two of your longtime contributors, Aram Bakshian and Tony Dolan, on our White House staff. *NR* isn't a favorite only because it's fought the good fight so long and so well, although that would be reason enough. It's my favorite because it's splendidly written, brilliantly edited, and a pleasure to read. In fact, I honestly believe even if I were to suffer from mental illness or convert to liberalism for some other reason—[laughter]—*NR* would still be my favorite magazine because of its wit and its charm and intellectual quality of its contents.

There's a problem, though, Bill, that I think you should know about. It's all that talk about your being aloof and insensitive and an out-of-touch editor. People are saying that you spend too much time away from New York. They're also saying you're being pushed around by your staff. [Laughter] And I understand there's a new button on the market: "Let Buckley be Buckley." [Laughter] Some people even question whether you're going to seek another term. [Laughter]

Now, of course, I don't believe a word of this myself. But let me give you one piece of friendly advice. Bill, I think it would be a good idea for you to make a definite statement about your intentions sometime before Labor Day. [Laughter]

But, this is a party, not a political rally. And I think I addressed most of the substantive issues on everyone's mind last Friday at the Conservative Political Action Conference. By the way, has anyone seen any of the poll results from this year's conference?

Let me just close by saying a heartfelt thank you to *National Review* for all you've done for the values we share and for sending reinforcements to Washington at just the right moment. I know that your heightened presence here will be an aid and inspiration to all of us in the movement in the years ahead. And just by being here you help to make the Nation's Capital a little less of a puzzle palace and a little more like our town.

So, thank you. God bless you all.

The Defense of Freedom and the Metaphysics of Fun

EDITOR'S NOTE: *This speech was delivered by President Ronald Reagan at National Review's 30th anniversary dinner in New York City on December 5, 1985.*

Ladies and gentlemen, I mean it literally when I say it is a delight to be here tonight. The editors, associates, and friends of *National Review* are celebrated not just for skillful argument and sound polemics, but for the wit, warmth—even merriment—of their gatherings.

I will admit that like most of his friends, I wonder if Bill Buckley's well-known regard for fun doesn't get a little out of hand. A couple of years ago, I made a congratulatory phone call to an anniversary party for Bill Buckley's telephone show. Now, as you know, *Firing Line* attracts many important guests, some of whom, however, are also very, very controversial. No sooner had I picked up the phone and said, "Hello," than Bill's voice came ringing through: "Mr. President, I'm standing here with Gordon Liddy on my right and Howard Hunt on my left, and we await your orders, sir."

And once when Bill was asked what job he wanted in the Administration of his friend the President, he replied in his typically retiring and deferential way: "Ventriloquist."

But when you think about it, the word "fun" really is important to the meaning of *National Review* and the conservative movement it fostered, a word, as Bill Buckley might put it, that is "transcendentally freighted, resonant with metaphysical meaning and overtone." By which he would mean (I got used to interpreting in Geneva—so with your permission, Bill) it is a word not very popular in our century. Especially those who preach the supremacy of the state, who think they can remake man and society in the image of a brave new world. For these serious people, earthly paradise is always just around the corner, and evenings like these are bourgeois distractions. Laughter itself is suspect; and even fun is an act of subversion. It is purportedly why Lenin refused to listen to music.

But it is also why all of us are here tonight—to celebrate thirty years of witty, civilized pages from our beloved *National Review* and the damage, the terminal damage, those pages have done to modern statism and its unrelenting grimness.

Since its beginning in 1955, *National Review* has argued that politics and state power—like all human endeavors—have their limitations, and that acknowledging those limitations is the beginning of political—even earthly—wisdom. It really is an acknowledgment that God means for us—at least sometimes—to take life as it comes: to woo, to laugh, to love, and to make room, as you have tonight and throughout the thirty-year life span of *National Review*, for fun.

If any of you doubt the impact of *National Review*'s verve and attractiveness, take a look around you this evening. The man standing before you was a Democrat when he picked up his first issue in a plain brown wrapper; and even now, as an occupant of public housing, he awaits as anxiously as ever his biweekly edition—without the wrapper. Over here is the Director of the Central Intelligence Agency, who, besides running a successful presidential campaign in 1980, is the same New York lawyer who drew up the incorporation papers for *National Review*. Or ask any of the young leaders in the media, academia, or government here tonight to name the principal intellectual influence in their formative years. On this point, I can assure you: *National Review* is to the offices of the West Wing of the White House what *People* is to your dentist's waiting room.

So in standing up, then, for what Russell Kirk might call the metaphysics of fun, I think history will show *National Review* also launched a spirited and decisive defense of freedom. *NR* taught several generations of conservatives that it is this recognition of a higher order that enables the individual to stand against the massed power of the modern state and say: No, there is more to life than your budget and bureaus, your camps and constraints.

All of this was against the trend of the time and drew its share of disapproving stares. Just when political commentary had become so ponderous, along comes this spirited, captivating little journal pledging in the now familiar words of its first issue: "It stands athwart history, yelling, Stop . . ."

Let me now simply and briefly do what I came here to do tonight, and that is, as President of the United States, to salute the editors, associates, and friends of *National Review*; and on behalf of America, the Free World—and especially the not-so-free world—to thank each one of you for your extraordinary work, your sacrifice, your daring devotion.

I want to assure you tonight: You didn't just part the Red Sea—you rolled it back, dried it up, and left exposed, for all the world to see, the naked desert that is statism. And then, as if that weren't enough, you gave to the world something different, something in its weariness it desperately needed, the sound of laughter and the sight of the rich, green uplands of freedom.

But if tonight we celebrate *National Review* as a force for change of hurricane force, we also note tonight that the eye of the hurricane is retiring. Priscilla Buckley is known for her adventurous spirit; nowhere has that spirit been better evidenced than in her willingness to be at the center for almost thirty years of the whirlwind at 150 East 35th Street. That she has come through all this with a reputation unchallenged for journalistic skill and professionalism, as well as the sweetest disposition on the Eastern Seaboard, is testimony to her work and to her life. Tonight, Priscilla, America and its President and all of us honor you and thank you.

Now, ladies and gentlemen, recently a message from Bill Buckley was sent through the White House staff about my remarks here—and I quote—"Bill says this is the thirtieth, and you should say something important like announcing a new Marshall Plan."

Well, we shall see about a Marshall Plan; but for the moment, perhaps a few concluding remarks on the future of this journal and the conservative movement it fostered are in order. I think most of you are aware that there is now in the nation's capital a consensus on the need for reducing marginal tax rates—even the Ways and Means Committee proposal, though it is not the bill we asked for, agrees that such high rates are an obstacle to economic growth and initiative.

On another front, not only has the House of Representatives agreed to humanitarian assistance to the Nicaraguan freedom-fighters, it has lifted, largely on its own accord, the ban against helping anti–Communist insurgencies in Africa. I think you will agree that it is a long way to travel: from "Dear Comandante" to spontaneous repeal of the Clark Amendment.

Believe me, there were few articles of faith in the liberal credo more fervently held than: First, a belief in government as the great redistributors of income through punitive tax rates; and second, an adherence to post-Vietnam isolationism and the adolescent notion that anyone brandishing a rifle, wearing green fatigues, and calling himself a socialist revolutionary was worthy of American sympathy and support.

Now the question I want to ask you is this: If at *National Review*'s last anniversary dinner someone had told you that in a little over four years tax rates could be cut from 70 per cent to nearly half of that and that we would be not only helping a growing anti–Communist insurgency in Central America but lifting the prohibition against such assistance in Angola—and that in both cases these changes would be effected by a House of Representatives supposedly dominated by liberal Democrats—wouldn't you have tagged him or her a hopeless optimist?

Yet it is all happening and will continue to happen. And for this reason: We have reached that point which military historians single out as critical to the outcome of any battle; the point at which one side begins to display a decisive will to win, a kind of psychological dominance over the consciousness of the other. The point at which the adversary is more preoccupied with countering our next tactical move than with changing a strategic picture that he does not even realize is shifting dangerously against him. How many Northern generals, preoccupied, in General McClellan's words, with what "Bobby Lee will do next," came to naught because they failed to do what common sense or their own strategic plan dictated? As Yogi Berra said once: "90 per cent of this game is half mental."

And today, the adversaries of conservatives seem sometimes more concerned with our agenda than we are ourselves. It is the kind of slide that, once it begins, is almost impossible to halt. Already some young members of the other party have had to face charges that they are "me-too" Democrats—what a refreshing ring that has to those of us who remember how a similar expression was used in the Fifties.

And I wonder if the day is not too far off when some Democratic presidential candidate sweeps the primaries by declaring, "We are all conservatives now." And then proudly boasts of his subscription to *National Review*. Again, without the wrapper.

Ladies and gentlemen, the strategic situation internationally is also changing, and decisively so. While democracies are growing in economic strength, the totalitarian world is in decay and disarray. We see that Marx was right: The economic order is making demands on the political order. But he was wrong about where it would happen. China is only the most remarkable and most recent example. Add to this the growth in democratic institutions around the world. In Asia, the realization that personal freedom means economic growth has made a number of small nations models of economic progress. Even Europe, the birthplace of socialism, is now catching up with the Laffer curve. And it is especially in Europe that we see one of the most important changes I believe this journal has helped to spark: Statism has lost the intellectuals.

So there is, after all, a Marshall Plan to announce here this evening—but not, this time, one confined to Europe or limited to monetary aid. A Marshall Plan of mind and heart and spirit—a Marshall Plan of ideas. Ideas that *National Review* first promoted: the worth of the individual, the value of personal freedom, the efficacy of the free market, the wisdom of representative, constitutional government, and the rule of law under God.

We know that the permanent things this journal stands for, if given only the slightest bit of breathing space, must and will triumph; it is this spark of life that this journal and the conservative movement have provided.

When he left Communism for the Western side, one editor of the magazine said he understood his defection meant he was joining the losers. I can think of no better way to pay tribute to his memory—and frankly nothing he would have liked better—than to say: We can affirm here tonight that Whittaker Chambers was wrong. That civilization will triumph. That freedom is the winning side.

One final note: I think eventually the pundits and analysts are going to catch on to the enormous force and deep roots of the conservative movement. Some of them even seem to have finally realized that I actually am one and that I mean it. And when that happens, they are going to realize something not only about this journal, but about its founder and editor: that Bill Buckley is perhaps the most influential journalist and intellectual in our era—that he changed our country, indeed our century.

While I am quite certain that this is what history will say, I also know you and I would add something, because you and I remember a time of the forest primeval, a time when nightmare and danger reigned and only the knights of darkness prevailed; when conservatives seemed without a champion in the critical battle of style and content. And then, suddenly riding up through the mists, came our clipboard-bearing Galahad; ready to take on any challengers in the critical battle of point and counterpoint. And, with grace and humor and passion, to raise a standard to which patriots and lovers of freedom could repair.

Like myself, many of you have known and been grateful for Bill's friendship—like everything else he does, he has made of that too an art form.

So, Bill, one last word to you. We thank you for your friendship. You are, of course, a great man. And so we thank you also for *National Review*, for setting loose so much good in the world. And, Bill—thanks, too, for all the fun.

God bless you.

The Record: Domestic and Economic Issues, and Campaigns

Ronald Reagan: A Light in the West

By Farley Clinton

EDITOR'S NOTE: *This article appeared in the June 28, 1966, issue of* National Review *following Mr. Reagan's victory in the California Republican gubernatorial primary.*

The Reagan landslide in California is certainly the most cheerful thing that conservatives, or Republicans, or believers in the two-party system, have seen for a very long time. At this juncture it looks as if he may well be the next governor of California.

"The Republican Party has conclusively shown its preference for the philosophy of Mr. Ronald Reagan over my own belief," the Liberal George Christopher remarked, in conceding the Republican nomination.

This significant admission was wrung from Christopher, not by the fact of Reagan's victory, which all the polls predicted, but the overpowering size of it. In Los Angeles County, where live three million of the state's eight million voters, there was a completely unexpected rush to the polls: there was wider interest, and participation, in this primary than any other election since Eisenhower's, in 1952. And Los Angeles County came on strong for Ronald Reagan, choosing him over Christopher by about 4–1.

It is noteworthy that all the polls have been predicting for some time that either Reagan or Christopher would defeat Brown in November. But nobody dared say that Brown's opponent, Los Angeles Mayor Sam Yorty (who ran on a straight, simple platform: "Turn Brown out!") could count on more than 20 per cent of the Democratic vote. He actually picked up about 40 per cent of the Democratic vote throughout the state.

Reagan's most impressive showing was that he actually drew more votes in the Republican primary (in which there are barely 3 million Californians registered) than Brown did in the Democratic primary (in which about 4.5 million, or half again as many people, are registered). In other words, Reagan had decidedly the largest popular vote of all gubernatorial candidates in either party; half the registered Republicans in the state went out to vote for him; not much more than a quarter of the registered Democrats paid that compliment to Mr. Brown.

And if it seems optimistic to count on a Reagan victory in November, even after this encouragement, let's look at it the other way and imagine what would be necessary for Reagan to be defeated. One of California's top Democrats, state controller Alan Cranston, has been trying to imagine that, and this is what he has imagined:

"I think virtually all the votes that went to Yorty in the primary cannot go to Reagan and will go to Brown in November. I think many moderate Republican votes cast for Christopher cannot go to Reagan and will go to Brown in November."

Brown's Long Hot Summer

One must point out that, since Reagan is ahead in the popular vote to start out with, if he holds the votes cast for him in the primary, he could afford to lose half the Yorty and Christopher votes to Brown, and still win; but will he lose them? Will Brown gain more than half the Yorty votes, which were cast as a gesture of open rebellion against him, and more than half the Christopher votes, some of which certainly come from ardent Liberals, but many of which simply represent the discipline and loyalty of the Northern California Republican Organization, which was politically indebted to Christopher? Everybody assumes (except Mr. Alan Cranston) that the logical direction for many of the Yorty and most of the Christopher people to move is into the Reagan camp.

As the votes mounted up through the evening of June 7, Governor Brown was heard to mutter: "It's going to be a long, hot summer." And indeed through the evening and the next morning, Mayor Yorty absolutely refused to concede the Governor's re-nomination by the Democratic Party, and he seemed to hint that he would not support Brown—just as he refused in 1960 to support Kennedy, and so contributed to Nixon's victory in California.

To the end the rambunctious mayor bluntly refused to admit defeat. "Defeat? Defeat? This wasn't a defeat, it was quite a victory," he cried. Would he support Brown? "I'll decide that later. I'll certainly never support some of the groups that support Brown."

As for Reagan, Yorty said: "I always felt that Reagan was the only candidate Brown could possibly beat. But in view of his tremendous showing, which I think was quite a surprise, I think he has a very good chance." It does not seem very likely, therefore, that Brown can depend on retrieving the 900,000 votes he lost to Yorty in the primary. And there are two factors which perhaps diminish the likelihood of that development even further.

First, many of Yorty's followers are really Republicans anyway, whom Yorty persuaded to re-register as Democrats so that they could support him. Secondly, Mr. Yorty is a man of burning ambition which he makes no effort to conceal. Many observers (check the *New York Times* on this, for example) felt that his entrance into the governors' primary was merely a preliminary to a more serious race for the Senate in 1968. Mr. Brown took the view, as a rule, that it was more dignified not to notice Yorty's savage personal attacks; when he did once briefly admit knowing of Yorty's crusade against him, he called Yorty a "paranoid." (Yorty wore this like a badge of honor. "He'll say anything," he cried on one of his TV shows. "The other day he got off a plane and he called me a paranoid.") Yorty had a few names for Brown, too.

It would seem likely, therefore, that Brown-Yorty relations have deteriorated beyond any hope of their being patched up. And it must strike Mr. Yorty, who is certainly no fool, that it cannot be too healthy for his political future in the Democratic Party in California if Brown does win re-election. Far from seeking any help from these quarters, he has spent his days and nights in denouncing the "Brown machine" and working for its downfall, and it is difficult to see what possible advantage he could gain by helping Brown or the Democratic Party in November.

Perhaps the most striking achievement of Ronald Reagan's is that he has unified the Republican Party of California behind him. He has done this without vindictiveness, without malice, without dogmatic insistence on any specific proposals. He has harped on the necessity for party unity, and he has been listened to in some quarters where many of his conservative ideas find little favor.

He did not betray conservatism or deny it, but he brought into its service some of the pragmatic sense, the charm, and the eloquence which in recent years articulate Irishmen have usually expended upon the causes of the political Left. In doing so, he has destroyed the idea that conservatism is doomed in the 1960s.

It was a quiet, non-controversial campaign. Reagan was seldom on television—seldom, at least, compared to Mr. Yorty and Mr. George Christopher—and his appearances were brief, dynamic, and confident, and his words conciliatory. "We assure you all that we have no quarrel with the humanitarian goals of the Great Society," he told the Californian public. "But we believe in government of, and by, as well as *for* the people." It was all in that vein. "Our organization has crossed all factional lines." And it did; he worked with Nixon and Rockefeller men as much as, or more than, the hard core of Goldwater supporters; he will work as graciously and cheerfully as possible with all the Christopher people, and all the Democrats, who jump on the bandwagon.

Consequently, he can reply calmly to Brown's rather desperate charges that he is an extremist. It must be admitted that the Goldwater victory in the California primary of 1964 left scars behind it, and a divided party. But Reagan's victory, even with the total loss of Christopher's city, San Francisco, and its suburbs, was not 51 per cent but 67 per cent, statewide; and the voters went out in larger numbers than in 1964. "Evidently," says Reagan, "the percentage of the Republican Party that has made this decision must [like our organization] cross all factional lines."

Reagan was helped by the fact that his opponent in the primary was not much of an opponent. He was Mr. George Christopher, a Greek from San Francisco, a very nice man, a businessman (dairies), chubby, irrelevant, totally unattractive to Southern California. He used to be mayor of the strange and charming seaport of San Francisco, most untypical of American cities. (Los Angeles is the most typical, the characteristic American city.) He had made two previous, painfully sincere tries for statewide offices; in both races he was loyally supported by San Francisco, and annihilated by the eight teeming counties (Los Angeles, San Diego, San Bernardino, Imperial, Santa Barbara, Orange, Ventura, and Riverside) which are known specifically as "Southern California."

In the election this June the familiar pattern was repeated. Christopher lost almost every county in the state from top to bottom, from Oregon to Mexico, except San Francisco and its immediate suburbs, Marin and San Mateo counties. In these three areas he defeated Reagan; he was 7,000 votes ahead in Marin, 15,000 votes ahead in San Mateo, 30,000 votes ahead in San Francisco. And that was it. Reagan ran very well everywhere else, sometimes by as much as 2–1. And in the heavily populated South the eight counties came through very nicely: Reagan led by 5–1 in Imperial County (that's 87 per cent of the vote), 3–1 in Riverside, 3–1 in San Diego, 4–1 in Orange, 2–1 in Santa Barbara, 4–1 in Ventura, 4–1 in San Bernardino, and very nearly 4–1 in Los Angeles, where essentially he picked up his tremendous statewide lead. He ran 654,000 votes *ahead* of Christopher in Southern California.

In the Democratic race. Brown managed to carry almost every county (not Orange County, of course) but his only really dramatic victories over Yorty were in— San Francisco, San Mateo, and Marin counties. There are some indications, therefore, that the election will simply be a North-South fight—or, rather, the San Francisco urban area against the rest of the state. Obviously anti-Brown feeling is strong not only in Southern California but in all parts of the state except San Francisco.

In preferring Brown and Christopher to Yorty and Reagan, San Francisco chose two Northern Californians over two Southern Californians. Christopher of course did not run as a man from the North, nor did he run as a Liberal; he didn't dare emphasize either of these things in Southern California. He appealed to the widespread discontent with Brown, to the Liberal belief that a strong conservative couldn't win a decisive vote, and to the moral certainty that any Republican without some great disadvantage (such as Reagan's conservatism was thought to be) would easily rouse the populace to turn Brown out.

Christopher's line ran thus: I am the only Republican candidate who can win in November and really defeat Brown. Hence a vote for Reagan is a wasted vote. Very few voters believed that; the measure of the general dissatisfaction with Governor Brown is really to be found in the 2 million votes divided between Yorty and Reagan rather than in the 600,000 secured by Christopher.

But oddly enough Governor Brown (who has a thoroughly conventional mind, and allowed himself to be governed by the newspaper polls which told him, for example, not to worry about Yorty) believed Christopher's argument. Accordingly, his aides (Brown's) drew the attention of columnist Drew Pearson to Mr. Christopher's arrest, 28 years ago, on misdemeanor charges concerning violation of the milk-price laws by his dairies.

Mr. Christopher was highly incensed and spoke his mind about Mr. Drew Pearson; leading to a number of libel actions all round. In the latest of these to be widely publicized, Christopher is counter-suing Pearson (who has for some reason, sued him) and is demanding $6 million.

It is universally admitted that the cunning of Brown's political hacks is entirely responsible for this shabby business. They were not cunning enough to have any idea of the enormous groundswell which had already gathered around Reagan, and they were anxious that he should win since (the polls said) he was less certain of beating Brown than Christopher. They did manage to send Christopher into a complete tailspin. He spent the last weeks of the campaign appearing on television to deny ill the charges against him—without stating what they were, so that he gave an impression that they were more serious and disturbing than was the case. Christopher soon lost heart completely; conceded the election, almost before the returns were in; announced his withdrawal from public life; and refused to speak to the press again.

All this has helped Reagan in a way no one had expected. His campaign has revealed his fundamental and convinced conservatism mainly by its strongly moralistic tone and the impression of sincerity and simplicity which he communicates even to his most convinced opponents.

Brown's best hope must come from the people who didn't vote at all on June 7. There may well be many of these, who took his election for granted and didn't bother to vote. Some observers will go so far as to say that his entire strength now lies with the Negroes and the unions—classes of voters who may have been underrepresented in the primary. There is, these people will tell you, simply no one at all in the middle and upper classes of Southern California who isn't thoroughly tired of Pat Brown and anxious to see the last of him. This may be so. It is certainly true that Mayor Yorty's votes came entirely from white people; this was only to be expected, after he had been loud, violent, and tedious in insisting that all the racial trouble which has disturbed Los Angeles is the result of agitation by Communists. I do not think it is fair to say that Yorty's vote was entirely, or primarily, an anti-Negro vote. He made many, many other points in the course of his week-long saturation of the air waves. But it is noteworthy that, after the entire Negro vote had been driven by force into Brown's arms, through Yorty's harangues, the Governor was still unable to do any better than he did. There cannot have been many white people in Los Angeles County who voted for him. Certainly they were few, compared to those who voted for anybody else, i.e., Yorty. Yorty may be said, not so much to defend conservative ideas, as (unconsciously) to caricature them. But nobody, except the Negroes whom he foolishly insulted, really minded. Reagan is not foolish, and he will not insult them; so why should they necessarily object to Reagan?

It's Paradise

Ideals of social protest, or of utopianism, were conceived in Berlin, or London, or in the rainy autumn of Paris. They have been transplanted to chilly Boston and its suburbs with some success. But they never existed in Naples; and they do not survive here, on the beaches, or under the orange trees. Southern California, to its inhabitants, is Paradise already; and no idea is more repugnant to them than change; change in any form, to Right or Left, for any reason. Even the French Communists do not try to make converts among the crowds at St. Tropez or Nice, and if they came to Los Angeles they would be similarly overwhelmed by the spirit of the place. Most people who have come to live in Los Angeles were fairly well off before they came. When they came, they conceived an affection and a sort of passion for the place that they never felt for Iowa or Kansas; and they forgot their troubles and their loyalties even if they came from New York, even if they were poor, or Catholic, or Jewish, or for some other reason bound by heredity and up-bringing to the Democratic Party. The social minorities, somewhat disdained by America as a whole, somewhat alienated, potentially radical, which have since the 1890s been bound together in the East and Midwest by the Democratic Party, simply do not exist here. There is no role for a political party with such preoccupations, and in fact all difference between the parties, all sense of loyalty to one party rather than another, has very largely disappeared.

One would expect, in the light of what we hear today about the threat of too rapid a growth of population, that Los Angeles and its environs would have sunk into the depths of poverty and malnutrition. For the population has increased by 7,000 per cent in sixty years, a city of 100,000 people growing to one of 7-million. But the opposite has happened. Everybody is richer than he ever was before and the sudden wealth of a lot of newcomers, in a very mild but sunny country, has created a society of almost complete social democracy. For this reason, also, there is simply no role for a strong party which dallies with socialist nostrums. It is true that the state government has gone very far indeed along a socialist path; but this only cuts off demand and desire for such things—reformers whose objects have been achieved have no place to go—and makes it still harder for anyone but a conservative to play a role in Californian politics. As California looms larger and larger in the life of the nation, as Los Angeles grows nearer and nearer to the rank of the first city in the nation, the effect upon national politics will unquestionably be to strengthen the cause of conservatism. California played a large role in securing the nomination of Goldwater in 1964, and it already seems very likely that, under a committed conservative governor, California will play a decisive role in the counsels of the Republican Presidential convention of 1968.

Reagan: A Relaxing View

By William F. Buckley Jr.

EDITOR'S NOTE: *This article appeared in the November 18, 1967, issue of* National Review.

In this here neck of the woods, there is some uneasiness in the air, and the reason why is Ronald Reagan. Here is how the nightmare goes. Romney does so-so in New Hampshire, not well enough to give him a solid lead, not poorly enough to dispose of him once and for all and leave time to build up another liberal. Nixon does poorly, maybe not so poorly as to make him withdraw either, but poorly enough to prevent the bandwagon's forming. On to Wisconsin. Same sort of thing. Then in Oregon and in Nebraska Reagan supporters submit his name, and without campaigning Reagan wins decisively. On to the convention. A bitter fight, but once again the liberals are disunited. George Romney has had a divine visitation telling him to stay in the fight, and he does: through the first or second ballots, fracturing the liberals. And—big difference from 1964—somehow the disparagement of the Reagan forces hasn't had the desirable effect on weakening the Republican Party so as to guarantee, at least, its ultimate defeat in November. Add to that the ecumenical goo that Ronald Reagan is so good at extruding—why you would think, sometimes, that Senator Kuchel was his best friend. So Reagan gets nominated, and then we all rush off to our artillery pieces, aim, pull the triggers and—typical nightmare— nothing happens; so that, smiling that confounding smile of his, he rides his horse right into the front lawn of the White House, dismounts, hands the reins over to the benumbed editor of the *Washington Post*, and proceeds to the throne, whence he judges over us all.

The nightmare peters out at this point, for one thing because it never is absolutely clear just how a political conservative is actually going to succeed in destroying the country—it is better for nightmares to end with such details unspecified (a haunted house should never be entered—no bad can come of it). Presumably, that which he would do which is undesirable is a projection of what he has done that is undesirable in California. And concerning what he has done in California, there is thoroughly mystifying disagreement in many quarters.

There is the opinion, for instance, of Mr. Hale Champion. Mr. Champion, who is now uncoiling at Harvard at what has been called the Center for the Advancement of the Kennedy Family, served Governor Pat Brown as State Finance Director (one thinks of serving President Kubitschek of Brazil as Budget Balancer). Mr. Champion undeniably earned a period of repose in the groves of academe, or even of a sanatorium. He suggested an appropriate structure for the criticism of the Reagan administration in *West* Magazine (April 23), in which he commented on the new governor's first 100 days. Governor Reagan, said Mr. Champion, (a) is "in deepening trouble with the legislature and with the public"; (b) has a "completely negative and destructive attitude [toward] higher education"; (c) has "accomplished" almost nothing "except the dismissal of Clark Kerr"; (d) is likely to be swamped by "the future consequences of [his] failure to work out solutions to problems" and (e) is aesthetically offensive, as witness "the loose bundle of social and moral pronouncements that constitute the governor's vague, historically inaccurate, philosophically sloppy, and verbally undistinguished inaugural address."

From this criticism we were all to infer that Mr. Reagan is quite as bad as it was feared by the most fearful that he would be. Well, perhaps not quite as bad as some of Governor Brown's campaign rhetoric predicted. After all, at one point in the campaign, Governor Brown, addressing a Negro child in a widely played television spot, reminded the boy that Ronald Reagan was an actor, and that it was an actor who had shot Abraham Lincoln—a sorites that Mr. Champion did not, at the time, identify as philosophically sloppy or even verbally undistinguished. On the other hand, Mr. Champion is in a position to point out that Reagan hasn't had the opportunity to assassinate Abraham Lincoln, and how can we know that, given the opportunity, he would not seize it?

Reagan Confronts California

But then, having prepared ourselves to think about Mr. Reagan the way Mr. Champion thinks about him, one is confused by the contradictory analyses of another very liberal critic of Mr. Reagan, Mr. Andrew Kopkind, who has kept in very close touch with Reagan over the years, and disapproves of him every bit as much as Mr. Champion—but for different reasons. He thinks that Mr. Reagan is a phony—that he isn't really conservative at all, just talks that way. Whereas Mr. Champion warned that precisely Mr. Reagan's difficulty is his genuine commitment to his atavistic ideas (a "surprising number of state employees, educators and members of mental health organizations . . . didn't really believe he meant what he said in the years before 1966"), Kopkind quotes an anonymous observer as remarking that "Reagan plays Pat Brown better than Pat Brown." "Reagan," he begins his recent analysis, "is selling out . . . He rationalizes his own position by calling himself a pragmatist, and may even believe that he is working from the inside. But he is out for himself alone." Once again he finds a useful anonymous observer to quote: "There are three big phonies in politics in this state—Sam Yorty, Max Rafferty, and Ronald Reagan."

Granted, there are people on the Right who also believe that Reagan has sold out. California has a state senator, Mr. John G. Schmitz, who is a member of the John Birch Society, and he says that Reagan is "a tragic end to the brightest hope on the American political scene today. Many of the best of our citizens may never again be willing to trust the word of a seeker or holder of high political office." On the other hand there have been no complaints from the conservative Californians who helped to finance the Reagan movement and who would presumably feel most deeply the weals of ideological infidelity, no complaints from Henry Salvatori, Holmes Tuttle, William Knowland. Moreover, they contend, and Mr. Kopkind would go along, that if the election were held again tomorrow, Reagan would win against Brown as triumphantly (one million votes) as he did last November.

All of this is very confusing to non–Californians. There are the liberals (e.g., Champion) who say he has done the state irreparable damage—and those liberals (e.g., Kopkind) who say that he has, as a matter of fact, administered a stoutly liberal government. How can you cause irreparable damage—in the liberal view of things—by taking militantly liberal action? There are those (e.g., Champion) who say he is losing popularity, and those (e.g., Kopkind) who say he is gaining popularity. Some say he is true to his conservative faith, others that he isn't. Some that he is sincere—that's his trouble: others that he is insincere, that that is his trouble. The Birchers (e.g., Schmitz) who are greatly disillusioned, and the conservatives (e.g., Salvatori) who are by and large elated.

What's he like personally? Ask Evans and Novak: "Naturally aloof. The thing Reagan needs to do [they quote an unnamed "Republican leader"] is to ask the legislators over to his house to play poker and drink some booze. But that's not going to happen any time soon.'" Fascinating. But—oops!—*Time* magazine quotes Assembly Republican Caucus Chairman Don Mulford: "I don't think there is a single legislator who doesn't like Governor Reagan as an individual." *Time* commented on Reagan's "success" at the end of his first session, which he accomplished "by holding frequent meetings with the lawmakers, infect[ing] them with his straightforward, purposeful approach." Champion insisted on the diminishing prestige. Now, William S. White observes that "no one who has recently been in California with eyes and ears open can doubt that Reagan is going from strength to strength. By every ordinary measurement he is both a popular and an effective state executive."

As far as the outer world can see, there have been three significant confrontations between California and Reaganism. They had to do with (1) education, (2) mental health, and (3) taxes.

The first was in two parts. There was, to begin with, the firing of Clark Kerr. In fact, Reagan's role in the dismissal of Kerr, while it could be held to have been psychologically critical, was insubstantial. It is true that the regents, execution-bound, addressed the freshly inaugurated governor at the regents' meeting in January and said to him: If it would be greatly embarrassing to you for us to proceed with the business at hand—which is to ask Clark Kerr for his resignation—we are willing to put off doing so for a few months. Reagan's answer was: Don't mind me, go right ahead, and God bless you. What happened then is instructive. In the first place, Reagan's siding with the majority of the regents, who after all had been named as such by his celebratedly liberal predecessors Brown, Knight, and Warren, ended him up carrying the onus of the entire majority. Thus Mr. Champion, relaxing in the scholarly detachment of Harvard University, refers to Mr. Reagan's having "accomplished" the "dismissal of Clark Kerr." In fact Reagan did vote for Kerr's dismissal. If he had voted against Kerr's dismissal, Kerr would nevertheless have been fired (the vote was 14 to 8)—unless one assumes that Reagan controlled the marginal votes, which why should one assume it considering that only a single voter directly owed his status as a voter to the governor? Never mind, Reagan was widely held to be responsible.

And secondly, one learns ever more about the powers of the Educational Establishment, and they are, of course, formidable. The rule of thumb is: Never disagree with the educators, never give them less than everything they want, and never act other than as a postulant at their shrine. It is all neatly put by Professor James Q. Wilson of Harvard University, who wrote recently a "Guide to Reagan Country" for the academically chic *Commentary* magazine in which he ventured a number of observations not entirely congenial to orthodox anti-Reaganism, and thought to protect himself winsomely by acknowledging: "I do not intend here to write an apology for Reagan: even if I thought like that, which I don't, I would never write it down anywhere my colleagues at Harvard might read it." No indeed: academic freedom is very broadminded, but it stops short of defending the position of Ronald Reagan. Stops short, that is, of defending the indefensible.

The Politics of Academe

It is a perfectly reasonable criticism of Ronald Reagan that he does not entirely understand the influence of the academic establishment. Not very many politicians do, and it is not enough merely to tell them that that influence exists. Barry Goldwater was scandalously late in harnessing what academic support was available to him for the asking. Richard Nixon's cheering squad always sounded rather like William Yandell Elliott plus the deans of the schools of business administration of midwestern Baptist colleges. Actually, there is a great deal of potential support available to a right-bent public figure, but he must know how to discharge the correct vibrations to shake it out, and Governor Reagan didn't know how to do that in January 1967, and does not know—and here is his most baffling dereliction of the moment—how to do so even now. It isn't really all that difficult. The supporters, as I say, are there: one has only to meditate on the silent vote against Clark Kerr among the chancellors of the individual university campuses in California who for years have deeply resented his importunate ways; and there are the others who recoil against the anti-intellectualist spirit of the Berkeley disorders, and even against the antipersonalist impulses of macro-education

But those folk need to be approached in just the right way, and it may be the single lesson—he gives signs of mastering almost all of the others—that Governor Reagan has not learned. So that when simultaneously Reagan voted with the majority to dismiss Kerr, and came out (via a subordinate who spoke out ahead of schedule) in favor of uniform reductions (10 per cent) in state spending, and in favor of charging tuition at the University of California and the state colleges, all the educators felt the tug of class solidarity that Karl Marx, Eugene Debs, and James Hoffa never succeeded in eliciting from the proletarian classes. It was a field day for the professors and the students, who delightedly burned their governor in effigy. The canny and brilliant Jesse Unruh, lord of all he diminishingly surveys in the evenly-divided state Assembly, quickly took his advantage. Only months before, because he had seen the necessity to deplore the excesses at the Berkeley campus, he, too, had been burned in effigy; but now, in gratitude for his scornful resistance of the governor's position that students should contribute to the cost of their own education, the placardists bore signs: "JESSE SAVES." The speaker was vastly amused, and vastly instructed: he knows, he knows, the strength of the Harvard vote.

And then Governor Reagan made probably the principal verbal faux pas of his career, a remark to the effect that the state of California has no business "subsidizing intellectual curiosity." The difference, Mark Twain reminded us between the right word and almost the right word, "is the difference between lightning and lightning-bug." Intellectual curiosity is a very good thing, intellectual frivolity is not. When asked to document his case against educational excesses Governor Reagan brightly observed that he did not see why the state should need to support courses in "how to burn the governor in effigy." An amusing response, the kind of riposte that an Adlai Stevenson or John F. Kennedy would make with pleasure and profit. But Ronald Reagan needs to remember that he is a Republican and a conservative, and does not have the ordinary man's license to exaggerate. In fact, industrious reporters discovered, the course in question was being offered by an organization adjacent to the state university, which teaches the theory of nonviolent resistance; and though to be sure the university was extending credit to students who took the course, it was technically untrue to say that the taxpayers were spending money to finance the burning of their governor in effigy. Just a little research would have armed the governor with copious examples of the abuse of education. It can be maintained (and is, by some people) that all of life is an education; in which case, as a matter of logic, one automatically loses any argument to the effect that training in this or that is a waste of money. But Reagan could have split the university community and got going a very useful debate by asking whether in fact all of the gentlemen and scholars in the university system were prepared to defend the notion that courses in home economics and fly fishing and hotel hygiene and life adjustment are a part of the life of the mind to the advancement of which the voters of California are dedicated.

Reagan on Mental Health

And then, too, Reagan should raise the question: granted the infinite desirability of more and more education, what are the practical limits that even an idealistic community should observe? During the past decade, enrollment in California state colleges is up 397 per cent, operating costs are up 260 per cent, capital expenditures are up 260 per cent—whereas population and hence the ability to pay is up only 39 per cent. Question: How much further? Here is a very serious question, which Governor Reagan has an excellent opportunity to probe. The society would be ideal in which everyone with a velleity to become a doctor of philosophy could proceed to stroll through the years of his early manhood in order to become one, at no expense to himself. But—as Professor Ernest van den Haag of New York University tartly pointed out a few years ago—isn't it a fact that the figures show that professors will earn more money than plumbers and taxi drivers, and that therefore to tax plumbers and taxi drivers to subsidize the education of professors is a form of regressive taxation, and therefore antiliberal, by a definition with which both Mr. Champion *and* Mr. Kopkind could agree?

Such questions as these Mr. Reagan has not asked, as yet; and, indeed, he has not perfected any line of communication to the academes. Meanwhile, the question rests. The case for the firing of Clark Kerr is at least defensible. Certainly it is true that he'd have been fired irrespective of Reagan's adventitious attendance at the regents' meeting on January 20, 1967; and, as regards tuition, the seed has been planted and voters are aware that a public question has been raised. The State of California provides, typically, more than one-half the expenses of the university. The university proposes a budget, the regents examine it, it is submitted to the governor, and he in turn submits it to the legislature. Reagan persuaded the regents this year to spend $20 million of their own reserves, and he vetoed a supplementary appropriation proposed by Unruh. And the university emerged from it all with $10 million more than it got the year before: but the percentage rise was reduced. And more important, heuristic questions have been raised, questions which should have been raised before, questions which quite properly relate higher state education to the total resources and needs of a community. The exact formulation of the ultimate questions neither Governor Reagan nor anyone else is ever likely to come up with. But Reagan has naysayed the superstition that any spending in the name of higher education ought (a) to be approved of, and (b) to be exempt from public scrutiny. And that, perverse though it may sound, is a contribution to public education.

Concerning mental health, it was widely disseminated that Reagan's superficiality caused him to ignore the salient point. True, the in-patient population had reduced from 34,000 to 20,000; and true, the state budget for the maintenance of the mentally ill had not reduced at all. Why not, asked Reagan, reduce it *pro tanto?* Because, his critics leaped, the fact of the diminution of in-patients is testimony to the effectiveness of the entire working force of the mental hospitals, and precisely the wrong thing to do under the circumstances is to reduce their total firing power. Reagan countered that that was supposititious, that he was quite prepared to reverse his recommendations in the event of a decline in the rate of the cured.

Economies Not Easily Effected

Sounds reasonable, one would suppose. But the point, of course, is that economies are never easily effected, and just about never effected when the emotional instrument at the disposal of the spenders is, no less, the mentally ill. Take the incidence of stricken mothers-in-law and multiply it by the prospect of their repatriation, and you have an idea of the size of the political problem. If President Eisenhower was unsuccessful, even during his relatively brief period of militant frugality, in eliminating the Rural Electrification Agency because of the lobbies available to agitate for its survival, one can imagine the difficulties in paring the mental health agencies of a single state of the nation. So Reagan yielded—actually he had no reasonable alternative than to do so. But again he had made a public point. And, as in the case of education, the point would yield dividends, or should at any rate, when the time comes, as routinely it always has, to augment the budget for mental health. Reagan's position is after all distinguishable from the position that says that the states should ignore their mentally ill. It is a position that says: if modern psychiatric advances, e.g., through the use of tranquilizers, permit a diminution of the problem, even as the Salk vaccine has diminished the problem of polio, oughtn't the states to adjust their budgets accordingly?

And then, of course, the big question of the budget. It is a matter of universal hilarity. The most economy-minded governor since the inauguration of J. Bracken Lee as governor of Utah in 1953 forward to the legislature the highest budget in state history! Loud guffaws. Not utterly wholesome guffaws, to be sure. Nelson Rockefeller, who at least noticed, though he did not precisely run against, the extravagances of his predecessor Averell Harriman as governor of New York, also proceeded to submit a higher budget than that of the Democratic Mr. Harriman. But in Rockefeller's case, that was considered an act of statesmanship, or at least it was considered as such by the same kind of people who have reacted so ardently against Ronald Reagan.

Reagan's reasoning can, of course, be made to sound disingenuous. He claims to have discovered only after achieving office the programmed deficit of Governor Pat Brown. Mr. Casper Weinberger, chairman of Reagan's Little Hoover Commission, likes to tell the story . . . "Hale Champion, outgoing director of the Department of Finance, cheerfully walked into the conference room, greeted [us] affably, and announced that while there would be a surplus available on June 30, 1967 (when the last of Governor Brown's eight fiscal years ended), there was going to be a problem starting in January 1968.

"The Department's best estimates showed, he said, that there would be a cash flow shortage in January, February, and March of 1968 amounting to $740 million. Champion added that approximately $340 million could be borrowed from other state funds, leaving the state's bank accounts short by $400 million of the amount needed to write checks covering the state's daily bills during those months. When the new tax monies came in April 1968, most of the cash flow problems would be behind us, added Champion, but of course there would be quite a big deficit by June 1968 if present rates of revenue and expenditure continued. In fact, the deficit by then would probably amount to over $350 million.

"After a moment's silence," Mr. Weinberger recalls, "somebody asked, 'Hale, what would you have done about this if you had been re-elected?' 'Well,' he answered with a slow smile, 'we've been telling you Republicans we needed withholding and more taxes, but you've always defeated them.'"

Brown Spent Contingency Funds

"We knew there would be a deficit during the campaign," Reagan reminisces. "But we didn't know how large it would be. Accountants told us there simply wasn't any way of ascertaining how much. Brown kept borrowing all over the place. The civil service people said there was a bare chance we could make it without raising taxes.

As we got closer to the election, it began to look as though there wasn't any chance. I said during the campaign that there would have to be new taxes. The constitution requires that you submit a budget right after you take office. I did. But the research hadn't been completed. And soon it became clear that even it we could effect $250 million in economies, there wasn't a chance for a balanced budget. We just didn't know the extent of the problem. We had no way of knowing that Brown was spending most of the contingency funds. I've now recommended that in the future, independent auditing firms be given a crack at the figures, so that how the state stands financially can be a part of the public knowledge."

He paused to wave back cheerfully at four college-types who had pulled their sedan alongside, driving 55 mph in tandem with the state trooper who was chauffeuring the governor and exactly observing the speed limit. A honey-blonde leaned smiling out of the open window, hoisting a cardboard square hastily improvised from a grocery box or whatever, when the party spotted the governor's license plates. Scrawled on it with lipstick was NO TUITION! Reagan laughed as the collegiates pulled away. "The faculties are mostly responsible for that," he said. "They tell you one thing, and then they tell the press another." He gave examples. "The No-Tuition bit is a local superstition. Even Brown said years before the election that tuition was 'inevitable.' Did they jump him? But it'll take time. Right now the point is to save money where we can. I'm a good person for people to trust their money with. I'm a good *manager*, and I'll treat their money as though it were mine. When we suggested 10 per cent across the board we knew some departments would have to expand, though others could trim back even more than 10 per cent. We won't make 10 per cent, but we will make about 8½ per cent. And remember, that's 8½ per cent of the spending we have control over. Two-thirds of the spending in California is fixed by the constitution or by statute and we can't do anything about it. It's bad enough to try to make economies when you need the help of a legislature that's controlled by the opposition party. We can't very well tackle the constitution at the same time. But what we're doing will take hold. What makes me mad is obstructionism that's clearly intended to screw up your program. For instance, I said no more new hiring. If one department needs another secretary, pull her from a department where there are surplus secretaries. So some of the civil service people got together and when you need a secretary for the most urgent job they tell you sorry, there isn't one available in the whole goddam state of California. You know there is, of course, but it's a problem of locating her, and that takes time, takes time to canvass the departments and identify those that have the excess people, and there are plenty around. It isn't any different from what you would expect. Why should the bureaucracy behave any different from the way I always said it did—protectively toward its own authority and vested interests? A governor can't do everything, he hasn't got that much authority, and maybe he shouldn't have that authority. I have only a psychological authority, because the politicians know that the people are with me, that they see a lot of waste, and they resent the taxes and the inflation, and that they'll support me. There are lots of things I just can't do, at least not for a while. Take judicial reform. You know how many judges Brown appointed as a lame duck?

Four hundred! I must be the only governor in the U.S. who can't fix a parking ticket. But in time there will be vacancies, and I'm trying to reform the system, but Unruh hasn't let the bill out of committee. You've got to be patient, and you've got to make a start. I'll be around for a while."

So the budget went finally to the legislature, a $5-billion budget, 8 per cent higher than his predecessor's. (By contrast, Rockefeller's first budget was 11 per cent higher than *his* predecessor's.) But, Reagan explained, the increase was almost entirely on account of Brown's commitments, plus the annual increase in California's population (2½ per cent in 1966). Assuming you merely want to stand still, you have to raise the budget 8 per cent to cover inflation, plus immigration. Reagan needed to cover the deficits of Pat Brown—and did so, raising the budget only the requisite 8 per cent. Up went the income tax, the sales tax and the so-called sin taxes. And on the issue of withholding—he was against it because, he said, "taxes ought to be out in the open. They should hurt, so that people know the price of what they're getting." Jesse Unruh was as determined that taxes should be painlessly withheld drop by drop as Reagan was that they should be collected in one painful annual extraction. Reagan held out, Unruh held out. But, finally, on July 28 the legislature approved within less than 1 per cent the figure Reagan asked for, and without the withholding tax. "All in all," Jesse Unruh, obviously taking another look at Reagan, concluded, "he did very well."

The Speech

The critics of Ronald Reagan are fond of quoting from his autobiography, *Where's the Rest of Me?* It is an unfortunate book, not at all for what it says, which is wholesome and intelligent, but for the way it is said. There is no doubting that it is primarily responsible for the insiders' assumption that the governor is a hopeless cornball. The opening passage of the book (it is Mr. Kopkind's favorite) is, well, disastrous.

"The story begins with the close-up of a bottom. My face was blue . . . my bottom was red . . . and my father claimed afterward that he was white . . . Ever since . . . I have been particularly fond of the colors that were exhibited—red, white, and blue."

I suspend the narrative in order to allow a minute for derision.

Now: the fact of the matter is that the book was co-authored, and co-authored "autobiographies" are, as a general rule, the stylistic work of the other guy. It is too bad that Mr. Reagan did not go further and publish it as an as-told-to-book, which is undoubtedly how the book was actually produced. Because the fact of the matter is that Reagan is not that way. "John Jones," I observed recently to him about a controversial public figure, "has the face of a bank teller." "Bank teller? Hell, he has the face of the neighborhood child molester." One cannot be as banal as (a), and as mordant as (b), and the circumstances clearly argue that the second, not the first, is the real-life Ronald Reagan. "Stand in front of the asparagus counter today," he told a political gathering, "and you discover that it's cheaper to eat money." That kind of crack, Made in America, unmakeable anywhere else, is a pretty big industry in California. But—good. And homemade. "Keeping up with Governor Brown's promises," he said during the campaign, "is like reading *Playboy* magazine while your wife turns the pages." Good. Very good. And they come effortlessly. They are a function of his vision. The perspectives are very good, the mind very quick.

I met him seven or eight years ago. He was to introduce me at a lecture that night at Beverly Hills. He arrived at the school auditorium to find consternation. The house was full and the crowd impatient but the microphone was dead—the student who was to have shown up at the control room above the balcony to turn on the current hadn't. Reagan quickly took over. He instructed an assistant to call the principal and see if he could get a key. He then bounded onto the stage and shouted as loud as he could to make himself heard. In a very few minutes the audience was greatly enjoying itself. Then word came to him: no answer at the principal's telephone, Reagan went off-stage and looked out the window. There was a ledge, a foot wide, two stories above the street level, running along the side of the window back to the locked control room. Hollywood-wise, he climbed out on the ledge and sidestepped carefully, arms stretched out to help him balance, until he had gone the long way to the window, which he broke open with his elbow, lifting it open from the inside, and jumping into the darkness. In a moment the lights were on, the amplifying knobs were turned up, the speaker introduced.

During those days he was busy delivering his own speech. *The* Speech, it came to be called: probably the most frequently uttered since William Jennings Bryan's on the golden crucifixion. All over the land, to hundreds of audiences, a deft and rollicking indictment of overweening government. And then the speech became the most galvanizing fund-raiser in political history. He televised it during the Goldwater campaign for a statewide showing in California. "And then, an hour before it was scheduled to go on, word came from Goldwater's headquarters to hold it—the boys at HQ had heard it rumored that it was 'too extreme.' I remember I went to the nearest pay booth, just by a gas station, and called Goldwater. There were only minutes to go. Luckily, he was on the ground. I reached him in Arizona. 'Barry,' I said, 'I don't have time to tell you everything that's in that speech, but you can take it from me, buddy, there isn't a kooky line in it.' Goldwater said: 'I'll take your word for it,' and I called the studio in the nick of time."

He Keeps on Improving

If Goldwater hadn't been at the other end of the telephone, Reagan would not have become governor. Because the speech was an incomparable success, statewide and subsequently nationwide. (It is said to have elicited almost $5 million in dollar-bill contributions.) It was on account of that speech that the Reagan-for-Governor talk began.

I saw him during a long evening a few weeks after Goldwater's defeat, when the Reagan movement was just beginning to stir. We talked about the national calamity for the conservative movement, and how it bore on his own situation. He was then quite positive that the Republican Party of California would not want him, especially not in the aftermath of so definitive a loss. But, he said, he wasn't going to say anything Shermanesque. He talked about the problems of California. The discussion was in generalities, very different from a second conversation a year later, in December of 1965, on the eve of the year when he would run. The change was striking. He knew a great deal about specific problems of California. But he had grown, too, in other ways. I remember being especially impressed when, looking out over the city from the elevation of Pacific Palisades, he remarked: "You know, it's probable that the cost of eliminating the smog is a cost the people who want the smog to be eliminated aren't, when it comes to it, willing to pay."

Still later, on a half-dozen occasions, I noticed the ongoing improvement in his personal style, particularly in his handling of the press. Last June in Omaha, after a press conference before his speech to the Young Republicans, the *New York Times* correspondent impulsively blurted out to a young correspondent he hardly knew: "I've never seen anything like it, I've been covering them since Truman. There isn't anybody who can touch Reagan." It's something people are going to have to get used to as long as Reagan's star is on the ascendancy. "To those unfamiliar with Reagan's big-league savvy," *Newsweek*, pained, dutifully pointed out last May after observing Ronald Reagan and Bobby Kennedy in a joint appearance answering student questions on Vietnam, "the ease with which [Reagan] fielded questions about Vietnam may come as a revelation . . . Political rookie Reagan left old campaigner Kennedy blinking when the session ended."

I mean, it is more than flesh and blood can bear. Reagan, the moderately successful actor, the man ignorant of foreign affairs, outwitting Bobby *Kennedy* in a political contest. It's the kind of thing that brings on those nightmares.

Richard Nixon was in the room. Who, someone asked, would the Republican Party consider as eligible in 1968? Nixon gave the usual names: and added Ronald Reagan's. I objected. It strikes me, I said, as inconceivable. "Why?" Nixon asked— "suppose he makes a very good record as governor of California?" (This was in December, just after Reagan's election.) Because, I said, he is very simply an implausible President. Anyone would be whose career was in Hollywood. People won't get used to the notion of a former actor being President. People are very stuffy about Presidential candidates. Remember what Raymond Moley said when someone asked him how to account for Kefauver's beating Adlai Stevenson in the Minnesota primary in 1956—"Did *you* ever tell a joke in Minneapolis?"

And then—I added, carried away by my conviction—how does one go about being a good governor in an age when the major moves are, after all, up to the Federal Government? Who last—I asked Nixon—can we remember, whose record as governor propelled him to the first ranks of the Presidential hopefuls?

Dewey, Nixon ventured—then corrected himself: Dewey became famous as a prosecutor, not as governor. Rockefeller was projected by the fact of being a Rockefeller, being personally able, being wealthy, and being governor of New York: not because New York had become a model state under his administration.

During the next year, California will spend, as we all know, $5 billion. During the next year the Federal Government will spend approximately $140 billion. Well over 17 billion of these dollars will be spent in California. But more important, it is the Federal Government that will decide how many California boys are drafted into the army, how much inflation there is going to be, how far the monopoly labor unions can go, whether there will be any praying in the schools, whether Californians can sell their property as they choose, where the main highways will come from and where they will go, how the water flowing in from nature is to be allocated, how large social security payments will be. Are there interstices within which, nowadays, a governor can move, sufficiently to keep himself in focus and establish his special competence?

Reagan clearly thinks so. After all, he has brought almost everyone's attention to the problems of California, even to some of California's problems over which, as in the matter of tuition, he has no control. Always there is some room. "To live," Whittaker Chambers wrote, "is to maneuver. The choices of maneuver are now visibly narrow. [But] a conservatism that cannot find room in its folds for the actualities is a conservatism that is not a political force, or even a twitch: it has become a literary whimsy. Those who remain in the world, if they will not surrender on its terms, must maneuver within its terms."

The knowledge of that is what causes Mr. Kopkind to call Reagan a hypocrite, a phony. Brings the Birch senator to consider him an impostor. Brings George Wallace to call him a lightweight. What did they expect? That Governor Reagan would padlock the state treasury and give speeches on the Liberty Amendment? They say that his accomplishments are few, that it is only the rhetoric that is conservative. But the rhetoric is the principal thing. It precedes all action. All thoughtful action. Reagan's rhetoric is that of someone who is profoundly committed, *mutatis mutandis*, to the ancient ways. His perspectives are essentially undoubting. Mr. Kopkind has recently written that the United States' venture in Vietnam is "the most barbaric imperialistic war of this century." If that is so, there are phonies in America by the scores of millions. Reagan would never get the Kopkind vote; Reagan is more inscrutable to Kopkind than the Aztec calendar. For the Kopkinds, America itself is inscrutable. Reagan is indisputably a part of America. And he may become a part of American history.

How Ronald Reagan Governed California

By Charles D. Hobbs

EDITOR'S NOTE: *This article appeared in the January 17, 1975, issue of* National Review.

An appraisal of Ronald Reagan as governor of California should start with the 1971 welfare reform negotiations between his administration and the liberal Democrats who controlled the California Legislature. The objective of the negotiations was to construct a welfare reform act, the legislative component of Reagan's celebrated welfare reform program. The Reagan team had just detected some legal "quicksand" in the language drafted by the Legislature's staff. If left in the bill, the language would undo a major element of the reform that Reagan had proposed and Assembly Speaker Bob Moretti, under tremendous public pressure, had reluctantly agreed to. The legislators and their staff members, opposed to any welfare reform at all and trying hard to soften its impact, argued that the language was inconsequential; the Reagan team insisted that the wording be changed to reflect the Reagan-Moretti agreement. An impasse was reached and one of the legislators, whose self-appointed role was to maintain an atmosphere that would encourage compromise, called for a recess and sent for food and drink. Warmed by his own hospitality and trying to put the situation in perspective, he commented: "It's too bad the people elect an ideologue like Reagan. They should stick with political whores, like me." His candor broke the ice and negotiations were resumed: the questionable language was redrafted to satisfy the "ideologue."

For anyone who takes seriously Ronald Reagan's 1965 statement that "nothing is more opposed to creativeness than bureaucracy," the chronicling of his governorship of California might be expected to recall the Battle of Gettysburg. That it doesn't is a credit to Reagan as a man. He had the best opportunity in our time to test the practical value of the conservative principles underlying the belief that uncontrolled growth and power of government is the greatest threat to our freedom and, therefore, to our nation and lives. He consciously strove to take advantage of that opportunity, and the future usefulness of these principles depends upon our willingness to examine honestly and critically the outcome of Reagan's eight years as leader of the largest and most typical of the United States. I hope that this article will serve as the beginning of that examination.

There are three impediments to such an examination. The first is the uncertainty produced, or at least reinforced, by the national events of the last six months—Nixon's resignation, his pardon by Ford, Rockefeller's ordeal as he sought the Vice Presidency, and the prospect of a full scale depression. It is an awkward time to analyze a current political career.

The second impediment is the budding crop of superficial appraisals celebrating the retirement of California's "citizen-politician." Clearly California and Reagan are parting friends, and the consensus, except at the raveled fringes of the political fabric, is that both have profited, but the state more so, from their eight-year association. California enters 1975 with a constantly decreasing welfare population receiving constantly increasing benefits: with financially and technically sound energy and water supply systems; with enforced environmental standards that are both lowering air and water pollution and preserving an extraordinary range of recreational opportunities; with a superb highway system that has become an orderly segment of an integrated transportation system responsive to both state and local needs; with $1 billion in property tax relief funds disbursed each year to local governments; with no more state employees than eight years ago, even though in that time state spending has doubled and state services have multiplied; with a public university system in which teaching, learning, and research have replaced violent confrontation and preparation for armed revolution; and with a $500-million budget surplus to buffer California against the coming hard times.

Even Reagan's enemies will agree, publicly if they can afford to and privately if they can't, that these assets are mainly the products of the personal and political strength, vision, and persistence of Ronald Reagan. That is why, as this article is being written, journalists like Lou Cannon of the *Washington Post* and Tom Goff of the *Los Angeles Times* have already published positive assessments of Reagan's performance as governor. Their theme seems to be that "he did a lot better than most of us thought he would." Heady praise from a generally liberal working press—unless one realizes that even the most liberal of the Sacramento press corps has succumbed to Reagan's unique combination of charm, intelligence, and integrity, and until one remembers that most of the people who try to mold others' opinions considered him, in 1966, a woefully inexperienced and unintelligent reactionary, preprogramed and made up to look like a gubernatorial candidate by Hollywood, Madison Avenue, and the money men of Southern California. Pat Brown, the incumbent governor, underestimated both the voters and Reagan and lost to him by almost a million votes. Only the people saw and understood in 1966 that Reagan wrote his own speeches and meant what he said. The opinion leaders are just now catching up with the people.

The third and most difficult impediment in appraising Ronald Reagan's performance is the conservative's desire to find his administration faultless or, avoiding that gross pitfall, to see what flaws there are through conservatively tinted glasses. Watching the rising tide of bureaucracy we are tempted to succumb to the vision of the man on the white horse. Mythology is full of such would-be national saviors, like the mad Irish hero Cuchulain who tried to beat back the sea with his sword. Reagan is Irish as well as conservative. Only four months ago he said: "I have also learned that politics, which is often called the second oldest profession, has a great similarity to the first."

We must ask the hard questions, not only about Reagan the man, but about Reagan the governor. How well did he put into practice the principles he enunciated so well just before the 1964 election in his famous "speech"? Did his accomplishments match his plans, or was he forced to bend principles to meet the political realities of a state that transacts more business than all but six or seven nations? Was he able to attract people to develop programs consistent with his principles? How often was he blocked from even greater accomplishments by people who, although personally loyal, either did not understand how or did not share the desire to reduce to practice his principles? How effective was he in the give and take of political warfare, where compromise is supposedly the only way to succeed? How well did he manage a large bureaucracy while admittedly holding views strongly antithetical to bureaucratic purposes and practices? Finally, is there any meaning in his experience for the future of conservatism and, if so, what is it?

Three facets of Reagan's personality have colored and often controlled his decisions and impact as governor. First there is his charm: very few people, alone or in a group, can meet or listen to Reagan without liking him. He is at once interesting and interested—as good a listener as he is a talker—and the effect of his personal magnetism cannot be disregarded.

The second important facet of his personality is his integrity in adhering to his principles, no matter what the circumstances. The Davis students who applauded him at a recent rally were also applauding Reagan's ability, courage, and readiness to express his principles, politely but firmly, to an audience he knew had been conditioned to disagree with him. In my research and experience there is no instance in which he has compromised his principles for personal or political gain. He came intellectually prepared to Sacramento, to the amazement of his critics and even some of his supporters, with a well thought out political philosophy and a matching set of principles from which he has never deviated.

Unfortunately, the third and least publicly understood facet of his personality has often undone the effects of the first two. For better or worse, Ronald Reagan is the most compassionate person I have ever met. Nor am I alone in this assessment: his closest advisers are both awed and dismayed by Reagan's inability to inflict injury on, or tolerate injury to, other people, except people who have harmed or injured a third party. Not only can't he hurt another person; he has great difficulty in withdrawing even a part of the complete trust he invariably places in those who work for him, even when their actions publicly embarrass him.

As a society we have come to expect our political leaders to be, to a certain degree, Janus-faced. Thinking it through, most of us would probably wonder how else a politician could both get votes and manage a government agency. Ronald Reagan doesn't change personalities when he turns from the TV cameras and enters his private office. Peel off the layers of formality that he adds for his public appearances and you find only an increasingly informal version of the same person. In fact, the more informal the setting, the more his natural compassion and consideration for others surface. That is why people who expect to hate Reagan find, on meeting him, that they like him. "He attracts all kinds of people," Jim Jenkins, one of Reagan's closest policy advisers, told me, and added that screening Reagan's visitors was important only because "we were always afraid the next one would come out wearing the Governor's shirt."

Reagan's undeviating loyalty to his subordinates, even to those who could not or would not put his principles into practice, has produced failures and missed opportunities that, in fairness, must be chalked up against him. On the other hand, when his subordinates have shared his principles and had the courage and ability to design and carry out programs based on those principles, Reagan has proved not only that conservatism in government can work, but that in practice it represents the will of the vast majority of Americans of all backgrounds.

In 1967 Reagan inherited an incredible fiscal mess: the product of clumsy attempts by Pat Brown's outgoing administration to prevent either a major tax increase or severe program cutbacks in an election year. Brown's director of finance,

Hale Champion, informed Reagan's incoming staff that the 1966–67 budget was running a deficit of $1 million a day, wished them good luck, and walked out. The entire Medi-Cal (California's greatly expanded version of Medicaid) budget for the year had been spent in the six months before Reagan became governor. The state-wide water system was severely underfunded because the value of the bonds to finance the project had been set at what Brown thought could win voter approval, a value far short of the actual construction costs of the system. In short, Reagan entered Sacramento, scalpel in hand, prepared to trim away the excess fat of government spending, only to find that he already had a $200-million budget deficit, a commitment for a water system that was underfunded by another several hundred millions of dollars, and a $4-billion potential unfunded liability in the State Teachers' Retirement System that, if not quickly corrected, would balloon local property tax rates.

In his first year as governor he was forced to raise state taxes by $900 million. But before he left office eight years later he had returned more than $1 billion of state taxes directly to the citizens of California and was providing another $ I billion per year in local property tax relief in the form of subventions to local governments to be spent for local programs. A miracle? Definitely not. A significant accomplishment? The answer can only be a qualified yes, considering that during the same period of time the state budget doubled and state spending grew at one and a half times the rate of state personal income. State taxes actually grew faster under Reagan than under Brown, but that was mainly the result of Brown's sleight of hand shift in the state accounting system from cash to accrual and toleration of a growing budget deficit during his last year in office.

Ronald Reagan wanted, much more than his predecessor, to control overall spending, but, like his predecessor, was unable to do so. For at least the past twenty years the governor and the Legislature have maintained only a semblance of control over the budget and expenditures of the State of California. Control has actually been balanced between two bureaucratic agencies, neither of which has been held directly accountable to the people. These agencies are the state Department of Finance, ostensibly reporting to the governor and charged with preparing the annual governor's budget for submission to the Legislature, and the Office of the Legislative Analyst, ostensibly reporting to the Legislature for the primary purpose of analyzing the adequacy and quality of the governor's budget. By playing off executive departments against each other, by helping to ensure that elected critics get enough funds, or economies, or programs to keep them happy, by maintaining staffs with superior knowledge of the budget process, these two agencies have acted as an informal coalition in controlling the lion's share of California's budget, and with it California's expenditures and taxes. The symbiotic relationship of the two agencies has made the Department of Finance bureaucracy so strong that, as Ned Hutchinson, Reagan's highly respected appointments secretary for six years, said: "Unfortunately, we never laid a glove on them." They gave the conservative governor what he wanted: tax refunds to the people and property tax relief for local government.

They gave the liberal Legislature what it wanted: more money for more state programs. But they kept effective control of the budget—their primary goal and the secondary goal thus defined itself: increases in taxes and government spending that would allow them to satisfy their "customers"—the governor and the Legislature.

Ned Hutchinson was drafted into the Reagan administration, as were many of those who became administration stalwarts, through the Businessmen's Task Force, Reagan's first major attempt at reform of the bureaucracy. Borrowing the idea from Governor James Rhodes of Ohio, Reagan recruited some 250 businessmen from the major industries of the state. Speaking to small groups of business leaders about the reforms he had promised in his campaign, he would wait until his audience began, one by one, to pull out their checkbooks. Then he would say: "I don't need your money, I need your talent. There's a sign-up sheet by the door. If you can spare a day, a week, a month, or more, please sign up as you leave." The response was overwhelming, and for ten months, from February to December 1967, the state's most successful businessmen looked critically over the shoulders of its civil servants.

It turned out to be as much an audit as a reform (although most of the task force's 1,500 recommendations were eventually implemented, and many resulted in substantial cost savings), but a greater benefit was the business community's better understanding of the problems and challenges of managing the nation's largest state. Many successful businessmen, like Hutchinson, stayed to be a part of Reagan's management team. In fact, Hutchinson first coordinated the implementation of the recommendations, and graduated from that laborious task to the even more difficult one of picking candidates for the 300-odd political appointments Reagan controlled. "There were always plenty of qualified and experienced people available," says Hutchinson, "but not enough of them also shared the Governor's conservative principles and zeal to implement those principles."

From the start Reagan operated through an executive assistant, who functioned more or less as assistant governor. The first of these, Philip Battaglia, a dynamic Los Angeles attorney, left less than a year after Reagan took office. The second was William Clark, also an attorney, now a justice on the California Supreme Court. Reagan and Clark began, in late 1967 and early 1968, to apply the business management techniques that Reagan had promised to bring to state government, and that the Businessmen's Task Force had given shape. Reagan and Clark set up a cabinet that would be a forum for threshing out policy positions on the multitude of expensive, complex, overlapping, and sometimes almost invisible state programs. Each cabinet member, except the executive secretary, was also secretary of an agency comprising several functional departments. There were four such agencies: Human Relations (later Health and Welfare), Business and Transportation, Agriculture and Services, and Resources. The agency secretaries usually exercised no direct-line management responsibility except when their programs were in experimental or developmental stages, when they would be most susceptible to technical and political criticism. Under the cabinet system the line departments would make their budget requests to the agency secretaries, who would then meet with the governor and argue the case for the fiscal needs of their agencies. Then the cabinet, headed by the governor, would set spending priorities and limits and instruct the Department of Finance as to what should constitute the governor's budget.

In retrospect, it appears that Reagan, Clark, and the other cabinet members did not know how strong a grip the old-line bureaucrats of the Department of Finance had on the preparation and enactment of the budget, or how close they came to breaking that grip with the establishment of the governor's cabinet. What saved the bureaucracy was its technical expertise. The new cabinet secretaries could not fathom the governor's budget, a document so esoteric that nowhere in it can be found the first requirement of any budget: single numbers representing the total projected expenditures of the state treasurer for the current year and for the projected year. Technical help obviously was needed: the director of finance was added to the cabinet as a full-fledged member and, properly briefed by his indulgent civil service staff, continued to call the shots. For the past five and a half years the director of finance has been Verne Orr a man who is universally liked and respected by the state legislators and in whom Reagan has always placed great trust. Orr has been totally loyal to Reagan but, like other directors of finance before him, has depended completely for technical support on the civil servants who have managed the budget for over twenty years.

The cabinet worked well in other ways, however. A cabinet secretary would act as a sergeant at arms and parliamentarian, keeping the discussion as close to the agenda topic as possible. The structured discussion of cabinet issues, summarized before the meetings in "Cabinet Issue Memos," and the open exchange of views among all of Reagan's top advisers, with his active participation, were a vast improvement on the practices of his predecessors, who had usually decided issues on the advice of whoever was present at the time—cabinet member, legislator, lobbyist, or old fraternity brother. The cabinet made a workable routine for the day to day policy management of the executive branch. Had Pat Brown had such a forum, some of the disasters that struck his administration might have been averted, or at least reduced in effect. One such disaster was the decline and fall of the University of California in 1964.

A question that conservatives should ask about Ronald Reagan is why the vast majority of college and university students in California think he belongs in one of the lower levels of the Inferno. Part of the answer may be that most college students don't want to like or believe any public figure, on the assumption that to be a public figure is probably to be a hypocrite. But then most people, including most college students, are hypocrites, and Ronald Reagan, despite the political cartoonists, is not.

In addition Reagan has made no effort to communicate directly with large groups of college students, mainly because some of the staff members who scheduled his speaking engagements felt that student audiences would invariably contain provocateurs, and most students wouldn't vote anyway.

But for one who knows what Ronald Reagan believes in and how close, notwithstanding the generation gap, his beliefs are to what most students say they want to believe in, neither answer is satisfactory. I think the larger part of the answer lies in the insecurity and paranoia of the University of California's administration and faculty, stemming from its public attempt at self-destruction as an institution of higher learning in 1964. The spectacle of the president of one of the most respected institutions of higher learning in the world bargaining away, in exchange for a campus police car, administrative control of the university to a few hundred radical faculty and student punks, destroyed almost instantaneously California's respect for its university. When, two years later, Ronald Reagan became the spokesman for a free society faced by a revolution fomented on the campuses, his targets, whether he willed it or not, were students. He realizes, and has said so over and over again, that the real culprits in campus unrest are a few students swayed by a radical minority of the faculty. But the wall between Reagan and students is there, and it is only recently that Reagan himself has shown the inclination to climb over or walk around that wall. The students, having more pride than experience, will stay on their side until he comes over to be tested.

Another wall is the wall between him and some members of the California Supreme Court, particularly the Chief Justice he appointed in 1970, Donald Wright. Soon after he took office, Reagan initiated a system by which candidates for judgeships would be pre-screened and evaluated by committees composed of members of the bar, judges, and laymen before he personally selected from among the candidates. He also applied a rule of thumb to his selection of judicial candidates: whenever possible, he would try to appoint judges who were younger than 55, so that the state legal system could benefit from the store of experience they would gather.

Reagan's system for appointing judges and his judicial appointments have been hailed as exceptionally good by conservatives, and even liberals admit that the quality of judicial appointments has improved under Reagan. For Reagan and other conservatives, however, Donald Wright has been a tragic disappointment as Chief Justice of the State Supreme Court, which had for years been somewhat to the left of even the Warren Court. Wright was expected to help remedy that tilt, and his conversations with Reagan prior to his appointment reinforced that expectation. Reagan fudged a bit on his rule of thumb: Wright was 63, but he had mentioned, in several conversations with Reagan's advisers, that he intended to retire on his twentieth anniversary as a judge, which would occur before the end of Reagan's second term and allow Reagan then to appoint a younger man. Reagan also thought that Wright supported the death penalty.

Reagan made Wright Chief Justice, and Wright changed colors overnight. He wrote the decision abolishing the death penalty in California, voted with the Brown-appointed liberals on most issues, and, instead of retiring, he sought and gained reconfirmation in the last general election. The wall between Reagan and Wright is probably a permanent one.

The cabinet, however valuable as a management forum and a stimulant to intelligent decision making, was still basically a reactive, not an innovative mechanism, and Reagan was more interested in changing government than in just managing it. He firmly believes that government should be out of most of the businesses it has gotten into since 1930, and that the private sector should be increasing, not decreasing, its role in solving society's problems. Before William Clark left to become a judge in early 1969, he fathered a Program Development Office within the governor's office, for the specific purpose of developing innovative programs that would lessen the intervention of the state government in people's lives and pocketbooks. The office generated many ideas, and went a long way toward explaining, in terms of specific programs, what the "Creative Society" government could accomplish. The office's proposals, however, were never equipped with implementing mechanisms.

In a more specific attempt at reducing government expansion, Reagan's staff took aim, early in 1970, at the California Rural Legal Assistance agency, a group of attorneys set up by the federal Office of Economic Opportunity (OEO) to give legal assistance to the poor, but under the administrative control of the state OEO, which was headed by Lew Uhler, a Reagan appointee. Uhler's aides began to build a file showing that CRLA attorneys were organizing protests against the government that was paying them, in violation of the regulations covering their scope of work. Reagan, relying on what seemed to be massive and well documented evidence presented by Uhler, vetoed CRLA funds for the coming year. In Washington, Frank Carlucci, then OEO director, holding that the Reagan charges could not be substantiated, indicated he would override the veto. Reagan sought the backing of President Nixon, and a thorough investigation of the charges ensued. As it turned out, the staff work done for Reagan was inadequate. A few of the charges held up, but most, although probably true, could not be substantiated by hard evidence, and Reagan was forced to back off. In a no-win, no-lose compromise, CRLA got half the money it had expected, and the other half went to the state to create a new legal aid program for the poor, which, however, never got off the ground.

Reagan was learning from these mistakes. He finally developed the mechanism that was to turn the thrust of his administration from simply improving government management to improving government itself when, in mid-1970, he found that uncontrolled growth of the welfare system threatened to bankrupt the state.

In the spring of 1971 Ronald Reagan singlehandedly cleaned up the federally created "welfare mess" in his state by (1) restricting welfare to those who really needed it, (2) increasing the benefits to those truly in need, and (3) requiring able-bodied welfare recipients either to take a job for pay or perform public services for their welfare grants. These simple steps, implemented through an elaborate, carefully timed series of administrative directives from his Director of Social Welfare, Robert Carleson, to California's 58 County Welfare Departments, produced immediate and, to the rest of the nation, incredible results: within thirty days the welfare case load, which had been growing at a rate of 25,000 to 40,000 persons per month, leveled off and began to drop. It has dropped ever since, and there are now 400,000 fewer people on welfare in California than there were in February 1971.

Savings in state and local taxes, by the most conservative estimates, are more than $2 billion, with another $2-billion saving in federal taxes. And, most galling to liberals who said it couldn't be done, welfare grants, after an initial 30 per cent increase as part of the reform, have continued to rise with the cost of living, so that no Californian on welfare will be penalized by inflation. Nor was this welfare reform fortuitous: every other large state's welfare case load continued to grow while California's fell until, one by one, the other states, led by New York, with Governor Nelson Rockefeller publicly toasting Reagan on his success, came to California to learn the formula for welfare reform. Reagan's welfare reform director, Robert Carleson, has since become Federal Commissioner of Welfare, and serves as HEW's representative to states with runaway welfare problems.

Many conservatives know about these simple and impressive results, but few know how the combination of knowledge, creativity, courage, and perseverance that produced those results was brought about. Even fewer realize that those results were achieved despite the active and concentrated opposition of the Nixon Administration, of HEW, of the organized federal, state, and local welfare bureaucracies, of the California Legislature, of every special interest group involved, and even of the bureaucratically controlled portion of Reagan's own administration.

The story really started in the early autumn of 1969, when President Nixon and his staff humanitarian, Pat Moynihan, were trying to sell the Congress and the governors on the Family Assistance Program (FAP better expresses the qualities of its subject than any other acronym in my experience). By then Ed Meese, an ex-deputy district attorney of Alameda County, and a man who, as legal affairs secretary, had already shown himself to be not only absolutely loyal to Reagan but a master at gaining consensus within the cabinet, had replaced William Clark as Reagan's executive secretary. At the Western White House in San Clemente, Reagan and Meese listened to FAP described in Moynihan's honeyed brogue. Welfare recipients would benefit; states would benefit; the "welfare mess" would be cleaned up once and for all, and by a national Republican Administration. Reagan and Meese were almost convinced.

In Washington, however, Jim Jenkins, then Reagan's "ambassador" to the Federal Government, was seeing a slightly different picture. Jenkins passed his information along to Reagan. Reading the reports himself and knowing the liberal crew that was writing the bill, Jenkins came to the conclusion that FAP would probably turn out to be another giant step toward state socialism in the form of a guaranteed federal dole to workers and nonworkers alike, sugarcoated with savings for the states but hiding an enormous price tag that would force a federal income tax increase or an expansion of the national debt. Jenkins flew to Sacramento, and briefed Reagan and the cabinet on what FAP would really be with Moynihan's rhetoric peeled away. Between Jenkins' briefing and the intensive discussion that followed, Reagan probably received more information about the potential effects of FAP than Nixon ever did. On the evidence, this time meticulously researched, Reagan concluded that California could not support the President and that FAP would, if implemented, be a burden the nation could not bear. A few months later, in the summer of 1970, Reagan made his first and only appearance before Congress as governor of California when he testified at length to Senator Russell Long's Finance Committee as to how and why, in his opinion, FAP would be a disaster for his state and for the nation. Even as he spoke, he realized that, as governor of the largest state, his best hope of stopping FAP would be to design a workable alternative. From this realization California's Welfare Reform Program was born.

Returning to Sacramento, Reagan formed a task force of experts in law, public administration, and business management, expressly picking people who had had no previous experience of, and therefore had no stake in, the current welfare system. Under the leadership of Ned Hutchinson, this team spent five months examining the welfare system to see if it could be changed to make people less, rather than more, dependent on government handouts. The Welfare Reform Task Force concluded not only that such changes could be made, but that simultaneously aid to the needy could be increased and the cost of the system reduced.

The welfare crisis had not only elicited a workable reform program but discovered a mechanism—the independent task force of experts relieved from day to day management responsibilities—for determining how to make those permanent changes in government for which Reagan had campaigned and been elected.

In laying out for Reagan their detailed plans for welfare reform, the task force members, to a man, expressed their doubts that the Legislature would enact the parts of the plan that could not be carried out by executive fiat. Reagan disagreed, knowing that in this matter he held a trump card—the support of the people. Gambling that the initial administrative reforms, which he could order on his own authority through Carleson as state director of social welfare, would cause a sharp and immediate drop in case load growth, he felt the people would then agitate to force the Legislature to complete the program.

Reagan won this one, but it was close. The attack began as soon as the Legislature got Reagan's proposed 1971–72 budget, with a marked decrease in funds for welfare. A. Alan Post, the Legislative Analyst, immediately dubbed the proposed budget "the Property Tax Increase Act of 1971." He was wrong. Welfare reform worked: 42 of California's 58 counties lowered their property taxes that year, and Post's reputation for objectivity and accuracy suffered a severe setback.

But the Legislature had other weapons. The annual legislative ritual of publicly massaging the governor's proposed budget for months and then appointing a six-man conference committee to formulate the Legislature's counter-proposals offered an excellent opportunity to sabotage welfare reform. An integral, in fact critical, element in the welfare reform program was the administrative reorganization of the bureaucracy. That reorganization depended upon Carleson's having discretionary power through the budget to separate certain people from their old functions. The night before the completed budget was to be presented to and quickly passed by both houses of the Legislature, so that it could be signed before the old year ended, members of the legislative staff changed enough of the budget control language to kill the reorganization. The new language was of a masterly obscurity, and its intent certainly would not normally have been noticed by members of the Legislature.

Fortunately for Reagan, however, two members of his welfare reform team were also working late that night and decided to drop into the Capitol office where the budget document had just been "put to bed." An ebullient Legislature aide, proud of the sabotage he and his companions had done to Reagan's plans, and thinking it too late for anyone to repair the damage, gleefully spilled the beans. Early the next morning each member of Reagan's welfare reform team approached key legislators, one by one, as they entered the budget session, pointing out the change in wording and the effect it would have, not only on welfare reform, but on future governors' abilities to organize the executive branch. Before the budget was passed, both houses had passed resolutions upholding Carleson's right to reorganize his department. One of the most liberal and influential of the Democratic senators took it upon himself to sponsor and personally ensure passage of a budget revision bill, undoing the sabotage and permitting the reorganization to be accomplished.

Finally, the efforts of the welfare reform team, combined with the overwhelming reactions of the public, brought Assembly Speaker Bob Moretti to the point of surrender. Appearing at Reagan's office door he held up his hands and said: "Stop the cards and letters. I'm ready to negotiate a welfare reform act." So, in August 1971, after Reagan had been in office four and a half years, the Legislature realized that Reagan was a governor as well as an ideologue.

Reagan had been reelected in 1970, beating Jesse Unruh by half a million votes. The margin would probably have been much greater had not Reagan, again showing the compassion that is, for him, a principle in itself, spent the last weeks of the campaign stumping for his old and ill friend George Murphy who, even so, lost his Senate seat to John Tunney. Reagan, who had always said that eight years was long enough for anybody to be governor, announced immediately after his reelection that he would not run for a third term. By then even legislators were beginning to understand that Reagan always keeps his word, so throughout the crucial days of welfare reform Reagan was acting from a lame-duck position.

Negotiations for the waivers of the Social Security Act that would give federal blessing to welfare reform were conducted principally with John Veneman, assistant secretary of HEW, a former California Republican assemblyman, and close friend of Robert Finch, Reagan's first lieutenant governor. Despite this, Reagan's welfare reform team got a cool reception from Veneman and other HEW officials, many of whom felt that performing a public service for one's welfare grant was "slave labor." The negotiations dragged out for seven months, until the obvious success of the California program and the public enthusiasm it generated convinced HEW it could no longer stand in the way. HEW Secretary Elliot Richardson finally granted the Social Security Act waivers on August 7, 1972.

But the most unexpected opposition to welfare reform came from within the Reagan administration itself. Nearly a year after legislative approval of the Welfare Department reorganization, the state auditor general and the legislative counsel, both employees of the Legislature, decided to investigate Welfare Department hiring practices. Charges of illegality against the Welfare Department during the reform battle were not unusual—Reagan, Carleson, and other officials had been defendants in some 140 suits filed mainly by CRLA attorneys—but in this case a new accuser was added. At a hearing called by the Assembly, the welfare reform team found itself accused of illegal and improper hiring practices, not only by the auditor general and legislative counsel, but also by representatives of Reagan's own Department of Finance, with the apparent knowledge and concurrence of Verne Orr, Reagan's appointed finance director. One of the members of the welfare reform team, remembering an old Pogo cartoon, muttered: "We have met the enemy, and they are us." The matter was resolved when State Attorney General Evelle Younger, independently elected and politically unaffected by welfare reform, ruled in favor of the Welfare Department. The last and crudest attack on Reagan's welfare reform had been overcome. Looking back, the entire set of reforms had been designed and implemented, against overwhelming odds, by fewer than ten people, including the Governor.

The welfare reform successes, precarious as they sometimes seemed to the small band of reformers, convinced Reagan that carefully constructed task forces, given the freedom and the authority to examine, could find conservative solutions to the problems of a large state government. In the spring of 1972, Reagan asked his cabinet to define the problems he should attempt to solve in his remaining three years in office. The cabinet decided upon three: crime in the streets, taxes, and the restructuring of local government. The Governor established two task forces immediately to address the problems of crime and taxes, and a year later created a final task force on local government.

The difference between the Task Force on Criminal Justice and the Task Force on Tax Reduction proved the diversity of the task force approach to government change. Reagan's executive secretary, Ed Meese, and his Criminal Justice Task Force produced a large number of relatively detailed and specific solutions that could be implemented, one by one, through legislation or administrative action by the state, or through individual actions by local governments. The recommendations ran the gamut from stiffer penalties for crimes of violence to methods of streamlining court procedures in order to reduce mounting case backlogs. This task force emulated the Welfare Reform Task Force in bringing together people from both inside and outside the administration, but differed slightly in its approach by recruiting individuals with extensive experience in law enforcement and court procedures. The positive impact of its recommendations, while not generating the publicity of welfare reform, will be felt for many years, at least in part because its goal—the reduction of crime and restoration of safety for all Californians—is universally accepted.

On the other hand the Tax Reduction Task Force, headed by Lew Uhler, was charged to meet a goal with which many people, among them the majority of the Legislature, did not agree: namely, to find a method for permanently reducing taxes and, coincidentally, the size and authority of government. One member of the task force, who had also been a principal designer of the welfare reform program supplied the answer: a constitutional limitation on the portion of the total state personal income that the state government could take as revenue in any year and, since the task force thought that the current percentage was already too high, a provision for a slow rollback of the percentage until it reached the level it had been when Reagan became governor.

The concept was simple, much simpler than welfare reform; but because it dealt with the very heart of governmental power—the ability to tax—the task force knew from the start that such a program would be even harder to implement than welfare reform. First, the change would have to be constitutional, requiring a vote of the people. Second, the simplicity of the concept itself exposed the complexity of the state budget and expenditure process. Some state revenues went to a general fund, some to special funds for specific purposes, and some to funds over which the Federal Government exercised control. In addition, the state AAA bond rating and various government-subsidized pension programs would have to be protected. Most importantly, local governments would have to be insured against the state Legislature's circumventing the revenue limit by transferring costs to local taxpayers. The problems associated with these complexities of the existing government structure would have to be resolved in the language of the proposed constitutional amendment, making it even harder for the voters to understand what they were voting for or against, especially in the face of campaign rhetoric.

Knowing these pitfalls, the task force sought the advice of more than two hundred economists, attorneys, political scientists, and other experts in national and state government finance to reduce the idea to its simplest workable form. Armed with the enthusiastic support of such eminent "government weight watchers" as Milton Friedman, Peter Drucker, C. Lowell Harriss, and James Buchanan, the task force presented its revenue limitation proposal first to a steering committee of administration officials chaired by Frank Walton, Reagan's secretary of business and transportation and one of the stalwart conservatives of the administration. With his enthusiastic endorsement, the task force presented its proposal to Reagan, in the form of a long memorandum, just as he left for a 1972 Christmas vacation. He returned not only ready to endorse the concept, but full of ideas for improving the proposal and presenting it to the Legislature and the public. In a series of special cabinet meetings with Reagan and the task force in January 1973, the details of the program were worked out. The task force, augmented by an expert in constitutional law and an economist whose specialty was taxation and government finance, was assigned to draft the legal language of the proposed constitutional amendment. The spirit of welfare reform was reborn.

The California Constitution can only be amended by popular vote at an election called for that purpose by the governor. A proposed amendment can be placed on the ballot either by vote of the Legislature or by petition of ten per cent of the number of voters in the last general election. Reagan found a conservative legislator, Senator Robert Lagomarsino of Ventura, who was willing to sponsor the amendment as a bill to the Legislature. While the Senate listened politely, the Assembly quickly made it clear to Reagan that it would not vote to put the revenue limitation program on a ballot, no matter how many cards and letters the people sent them. Bob Moretti listened to ten minutes of a briefing on the program and walked out, leaving his staff to produce and distribute a press release which declared that the program would mean the end of representative government in California. Finally, the defiant stance of the Legislature left Reagan no choice but to try to get over 500,000 registered voters to endorse a vote on the program. In the record time of three months the signatures were obtained, and Reagan called a special election for November 6, 1973. The revenue limitation program would be the only statewide issue on the ballot and so was entitled "Proposition 1."

In that first blush of enthusiasm for a workable permanent tax reduction program and the delight engendered by the speed in getting the necessary petition signatures, a few dissenting voices and several ominous signs were overlooked or, at least, undervalued. First, most of Reagan's advisers, not having worked directly on welfare reform, did not know how tough that fight had been and how close the welfare reform team had come to losing on several occasions. Furthermore, the polls showed that the tax burden, while unpopular, was not nearly as unpopular as welfare had been. Second, the opposition to Proposition 1 would undoubtedly be stronger than the opposition to welfare reform since virtually all public employees would probably not only vote against it but also contribute to the opposition campaign. Third, Verne Orr, Reagan's finance director, opposed the concept of a tax limitation. His argument was that the growth of government was inexorable, because the people wanted it that way, and that the best that elected and appointed government officials could do was try to spend the money wisely. Although, out of loyalty to Reagan, he actively supported Proposition 1, his support lacked conviction. Fourth, winning a statewide election would cost money. Fifth, in order to establish a campaign organization, half of the governor's office, including Mike Deaver, Reagan's closest political adviser, resigned their state positions and moved six blocks down the street to join the campaign, which Deaver chaired. Thus, for three months the governor's coordinated team was split in half, physically and operationally. Sixth, Reagan himself was forced into a difficult posture. The task force had recommended a grassroots campaign in which Reagan would support, but not lead, the thrust for change. Unfortunately, the early need for the use of Reagan's personal political strength to stimulate the signature petition drive foreclosed the use of a grassroots strategy. For better or for worse, to the public, Proposition 1 belonged to Ronald Reagan. Finally, and probably most importantly, Proposition 1 was long, complex, and written in the legal jargon that has replaced English among lawyers. Trying to read it confused most of the people, and confused people usually vote no. In a post-election survey 69 per cent of the people who said they voted no said also that they thought Proposition 1 would increase taxes.

The opposition campaign was, as expected, funded heavily by public employees, and the Legislature, taking advantage of the fact that Reagan had also submitted

Proposition 1 to them in legislative bill form, trotted out its fiscal howitzer, Legislative Analyst A. Alan Post, to blast holes in Reagan's contention, backed up by task force data, that future revenues under Proposition 1 would be more than sufficient to meet the state's real needs. Post produced a large volume of statistics showing that local taxes would skyrocket under Proposition 1, even though the Proposition contained elaborate protections against local tax increases.

Post's figures were disputed by the prestigious National Tax Foundation, but they were not refuted, as they could have been, by the agency that had the greatest capability and credibility—Reagan's Department of Finance. Director Verne Orr denied a request from the Tax Reduction Task Force for his staff to estimate the next five years of state revenues if Proposition 1 were to pass, on the basis that no five-year projections could be considered reliable. The damage done by Post went unrepaired. Across the state local officials, who could no more understand the legal language of Proposition 1 than other citizens became queasy at the thought of having to raise local taxes, and their confusion and concern was passed on to the electorate by a very effective propaganda campaign conducted by the firm which, ironically, had managed Reagan's 1966 gubernatorial campaign. When the votes were counted. Proposition 1 had got 46 per cent yes votes to 54 per cent no votes. Reagan's most significant attempt to keep his campaign promise to reduce the size and influence of government had failed, principally because the people, confused by propaganda, a barrage of problematical statistics, and legal jargon, did not understand what he was trying to do.

Reagan was mad, at the opposition and at himself, but not at his staff or at the voters. He hopes, as do many of us who worked on Proposition 1, that it will reappear, in simpler and more understandable form, in California and other states, and will one day redeem his vision of government growth controlled by the people.

During the Proposition 1 campaign the last major task force—the Local Government Reform Task Force—was organized and began to investigate whether some structural improvement could be devised that would lead to the restoration of a less costly and more effective form of local control. Under the leadership of Robert Hawkins, the man who had restored order to the state OEO after the CRLA battle, this task force carried out the most exhaustive research of any of the task forces and arrived at the simplest conclusion. Its conclusion was that almost all of the problems of local government originated in the statutes and regulations which emanated from Washington, D.C., and Sacramento, and that the best way to improve local government was to leave it alone. Among its recommendations was the abolition of most of the state's restrictions on the formation of local governments; the establishment of an optional local income tax, deductible dollar-for-dollar from state income tax, to relieve the pressure on the property tax; and the encouragement of joint powers agreements to solve problems among local governments, in preference to consolidation or state intervention.

The Legislature was in no mood, after beating Proposition 1, to consider any more of Reagan's reforms, so the report of the Local Government Reform Task Force remained in limbo until after the final date for introduction of new 1974 bills.

The report was then released, with no fanfare or call for action. The innovation-by-task-force train had run out of steam, at least for the Reagan administration; which was too bad, for this latest report was in some ways more valuable than anything the other task forces had done. For one thing, the Local Government Reform Task Force report debunked the myth that the application of a "business" model to local governments would automatically improve cost-benefit ratios. On the contrary, the report demonstrated that in function after function, per capita costs of service increased dramatically where the population per governmental unit exceeded 250,000, exploding the analogy from business that consolidation of government functions and units would produce economies of scale and lower taxes. The task force proved that exactly the opposite is true: the smaller the population served, down to about the level of 25,000 people, the more satisfied the people and the less expensive the service.

Secondly, the report catalogued exhaustively the bureaucratic sins inflicted by larger governments on smaller governments that Reagan had talked of in 1966. Statistics on local government expenditures in California between 1950 and 1973 showed that, despite the much ballyhooed subventions of federal and state funds to local governments, the percentage of local expenditures that come solely from local revenues had risen, not fallen. In other words, federal and state policies had caused local governments to raise their taxes even faster than state and federal governments. The recommendation drawn from the evidence—get higher governments off the backs of local governments—was exactly in line with the instinctive reaction to intergovernmental relations which Reagan had enunciated when he first became a candidate for governor.

There were two major issues that Reagan never resolved as governor of California. One is the quality of lower education, which he purposely avoided trying to reform because California has a constitutionally and independently elected superintendent of public instruction. Reagan offered his support to the superintendents who were in office during his two terms as governor, but no major workable reforms were attempted, at least not in the opinion of conservatives who would like to see their children learn to read, write, add, and substract as well as the children in Ohio or Virginia or any of about twenty other states. Some day soon California may have to face up to the fact that its public education system is bureaucratized into immobility. Reagan did not try to stimulate that awareness.

The other issue is the power of the state over the use of land, relative to the powers of local governments and landowners. This issue is also tied, of course, to the general concern about the environment. Reagan's cabinet split constantly on specific issues, and Reagan's actions often reflected that split. He personally remains a strong advocate of the rights of individuals to use their land as they wish, as long as they are not harming their neighbors, and he has continually restated his belief that government, although it has the right to take land, must pay a fair price for it. In specific cases, however, he has come down in different places at different times. He personally canceled construction of a dam that would have flooded an Indian

Reservation, and he canceled, after a horseback visit to the Minaretes Wilderness Area, construction of a highway which would have defaced the wild country that he feels must be preserved. On the other hand, under pressure from a part of his staff oriented toward increased state intervention in local affairs, he came uncomfortably close, for a conservative, to endorsing state takeover of zoning control and increased use of police power, instead of eminent domain, in preserving open space. He also signed the bills and disseminated the regulations that have substantially delayed California construction starts by requiring elaborate environmental impact reports; allowed regional agencies to be set up for the control of such regions as the Tahoe Basin and San Francisco Bay shoreland; and established state control over the locating of power plants. To the extent that these are inconsistencies, however, we must recognize that the issue is one on which conservative philosophy is not at present clear enough to buttress a consistent position in practice.

Conservatives are an irascible breed: seldom satisfied with anyone or anything, and then not for long. They are, unless distracted, congenitally suspicious of the ability of another person to make him or her like him. They discard heroes at the drop of a minor principle, and tend to carry grudges for life. They love their country as they love themselves, for whatever is left of its independence and integrity. Being a conservative, I know how easily we magnify flaws in others, even those we admire.

Ronald Reagan was not a perfect governor, and I have been blunt in pointing out what I think were imperfect actions. But both his principles and his achievements place him far enough above his contemporaries for us to ask whether anyone else has his combination of dedication to conservative principles, the integrity to adhere to those principles in the face of overwhelming challenges, the perseverance to carry through to the ultimate possible extent what he promises to do, and the magnificent personality to explain himself candidly and clearly to anyone who will listen. In the Sacramento Public Library there is in the card catalogue a card which reads:

REAGAN, RONALD
Biographical material on
artists, actors, and musicians
will be found in the Art Room.

That card immediately conjured up for me the vision of Reagan, card in hand, asking politely of the librarian: "Where's the rest of me?" I think I know. George Steffes, now one of Sacramento's most highly respected lobbyists and the man who, more than any other, brought Reagan, and the Legislature together, told me the story. It happened in the California governor's office in 1967, when Reagan, faced with a $200-million budget deficit, was handed a bill just passed by the Legislature appropriating $57,000 to add hemophiliac children to the State Crippled Children's Program. All of his advisers told him to veto the bill: there was no money for any purpose, even one as worthy as this. But Reagan signed the bill without hesitation, saying simply: "If we are going to have a Crippled Children's Program at all, how can we keep these kids out?"

Slipping Landslide

By John Coyne

EDITOR'S NOTE: *This article first appeared in the April 2, 1976, issue of* National Review.

Miami, March 4—If you're a sports fan, you watched the last Super Bowl, one of the best of the series. The Dallas Cowboys were the underdogs, a team with neither the depth nor the experience of the Pittsburgh Steelers, the incumbent NFL champions.

What the Cowboys did have, however, was an explosive offense led by quarterback Roger Staubach, who in the crucial games of the season had consistently stunned opponents with unpredictable plays and sudden long scoring passes. It was this ability to strike quickly, to dazzle, to keep the other team off balance, that brought the Cowboys to the Super Bowl. And it was this offensive ability that gave the Cowboys a lead over the Steelers at half-time. The famous Steeler defense just didn't seem able to diagnose the Cowboy plays, and Terry Bradshaw, the solid and accident-prone Steeler quarterback, was stumbling, uncertain, blundering.

And then came the change. The underdog Cowboys, with nothing to lose and everything to gain, were loose and daring during the first half, seeming almost able to score at will. But then it happened. They took a lead, and suddenly they realized that they could, against all odds, actually win. And so they began to play very cautious, conservative football, sitting on that lead, fearing to make mistakes. And that was the biggest mistake of all. Now they were playing the predictable, safe sort of game the Steelers understood. Bradshaw settled down and began to perform with aggressive competence, and the Steeler juggernaut began to roll. Toward the end of the game Staubach tried to play with that old abandon again, but by then it was much too late.

In retrospect, even the Cowboys's coach admitted that they might well have won big if only they hadn't decided to sit on that lead. If you don't have the depth and the troops, but you do have dash and speed, then the best defense must necessarily be total offense. This is true of football, warfare, and politics.

And this explains, I believe, what has happened to the Reagan campaign in Florida. Reagan is sitting on a melting lead, denying and explaining, campaigning defensively rather than offensively, answering charges instead of making them, letting Ford take the game to him. The Reagan strategy might have worked, had Ford kept falling down stairs. But he didn't. Somewhere along the line Ford got mad, and the decision was made to try to take Reagan out quickly. And it appears to be working. Ford has been allowed to go on the offensive, and with his formidable resources—Cabinet surrogates, Executive branch experts, White House staff, the pork barrel, the bulk of the Republican leadership—it is a very potent offensive indeed.

When I joined the Reagan tour as a reporter for several days at the end of February, it was obvious that the campaign had been knocked off stride by the New Hampshire primary. Reagan's supporters, along with much of the national media, had expected a victory. A poll taken a week before the voting showed Reagan with a comfortable eight-point lead, and despite the size of the uncommitted vote, the Reagan high command was sufficiently confident to leave New Hampshire two days before the primary to campaign in Illinois. On primary eve the Ford camp seemed sunk in despair, the atmosphere of gloom so pervasive that Stuart Spencer, Ford's professional political manager, went to the unprofessional length of publicly blaming Ford's anticipated poor showing on a conspiracy between Richard Nixon and John Connally to knock Ford out of the race.

But when the dust cleared the day after, the Ford people couldn't quite believe their eyes. A post-New Hampshire political cartoon seems to sum it up. A slightly dazed sheriff in white grins uncertainly down at a smoking six-shooter held uncertainly in both hands. Sprawled in the dust is a lean gunfighter in black, his two drawn guns beside him. The befuddled sheriff says, "Well, I'll be darned."

No one yet quite understands how it happened. But it did happen. By most political standards, Reagan's narrow loss would be considered a moral victory, as was Eugene McCarthy's loss when he polled 42 per cent to Lyndon Johnson's 48 in 1968. But because Reagan out-organized and out-campaigned an apparently ineffectual and disorganized Ford, and because most accepted indicators signaled a win, Ford was considered a distinct underdog, and his victory therefore a genuine upset.

As a result, the whole Reagan game plan is now in doubt. The idea had been to strike quickly by taking Ford out in New Hampshire and Florida. These victories, it was believed, would have a snowball effect, influencing the results in Illinois, where Reagan is presently running from seven to ten points behind, and encouraging regular Republicans to defect from Ford in droves. With Ford rapidly losing support, and with John Connally apparently ready to enter the race after Illinois, thereby siphoning off votes from Ford, Reaganites hoped to have a clear field by April.

But all that may be academic now, and in Florida, just days before the voting, the Reagan camp is desperately trying to come up with a new game plan. No one is quite sure what the new plan will look like, or whether it is even possible to develop a new plan at all. Everyone agrees that if Reagan is to hold on to his dwindling lead in Florida, he's going to have to come out swinging. But the problem is, swinging at what?

St. Petersburg, March 1—It's a defensive Reagan that I cover during the last days of February. On the first day of campaigning in the Tampa-St. Petersburg area, the atmosphere in the Reagan camp is uneasy, uncertain, Reagan himself bone-weary, having arrived in Tampa late at night, straight from a full schedule of campaigning in Illinois the day after the New Hampshire primary. Reagan is somewhat testy upon arrival, as is the press contingent traveling with him, and aides agree that the day would have been better spent resting and reassessing strategy.

The first event on the 27th is a noon rally in Williams Park in St. Petersburg, a city which literally swarms with old people. Thirty-five per cent of the citizens are over 65, a Reagan aide tells me, as are 60 per cent of St. Petersburg's registered Republicans. Pinellas County is a mecca for Midwestern retirees, many of them living on Social Security and pensions; it is one of Gerald Ford's strongholds.

We are in the land of the very old. About 8,000 of them sit on wooden benches or stand at the rear, chatting, tapping their feet, some of them singing along as a band plays Yankee-Doodleish tunes, many of them eating box lunches.

There are several hesitant preliminary speeches. Reagan finally arrives late, running just ahead of heavy rain clouds. The audience groans when it's told that neither James Stewart nor Efrem Zimbalist Jr. will appear after all. But they give Reagan a good, though not a rousing, welcome. He launches into an abbreviated version of The Speech, flipping through his pile of cards, hitting all the familiar points— bureaucracy, taxes, deficit spending, federal paper-shuffling, federal inefficiency, vacillating foreign policy. Cuba, Russia, Panama, détente, Helsinki. He is interrupted once by a spaced-out blond in blue sunglasses, carrying a baby and screaming, "Don't hurt me!" as the Secret Service and the police hustle her out of range. Otherwise, there is little crowd noise, the applause polite but never wildly enthusiastic. Reagan is slightly hoarse, his timing uncharacteristically off as he runs rapidly through the figures that document federal waste and inefficiency.

Each point is well taken. During the speech, however, and during the following question-and-answer session, it's obvious that the real topics of interest are the New Hampshire primary and Social Security. The charges made by Ford have clearly hurt, and it appears that Reagan now believes they lost him the primary. A great deal of his time is spent attempting to clear up the record. Ford has accused Reagan of advocating a voluntary Social Security system and of intending to invest Social Security funds in the stock market.

Reagan denies both accusations hotly, and launches into a detailed explanation of his plan for Social Security reform. He intends to appoint a "presidential commission of the most expert insurance, pension, and actuarial people in our land." The commission will study the program and make recommendations on how to put it on a sound financial basis—an idea based upon the success of the Citizen Task Forces he established in California ten years ago.

But presidential commissions tend to lack sex appeal, and the program sounds somewhat abstract and complicated. People begin to shift around and talk, their attention wandering, although they snap back when Reagan assures them that no matter what the final shape of his proposals, there will be no interruption in payments. And anyhow, he adds, it would all take about thirty years to bring about. They applaud, apparently secure in the knowledge that by that time most of them will be rejoicing in heaven.

No doubt it's a good and necessary proposal. But is this really the time and the place to be talking at length about reforming the Social Security system? Should he be talking about Social Security at all? David Keene, a top Reagan aide, likes to tell one of Lyndon Johnson's favorite stories. A Texas congressman told his press aide to spread the word that his opponent fornicated with pigs. Can we prove it? the aide asked. Of course not, said the congressman. But it's a hell of a charge to have to spend your time denying.

Reagan also spends a good deal of time responding to the doubt planted by Ford's assertions that no one to the right of him can win a national election. Reagan points out that he won twice by landslides in a 3 to 2 Democratic state, and he insists he proved his broad appeal in New Hampshire by getting 1,500 Democratic write-in votes.

Perhaps. But he's definitely playing the game on Ford's terms, trapped into talking at length on non-issues. And it's dangerous for an insurgent candidate, this late in the game, to be so obviously on the defensive.

As the rally begins to break up, I ask an elderly couple if they intend to vote for Reagan. No, they say. Ford? No. "Actually." says the man, "we're going to vote for Jackson. We just came over to see the fun."

"That's the trouble with crowd estimates in Florida," a reporter from the *Miami Herald* tells me. "You can't tell the residents from the tourists, and in a retirement town you can't tell a candidate's supporters from the people who think of these things as social events."

We cross the street to a retiree recreation center called Social Scene, Inc., where we are served Colonel Sanders and Pepsi, and where L. E. (Tommy) Thomas, Reagan's ebullient Florida campaign chairman, tells several of us that he has revised his estimate of the winning margin. A few weeks earlier Thomas had been predicting a 2 to 1 Reagan victory. Now he's predicting 55 per cent, a figure that makes Reagan aides wince. Governor Meldrim Thomson had been trumpeting the same figure around New Hampshire the week before.

"I'd hate like the devil to do less than 50 per cent," says Thomas. Anything in the 40s would be "damaging," he continues, and a flat 40 per cent or less would be "a disaster."

Later, as we board the press bus for an hour-and-a-half motorcade to a shopping center rally in Pasco County, a reporter calls it "the slipping landslide."

Several thousand people pack into a parking lot to hear Reagan. Again, sections of "The Speech" from cards, and again, a detailed discussion of Social Security and electability. Reporters, who have been waiting for something signaling a shift in strategy, perk up when a questioner in the crowd asks, "Do you think Mr. Ford is a good President?" Reagan pauses, then pleads the 11th Commandment.

"Where's Jimmy Stewart?" several ladies ask me as the rally breaks up.

That night, a talk, billed as nonpolitical, to a group called the Sales and Marketing Executives of St. Petersburg. This is a Reagan crowd, middle-aged, well-dressed, happy. He gives "The Speech" again, this time in its entirety, only the overt political references excised. He's at the top of his form, he likes this audience, and they punctuate every paragraph with applause, with a standing ovation at the end. Peculiar. Reagan is one of the few politicians in the country who seems at his best giving a non-political speech.

It's wasted on much of the press corps, however. Most of them aren't there. Many of them who follow a candidate around have to file several times a day. And if you give them precisely the same speech at each event, they run out of material to write about. The set speech has its advantages. The material is tested so you don't stir up any unexpected controversies, as was the case, for instance, with the $90-billion transfer speech. A set speech with no fresh news content is fine if you're running serenely ahead. But it's also completely defensive.

And so, when the day began with Reagan's poorest performance, at Williams Park, there was standing room only on the press bus. When it ended in Tampa with Reagan's finest effort of the day, the press bus was half-empty.

The next morning to Sun City, a retirement community, for more Social Security, then to Tampa for a lunch—ham, yams, and limas—sponsored by the Hillsborough County Citizens for Reagan. More of the same. "The Speech." Social Security. Electability. He talks about reforming the bureaucracy, about bringing in experts as he did in California, where 250 citizen volunteers devoted 117 days without pay, developing 1,800 recommendations for streamlining government, 1,600 of which were adopted. The result: he balanced the budget, wiped out a huge deficit, left his successor a surplus, and today California enjoys a triple-A Moody's bond rating.

During the question period he is again asked to comment on Ford, again refuses. Many in the audience are puzzled. "Why should he expect people to throw Ford out and put him in if he won't tell us what the differences are?" one woman asks. On the way out I ask another woman if she's going to vote for Reagan. She tells me she prefers Carter because he's cute.

Then to WFLA-TV, Tampa's NBC affiliate, for a press-conference taping. Détente? He approves of the concept. Should we break off SALT? No. (Why not, I wonder.) Should we withdraw from the UN? "We should not forsake that dream." (Did *Ronald Reagan* say that?)

Obviously, he wants to convince voters that his views are moderate. And that's understandable. But with a surging incumbent and a slipping lead, it's nearly past time to begin to crank up that offensive game.

"If we're going to go, we might as well go with a bang," says a Reagan aide. And meanwhile, on the last day of Reagan's penultimate swing through Florida, as he spoke to a crowd in a half-empty baseball park, Gerald Ford hit the state with a big bang indeed.

Tampa, March 3—"We've got the momentum," said Ford, motorcading down the condominium strip between Palm Beach and Miami, "and we're going to move and move and move." And move he did, swinging south and then north to Tampa, addressing 80,000 people in two days.

This was the new Ford, the President who suddenly understood the power of his office. As the columnists like to put it, Ford has discovered the value of the incumbency, and he is maximizing it.

"I'm not a part of the Washington establishment and I don't think that's a disadvantage," Ronald Reagan is fond of saying. Perhaps. As the think-piece writers like to tell us, the mood of the country is anti-Washington. But while non-membership may not be a disadvantage, there are still certain advantages to membership, especially when you're presiding officer and thus in a position to hand out the goodies.

And Ford has been handing them out right and left. On his first swing he landed in Orlando and promised that city it would host an International Chamber of Commerce convention, easily worth a cool million. In Bay Pines he visited a veterans' hospital and promised to build a new one. Then he tapped Jerry Thomas, the popular conservative who was Republican gubernatorial candidate in 1974, for a cushy post at Treasury. And the rumor is that he has promised Miami a mass transit system.

On this second swing he outdoes himself. In Miami he brings a predominantly Cuban audience roaring to its feet at Dade County Auditorium by branding Fidel Castro, the man the Administration had been playing footsie with, "an international outlaw," with whom he swears he'll have nothing to do. He personally greets 1,161 Cubans who have just become citizens, and he promises Miami's Cuban community that he will speed up the process by which refugees become citizens.

Those new citizens don't vote. But their friends and relatives do. Before Ford's rather tardy renunciation of Castro, they were expected to vote 5 to 1 for Reagan, whose consistent hardline anti–Castro position had made Miami one of his strongest centers of support. Of the 118,000 Republicans registered in Dade County, 27,021—or 23 per cent—are Latin, mostly Cuban. Before Ford's new hard line, it was estimated that he'd have to pull a good 60 per cent of the non–Latin vote to carry Dade. But now, Reagan backers concede, he has made significant inroads into Reagan's Latin support.

And just to make sure that the Cubans got the message, Ford, upon returning to Washington, gives an interview to a Miami TV reporter, in which he solemnly says, "I don't use the word détente any more."

It was one of the crassest and most obviously political ploys of the decade. But it points up one of the problems in challenging an incumbent President. A challenger can attack a policy successfully, as Reagan has done with détente. But a President, if he decides that the policy is a political liability, as détente is among Cuban refugees, can simply label it inoperative.

Ford is making maximum use of the White House. A Florida campaign flyer reads, "Come Out and See Air Force One." The *Sarasota Herald–Tribune* bannered its Sunday edition during Ford's visit with the headline, "Sarasota: White House for a Day."

"Ronald Reagan brings a political campaign to town," says one veteran reporter. "Gerald Ford brings the White House."

"Ford was one of the first to be critical of CREEP and the way it blew up the Presidency," says a frustrated Reagan supporter, bitter over what he believes to be Ford's duplicity. "Now it's the same thing again, it's the White House instead of the man running for office."

Is it working? Although Florida's Republican State Executive Committee still believes Reagan to be running slightly ahead, a top Reagan aide told me on March 1 that if the election were held on that date, he thought Reagan would lose by one or two percentage points.

As it now stands, Ford is expected to make one more last-minute visit, and Reagan will put in five final campaign days. If Reagan goes on the offensive, many of his backers believe, he can still pull it off. And if he does, he will go to Illinois with the same sort of momentum that carried Ford into Florida.

Gerald Ford has laid it on the line. At the end of his last campaign swing, he said: "Florida is really the key. If we win and win very well in Florida, they [Reagan's supporters] ought to know they can't win."

That's undoubtedly true. But Reagan is now in precisely the position that Ford found himself in in New Hampshire. The Ford camp, the press, and even many Reagan aides believe that a Ford victory is inevitable. Reagan has become the under-dog, and a win of any size would be seen as an upset.

"Florida's the whole ballgame," says one Ford staffer. And it very well may be the whole ballgame—for both candidates.

Miami, March 5—The situation among the Democrats in Florida is totally unclear, the whole thing having been thrown completely out of whack by Henry Jackson's stunning upset win in Massachusetts, where in 1972 he had finished in eighth place, behind Wilbur Mills.

During my visit to Florida, things still seemed relatively predictable. Of the three candidates who have made full-scale campaign efforts there, the order of finish was expected to be Wallace, Carter, and Jackson, the only real question being one of percentages.

Wallace, it was believed, would not equal his 1972 mark of 42 per cent. For one thing, his physical condition has persuaded many former supporters that he wouldn't be up to the demands of the Presidency. And unlike 1972, when busing was the subject of a ballot referendum, there is no single red-hot social issue in Florida of the sort that Wallace speaks to so eloquently.

Instead, this year, the issue among voters is unemployment, which has hit Florida with special severity. Wallace is seen by many as the ideal protest candidate, but most of his supporters know that he has no real chance at the White House, and on a gut issue like jobs, many of them are inclined this time around to vote for someone they feel actually has a chance of getting to Washington and putting programs into effect.

Jimmy Carter's support is seen as center-liberal, the latter a gift from the other liberal candidates, who decided not to campaign in Florida in hopes that Carter could take Wallace out, a move they now regret having made.

Floridians say that Carter's organization is the best of the three, made up primarily of McGovern–style volunteer youth squads, who have been knocking on doors since last year.

Florida newsmen also say that Carter shows surprising strength in the Wallace territory of north Florida, where he comes on as a good ole farm boy from Georgia. Carter's support is strange, however, shapeless and difficult to diagram. His position on the issues is still essentially unknown, and the assaults of the doctrinaire liberals are having an effect. Birch Bayh accuses him of "advocating Republican principles," and conservative Democrats in Florida seem to catch a whiff of radicalism in his proposals. In addition, the momentum from New Hampshire has been greatly dissipated by his disappointing showing in Massachusetts. Carter has also for the first time displayed a tendency to make mistakes, publicly implying that Scoop Jackson's win in Massachusetts came about as a result of a racist position on the busing issue, a charge that does not go down well in Florida.

And finally, here's Scoop, for real this time, finally proving that he can win a major primary, and win it in a big crowd. As a result there's a whole new view of Jackson's chances. A week ago the betting was that he'd finish right around 20 per cent, but now that estimate is being revised sharply upward, and Floridians are talking not only about his chances of beating Carter, but about edging Wallace himself.

The latter probably isn't a real possibility, but Jackson's support is solid and much more impressive than pre-Massachusetts analyses tended to indicate. For one thing, he is heir to the large Jewish vote on the southeast coast that went to Hubert Humphrey in 1972. Shapp will get a bit of it, but Florida's Jewish voters understand politics and don't believe in political waste. Jackson has a consistent record of concern for Israel, and the endorsement of Daniel Moynihan, a strong champion of the Israelis, will count for a good deal in Miami, just as it did for slightly different reasons in Boston.

Jackson's proposals have also been particularly appealing to Florida's massive retirement population, especially his call for national health insurance. His views on a strong national defense combined with his demonstrated distrust for détente are widely applauded among the Latins in Miami and Tampa. And, of course, alone among the three candidates, Jackson enjoys the organizational and financial backing of big labor.

There may indeed be an anti–Washington current running everywhere, including Florida. But there is also a strong desire for level-headed competence, a quality that many are suddenly discovering in Jackson after his performance in Massachusetts.

Miami, March 10—Jackson's 24 per cent was respectable, at least four points better than the showing predicted for him before Massachusetts. But given that Massachusetts momentum, and given the overwhelming support of the Democratic establishment, Jackson's percentage, though adequate, was less than astounding.

What did astound, of course, was Carter's TKO of George Wallace, who now finds himself in the same boat as Ronald Reagan—if they can't win in Florida, say the commentators, they can't win the big ones anywhere.

Carter's victory over Wallace took many of us who claim to know something about national politics by surprise. In Washington, where politics is the only subject of conversation, Carter's candidacy was, until very recently, expected to evaporate by the end of March. The Democrats, according to the conventional Washington wisdom, were determined to flush the last traces of McGovernism from their party's system and to go this time round for an old-line liberal centrist—Humphrey probably, Jackson perhaps, Muskie just possibly. Carter, the argument ran, was an unknown quantity without the support of the traditional Democratic power groups; party regulars weren't about to take a chance on him. And on the other side, also lined up against Carter, were the Wallace supporters, viewed by most observers as unflinching in their loyalty, a rock-solid constituency.

But all that, as a Nixonian would say, is now inoperative, and the political analysts are scurrying around attempting to find a frame of reference in which to place Carter, a candidate whom even the astute John Osborne has called "unclassifiable." And the Florida results do little to clear things up. Carter took a large share of the identifiable liberal vote, as expected. But he also scored respectably among conservatives. He did well with young voters, but also took an unpredicted share of the retiree vote. He cut into Jackson's relatively affluent Jewish constituency and also attracted a surprising number of Wallace blue-collar types, who were expected to defect to Jackson. Women supported him heavily, as did blacks. Carter's black vote stands at roughly 70 per cent—a total that, as one commentator put it, provides him with a "passport to liberal legitimacy."

That passport will now have to be validated in at least one Northern industrial state if Carter is to establish himself as a totally convincing candidate. The opportunity will come first in Illinois, where Mayor Daley is supporting Senator Adlai Stevenson III as a favorite son candidate. If Carter can run well against the Daley machine and the Stevenson name, then he will rate at least one unarguable classification—that of a winner.

As the Democratic leadership races to catch up with the voters, the Republicans now seem resigned to settling for Gerald Ford as the party's nominee. The Reagan candidacy is still alive, but with four straight wins under his belt, Ford is rolling. In Illinois, according to one top Reagan campaign official, former Reagan supporters are now defecting to Ford in droves. And if Ford wins big there, as it now seems he will, few Reagan supporters will have the heart to continue the campaign.

What happened? As pointed out above, Reagan was badly undercut by the power of the incumbency and Ford's sudden discovery of how that power could be used. He was also the victim of overconfidence. "They set themselves up," said one Ford staffer, referring to the predictions of landslides that were carelessly tossed around during the early days of the campaign, when Ford seemed most vulnerable. Because of those predictions, Ford was widely perceived as the underdog in New Hampshire and Florida, his first narrow win thus viewed as an upset, eclipsing the fact that Reagan's showings in both New Hampshire and Florida were, indeed, phenomenal political achievements.

The Reagan campaign strategy, examined in retrospect, was also seriously flawed. It is easy to criticize after the fact, of course. As someone once said, journalists analyzing political results are like people visiting the battlefield after it's all over, to shoot the wounded. Had that strategy led to the narrowest of wins in New Hampshire, its architect, John Sears, would now be acclaimed as a political genius.

But it didn't work. Reagan, by avoiding the tough infighting required to beat Ford, raised doubts about the depth of his desire for the Presidency. On the issues, he was disappointingly vague, fuzzing over the conservative image, thereby leaving real doubt in the minds of many grassroots Republicans as to why they should replace a President they perceived as essentially conservative with a man who seemed at times, surprisingly, even less conservative.

In brief, the Sears strategy was based on the assumption that this time round the voters were ready for a campaign of personalities and images rather than a campaign of issues. Perhaps. The Carter phenomenon lends credence to that view. But even here the strategy seems questionable. There is no doubt that from a conservative point of view Reagan could have out-issued Ford. But could he really out-personality him? There is something a bit Ikeish about Ford's image, and that's a quality that regular Republicans have always liked.

So, in the end, Reagan was as much a victim of his own strategy as he was of Ford's attacks on him. As one analyst put it, Reagan was trying to win the general election before he won the primary.

With Ford steamrolling toward a first-ballot victory, the questions that will now be asked are questions about his electability. He has demonstrated unexpected political strengths during the first three important primary campaigns. He has also managed, despite formidable advantages, to capture the allegiance of only about half of the voting members of a minority party. As the Ford people liked to ask about Reagan, does he have sufficient support to win a national election?

Where's the Rest of Him?

By Richard Brookhiser

> EDITOR'S NOTE: *This article first appeared in the February 22, 1980, issue of* National Review.

Two days after the Iowa caucuses, the press is waiting for Ronald Reagan in the Aloha Lounge at O'Hare airport, a room decorated with orange, yellow, and pink pineapples and volcanoes. Advance men have hung a red, white, and blue "Reagan 80" banner from the wall, and there are a number of good-looking men in three-piece suits with wires running out of their ears and bulges on their hips.

Reagan appears in a dark blue checked suit, a blue necktie, and shoes like mirrors. Whenever he speaks at press conferences, he places both hands on the lectern, and occasionally cocks his right foot and points a toe on the floor. This afternoon, he seems . . . *bleak* is too strong a word; *subdued* will do.

The press wants his thoughts on two battles, Afghanistan and Iowa. The invasion of Afghanistan, he says, represents "a new arrogance on the part of the Soviets. . . . It is time the U.S. takes a position. I've recommended bases in Oman and Somalia. I've recommended arms, possibly an American presence, in Pakistan. It's time to have a plan."

But the press is more interested in Des Moines than Herat. Reagan fields the questions, by turns gracious to enemies, protective of underlings, defensive of himself. "I'm quite sure George Bush succeeded in the strategy he aimed at. We knew he had a great organization" (all the bitter words Reagan has ever said about fellow Republicans could probably be inscribed on one of his three-by-five cards; over the next three days, Bush will be "George," or, at moments of exceptional stress, "George Bush"). No, Reagan has not lost faith in his planners. "If I did that, I'd lose faith in myself. We've been campaigning harder, working harder than some of you have been suggesting in your stories. These trips have been organizational—getting in to stimulate the local organizations. It gets pretty hairy."

Is Bush now the front-runner? "Why don't we wait and see the polls?" Do you regret not going into the Puerto Rican primary? "No." How do you expect to do in the Arkansas caucuses? "I don't know. I did pretty well in Arkansas in 1976, but they've gone back to guys in a room sitting down and picking" (he evidently suspects he might do badly).

An aide announces the press's thanks, and Reagan is off, through O'Hare in a brisk wedge of secret service men (heads turn, who's that? must be somebody famous), into a motorcade. The cars pull out from the black glass buildings, beneath the planes dropping in like bats, into a slate and orange colored sunset. Flat buildings, flatland-corporate headquarters, suburban ranch houses, ghosts of barns. State police cars with gumball machines flashing block every intersection as the motorcade passes. In 45 minutes, the cars come to the Pheasant Run Inn in St. Charles, Illinois—"The midwest's finest resort hotel."

Reagan is addressing a $50-a-plate fundraiser for Representative Tom Corcoran of Illinois' 15th District. He sits at a head table with Mr. and Mrs. Corcoran, the chief operating officer of Aurora Industries, and eleven Republican county chairmen. While the waitresses pass around a Grand Old Party dessert—ice cream with strawberry sauce and American flag pins—the dinner chairman introduces Corcoran, Corcoran introduces Reagan (citing his "ability to articulate Republican principles of government"). Reagan returns the compliments, gives some GOP rah-rah, then goes into a full-length speech.

Critics complain of Reagan's one-liners and, relatedly, of his giving simplistic answers. The second charge is mostly spite; what the people who make it usually mean to say is that they don't like Reagan's particular answers, or the definiteness of any answer at all: a clock chime like "We must not negotiate from fear, but we must not fear to negotiate" soothes a certain type of mind in a way that a thumb-nail program—"We bought it, we built it, and we're going to keep it"—can't. As for one-liners, Reagan is avoiding them tonight. If anything, the speech is pedagogic. He explains bracket creep. He asserts that the energy crisis is caused by government, not waste, and cites the 1978 fuel shortage in California caused by a reliance on the 1972 allocation system. He plugs the Kemp-Roth tax cut, and notes the salubrious effects of the tax cuts of Andrew Mellon (Jack Kemp clearly brought along a couple of copies of Jude Wanniski's *The Way the World Works* when he signed up with Reagan). He pins teenage unemployment to the minimum wage. He gives a post-mortem on Proposition 13: 100,000 fewer public employees, but 532,000 more pri-vate sector jobs. He lists his accomplishments in California: volunteer task forces formed, 16,000 recommendations implemented, $5.7 billion returned to taxpayers, bond rating up to Triple A.

And, as always, he ends with questions from the floor. *Iran*: "There isn't any-thing the Administration has done that they couldn't have done in the first 24 hours." *Windfall profits tax*: "It's not a windfall profits tax, it's an excise." He ex-plains—the first explanation of the evening that was not utterly lucid—that domes-tic oil regulations subsidize OPEC imports; charges that the oil industry has been virtually nationalized. *ERA*: (posed by the sweet-voiced female editor of the St. Charles high school paper) he opposes ERA, but rattles off a list of statutes passed during his term as governor removing legal burdens on women in rape cases, in the management of savings accounts, in various other economic matters. He doesn't have his card on this subject, he confesses disarmingly, and apologizes for the list's incompleteness. "Thank you," the editor chirps, "and I want to say, women are doing just fine without ERA." A blunder: it's bad form to tip your hand so obviously when asking a friendly question. But Reagan smiles and retrieves it all: "Well, I could have saved all that talk." He makes a last pitch for Corcoran, then adds, almost as an afterthought, "I'll be honest—-I'd like to be his neighbor in Washing-ton." There is a brief standing ovation, and most of the audience crowd around to shake his hand. In the hall, Illinoians position themselves shyly to get a look at him.

Back to the cars, back to O'Hare.

The Hyatt Regency O'Hare gives a credible impersonation of a palace in a desert. Breakfast costs a fortune, a pianist supplies the muzak, and the ivy trailing neatly over the balconies on the interior courtyard gives it the appearance of a crew-cut hanging garden. If you have to spend the night at an airport, and you have $80, there's no place else to go.

Reagan comes down the main escalator next morning at 8:15. The TV camera-men come down before him to set up ambush in the lobby and test their lights by flashing them into the eyes of innocent businessmen. Overnight the weather has gone from foul to vile, and Reagan's chartered 727 takes off late.

The sun comes out somewhere over Kentucky, and by the time Reagan lands in Florence, South Carolina, it's up to 45 degrees. South Carolina has the first South-ern primary this year; Senator Thurmond and Governor Edwards have come out for

Connally, and Reagan is showing the flag. The local advance people seem harried. A young lady hassles with a reporter in the Florence airport. *"What's* your name?" "Rowland Evans." "Where you from?" "Never mind."

Reagan begins this press conference with a statement:

> Having reviewed Mr. Carter's State of the Union address last evening, I must today speak out strongly on the crisis in Iran and Afghanistan. Mr. Carter terms the Afghan crisis "the most serious threat to world peace since the Second World War," yet he is willing to accept the Soviet presence in Afghanistan with a vague threat that if further aggression transpires in the Persian Gulf we may do something. I wonder how the Pakistanis feel about American resolve when they have, in effect, been excluded from the protection of even this vague threat of American action. And how seriously will the Soviet Union treat Mr. Carter's threat . . . when it is accompanied by his voluntary pledge to observe unilaterally SALT I and SALT II. . . .
>
> It is time for him to make our resolve clear in terms that are specific.

He reads it shakily, pausing in mid-sentence and hobbling words (he has never been able to talk from a manuscript; in 1937, he almost washed out of his first movie at the preliminary script reading, and all his major speeches are delivered from note cards). The baritone voice also sounds about half an octave lower—perhaps a touch of sore throat coming on.

The press wades in and Reagan perks up. What specific things would *you* do? He has already made suggestions, he answers—bases in Oman and Somalia, and an American "presence" in Pakistan. What about draft registration? Reagan cites his long opposition to a peace time draft, and calls registration a "meaningless gesture. It doesn't make us more able to respond." America needs instead a "strong active military reserve," built up by "promotion, incentive, and appeal to patriotism." Which does Reagan think Carter is—deceitful or a fool? "I wish I could say he was a fool."

But Reagan has not come to talk in airports. There's a crowd at Francis Marion College, and they've been waiting an hour and a half. The auditorium of the science building seats two or three hundred, and people are lining the walls. Many of the faces in the audience belongs to students, and they're clean and shiny as milk (Southern girls may not be any prettier than their sisters elsewhere, but they work a lot harder at it). The arrival of the press creates a stir—is Reagan far behind? Suddenly, the clarinetist, drummer, and pianist cut short the light swing and polkas with which they've been nibbling at the boredom and start "California, Here I Come." The crowd stops gossiping and springs up, some stand on their chairs, yelling, clapping, flapping hand-made signs. Reagan smiles, and waves relaxedly. A young man in a premature three-piece suit presents him with a Francis Marion jacket. Bobby Richardson, pride of the Yankees, noted Christian layman, and co-chairman of the Reagan for President Committee in South Carolina, waves from a chair on the stage. Patrick Brian, state commissioner of agriculture—there to offset Edwards and Thurmond—introduces Reagan as "a great American, a man of high moral character, and a great friend of mine."

Reagan apologizes for the rasp in his voice, blames it on the LA smog, and goes into his speech. He still gives two-minute treatises on the oil industry and inflation, but there are more applause lines this afternoon, and questions come sooner. He laughingly concedes that, yes, "George" did well in Iowa. He calls for getting rid of inheritance taxes that strike against "the small business, the family farm" (applause). He supports balanced budgets as well as Kemp-Roth—"balancing the budget is like protecting your virtue—you have to say No" (applause, students included). He works the questions so that he can slip chunks of his speech into the answers, concludes by observing that the real immorality of the Vietnam War was "sending 50,000 American boys to die in a war we didn't have the courage to win" (tremendous applause), spoils the effect by talking past the line, but it was still a good job, his best so far.

At VFW Post 3181, off the main road in the pine trees, the cars are backed up to the highway. This is a rally of Reagan workers, over a hundred of them, milling in an all-purpose room—rowdy men, some young people, some ladies, middle aged and up, four blacks, two of them aged (what electoral storms they have weathered!). Reagan makes a semi-circle through them, clambers up on a small stage, receives a toy bear from the student body president of a local college, and starts again. He warms up with a bit of history: during the Greco-Turkish war after World War I, the USS Arizona docked in embattled Constantinople, where, every morning, a sailor with a flag, a Marine with a mailbag, and a Marine with a rifle would march to the American legation and back, untouched, unmolested: "we can have that kind of America again," he assures them. Carter says a man in a plaid work jacket and a green shirt has been talking a lot about poor people; what do you say? "We Republicans have to show people we're not the party of big business and the country-club set. We're the party of main street, the small town, the city neighborhood; the shopkeeper, the farmer, the cop on the beat, the blue-collar and the white-collar worker. Now, a word we hear a lot is compassion. If someone is genuinely helpless of course we should be compassionate, and Americans are the most compassionate people on earth. But what about the man who gets up every morning, gets his kids off to school, goes to work, pays his bills, supports his church and charity, and pays his taxes? We have some compassion for them." Question about Iran. "The policies of the Administration," says Reagan, "made Iran possible." Cheers of A-men. The entourage wants to leave: the candidate wants to take two more questions. SALT II? "Ship that thing back to the Soviets in Moscow." Do you believe in God (asked by the younger of the black men)? "If I didn't think I could turn to God for help, I wouldn't be running for this office." Reagan workers stand at the door as the crowd leaves, holding buckets for contributions.

No buckets will be needed to collect contributions at the next stop, only envelopes. The 727 sails from Florence to Miami for a $250-a-person party in the Tropic Room at the Intercontinental Hotel. It's freezing in Miami, maybe 65 degrees, and a number of the bare female arms and shoulders take refuge under furs. Some of their contributions this evening will undoubtedly go to defray the cost of the violinist and the accordionist, the carvers in chefs' hats at the side tables, and the ice sculpture of an angelfish. The press find themselves cordoned off from this magnificence behind a velveteen rope, but some kindly bare arm passes in a tray of sandwiches which the reporters surround like goldfish diving after breadballs.

Reagan acknowledges the cost of the affair—"If we don't win, that's gonna be a regular price for a drink"—and goes immediately into questions. Tell us you *are* saying the same things you said in 1964, a woman asks him. "It wasn't exactly a question," Reagan observes. Are you moderating your views, someone else pursues. "The hell I am." What about Social Security? The system is now several trillion dollars out of actuarial balance, he says; he would appoint a task force to suggest reforms. A Cuban wants to know about Cuban freedom. We have to "get back to the Monroe Doctrine that there are no foreign colonies in this hemisphere." Age? Phil Crane, Reagan notes, has been saying he is Reagan, only twenty years younger: "That's too bad," Reagan adds, "because twenty years ago I was a New Deal Democrat." (Reagan, be it noted, refers to Crane only as "another candidate." Let no Republican's name be coupled, even in jest, with "New Deal," though the heavens fall.)

Hands clap, furs leave, and outside the silver moon slides to the zenith.

Reagan slightly misled his Miami audience. Twenty years ago his conversion was already complete.

Ronald Wilson Reagan was born February 6, 1911, the second of two sons, in Tampico, Illinois. He remembers (as people born in a thousand other such towns remember) a park, a Civil War cannon, stacked cannonballs. Before he was nine, the family had moved to Chicago, to Galesburg, to Monmouth, back to Tampico, and finally to Dixon. The Rock River runs through the middle of Dixon, and when Reagan turned 15 he began spending his summers there as a lifeguard at Lowell Park. He recalls saving over seventy people, though the only gratuity he ever earned was $10 for retrieving an upper plate.

John Edward (Jack) Reagan, Ronald's father, made a slender income from shoes—clerking them, selling them. He was an Irish Catholic and a confirmed Democrat, Northern style: he forbade his sons to see *Birth of a Nation* because it was sympathetic to the Ku Klux Klan. He was also an alcoholic. Nelle Reagan (née Wilson) bore with her husband's periodic benders, acquiesced in his politics, and devoutly attended the Christian Church. Neither of the Reagans had gone beyond grade school, but they enjoyed books, and Nelle led the dramatic readings in the local ladies' societies.

In 1928, Reagan entered Eureka College, a small, Christian, coed school twenty miles south of Dixon. Eureka gave him a scholarship for half his tuition, and a job washing dishes in the girls' dormitory to cover his board. Reagan gave Eureka three years, starting at right guard on the football team. He also lettered in swimming and track, and joined the dramatic society. In his junior year, Eureka entered the Eva La Gallienne Competition for one-act plays sponsored by Northwestern University. Eureka's production of *Aria da Capo* took a second, and Reagan was one of six actors singled out for a good performance.

He didn't act again for five years after leaving Eureka. "Broadway and Hollywood," he has said, "were as inaccessible as outer space," and he went to Davenport, Iowa instead, broadcasting the games of the Chicago Cubs for Station WHO. His break came in 1937, when he went with the Cubs to spring training on Catalina Island. A former colleague at WHO, living in California, recommended a screen test with Warner Brothers (provided he took off his glasses—Reagan has been badly nearsighted all his life). Warner took him, at $200 a week.

There followed 51 movies, some still leading a flickering TV afterlife in the small hours of the morning. His best-known role was George Gipp (whence "Gipper," as in *Let's win this one for the*), but his best was Drake McHugh. a small-town playboy in *King's Row* whose legs were amputated by a vengeful doctor. Reagan had to wake up, discover his mutilated body, and cry, "Where's the rest of me?" For the rest, he played engaging characters who sometimes did, sometimes didn't, get the girl. ("Reagan for governor?" Jack Warner is supposed to have asked in 1966. "No. Jimmy Stewart for governor, Ronnie for best friend.")

More important, Hollywood gave Reagan his first push toward conservatism. Reagan had inherited his father's Democratic loyalties, and added an idealistic, liberal overlay of his own: after World War II, he joined the ADA, the United World Federalists, and the American Veterans Committee. He was also, however, elected president of the Screen Actors Guild, from which position he observed Communist tactics firsthand.

From 1945 to 1947, Hollywood suffered a crippling series of strikes. The question at issue was ostensibly jurisdictional: should stagehands be organized by the International Alliance of Theatrical Stage Employees (IATSE), or by a variety of craft unions? In fact, the craft unions were being egged on by Communist organizers. "The Communist Party in Hollywood," concluded a committee of the California Senate in 1959, "wanted control over everything on wheels. . . . They moved Communist units into those unions having jurisdiction over carpenters, painters, musicians, grips, and electricians. To control those trade unions was to control the motion picture industry." The AFL soon disavowed the craft unionists, but their strikes persisted. Cars were trashed, strikers rioted in front of Warner, IATSE members were mugged, their houses bombed. Wages totaling about $28 million went down the drain. Some of the ugliness washed over Reagan, who, as president of the actors' union, had been trying to mediate. While filming *Night unto Night*, he got a call on the set threatening that he would be "fixed" so that he would never act again. The police issued him a .32 Smith & Wesson, and put a guard on his house.

Reagan's conversion continued, more subtly, during his next career. In 1954, with decent movie offers becoming increasingly scarce, he accepted an offer to host a television anthology sponsored by General Electric. The deal also included speaking tours to GE plants as part of the company's employee- and community-relations program. Reagan began by talking mostly about Hollywood, but the GE audiences wanted to hear more, and he found himself developing opinions on other subjects.

The final influence on Reagan's ideas was his wife Nancy. Reagan met Nancy Davis in 1951 on Guild business, and married her a year later. Nancy had gone to Girls Latin School in Chicago, and to Smith, and had been introduced to conservative opinions by her father. Her political instincts still come in handy; some reporters claim she recommended the TV blitz that won the North Carolina primary for Reagan in 1976.

In the Sixties, Reagan began putting his ideas to work politically. He campaigned for Richard Nixon in 1960, and switched his registration from Democrat to Republican two years later. He taped a television appeal for Barry Goldwater in 1964 which nearly failed to run. Reagan had to call Goldwater at the last minute and assure him that it was not extreme; and the Goldwater campaign grossed $600,000 in contributions.

The rest of Reagan's political career can be found in Teddy White. Reagan challenged Pat Brown for the governorship of California in 1966. Brown, in a famous enthymeme, noted that both Reagan and John Wilkes Booth had been actors; Reagan buried him by nearly a million votes, and proceeded, contrary to certain fears (and hopes) neither to destroy the state university system, nor to sell the streets. Reagan raised taxes to balance the state budget, but returned several billion dollars, in rebates and left Pat's son, Jerry, with the surplus which now takes up the slack of Proposition 1, a proposal to limit the percentage of income the state may take in taxes, now being pushed on the national level by the Tax Limitation Committee. Reagan entered the 1968 presidential contest too late to do anything more than exert a rightward pressure on Nixon. He supported the President loyally in 1972, and bolted against his successor in 1976.

Since his whisker-thin loss in that campaign, Reagan has moved with the deliberation of a battleship. Citizens for Reagan became Citizens for the Republic; the money left over from the presidential bid went into hundreds of Republican coffers in 1978. Reagan wrote a column, taped a radio show, and earned several hundred thousand dollars from speaking engagements. Reagan's 1980 game plan, as it developed, was grand and simple: to woo the Party's "moderates"; to generate a *force majeur*; to become the heir apparent. Critics would be ignored; challengers would simply wear themselves out. The strategy worked like the clockwork it resembled: IOUs accumulated; Reagan led in every conceivable poll; brushfires in California (an attempt to break the state's unit rule) and Florida (an early straw poll organized by the Crane camp) were extinguished. Until Iowa . . .

A correspondent lured campaign strategist John Sears from his crossword puzzle between South Carolina and Miami long enough to ask him what happened. Sears's explanation sounded ingenious. We had expected, he said, a large caucus vote—say, 50,000 people. Instead, we got twice that number—a small primary vote. The two, Sears went on, are qualitatively different. If you expect a primary-type turnout, you invest in certain things which caucuses do not warrant—direct mail, television spots. Bush invested; Reagan didn't. Therefore, Bush won.

Will the strategy change? No, Reagan had answered back in the Aloha Lounge; there is no need, Sears added now. There are still 35 primaries to go. They will use in New Hampshire all the days they had kept open in the schedule; but "it doesn't seem to be a matter of doing more than that."

Conservatives have spent many man-hours debating whether John Sears is a demon. It seems to be a futile exercise. Reagan retains him because he agrees with him. The campaign will go on, largely as it has been going—largely, though not exactly: for now it will be urgent. Losing Iowa, instead of winning by a few percentage points, may be one of the best things that happened to the Reagan campaign so far.

Reagan leaves Miami the morning after the fund-raiser and lands in a drizzly New Orleans. He is addressing the Southern Republican Leadership Conference in the starched and frosted Fairmont hotel. This is the big event of the trip; Connally has rented a riverboat for the weekend, and Crane will also be present later. Reagan has a new speech for the occasion, concentrating heavily on foreign policy.

His reaction to applause is unusual; the words that come to mind are "gosh" and "shucks." He grins, raises his eyebrows almost in surprise. His wave suggests thanks and embarrassment; he nods deferentially. He ends with the trope he used in 1976, the challenge that America be as a "shining city on a hill," "city on a hill" courtesy of John Winthrop, "shining" courtesy of Ronald Reagan.

He gives the speech again that night, in Stem Hall in St. Paul Minnesota. There are storm warnings in Minnesota; Connally finished only 11 percentage points back in a straw poll of the state central committee, and Bush claims rashly that he will get a majority of the delegates (he *will* clean up in the Twin Cities, where his strength is concentrated). So while Reagan reads the entrails at the Minnesota Club, the rally falls behind schedule, and Rick Teske, the warm-up speaker, labors earnestly to fill the gap. "A political speech with jokes and homilies wouldn't seem quite right" in this time of crisis, he says, so he cites Milton Friedman, the ancient Greeks, and poor Santayana on history instead. The audience, for its part, applauds only for Reagan. The weather bureau is predicting a high of zero, and these people are wearing scarves, tweeds, wool shirts, fur and felt hats (as well as plastic boaters with Reagan bumper-stickers pasted on them). It's a rural-looking crowd; some have come from Wisconsin, and Mr. and Mrs. Buddy Jensen have driven one hundred miles from upstate. Three clarinets, eight brass, and two laconic men behind a bass and snare drum await Reagan's entrance. Teske finishes, and they play "'There'll Be a Hot Time in the Old Town Tonight," two, four, six times. The crowd looks puzzled. Finally, he comes; the band gives it another shot, balloons fall and float up again to the ceiling, people wave their boaters.

It has been Reagan's strength, more important even than his industriousness in the service of fellow Republicans, that he can deliver a speech as convincingly to a crowd like this as he did to the crowd in New Orleans. Reagan believes his "party of main street" talk, and proves he believes it by acting on it. Republicans, a minority party for thirty years, desperately need that kind of an infusion. Nevertheless, if Reagan does badly in New Hampshire, and loses South Carolina and Florida, all that and seven hundred dollars will get you an ounce of gold.

He finishes with the Winthrop-Reagan collaboration; the band plays "The Battle Hymn of the Republic," and the campaign boards the plane for Los Angeles.

The Real Reagan Record

By Alan Reynolds

EDITOR'S NOTE: *This article first appeared in the August 31, 1992, issue of National Review.*

The economic policies presided over by Ronald Reagan were stunningly success-ful—except to informed opinion, as represented by the academy and the major media. The principal charge against Reagan has become almost a chant: The rich got richer, the poor got poorer, and the middle class was squeezed out of existence.

A key player in the campaign to popularize this view has been Sylvia Nasar of the *New York Times*, who relied on statistics concocted by Paul Krugman of MIT, who, in turn, garbled some already disreputable estimates from the Congressional Budget Office (CBO).

The purpose of the crusade was obvious. Mr. Krugman has been advocating that we somehow double tax collections from those earning over $200,000, so as to greatly increase federal spending. Miss Nasar openly boasted about "supplying fresh ammunition for those . . . searching for new ways to raise government revenue." Governor Clinton immediately seized upon the Krugman-Nasar statistics as the rationale for his economic plan to tax us into prosperity.

Since the question is what happened in the 1980s, after the Carter Administra-tion, it makes no sense to begin with 1977, as Mr. Krugman and Miss Nasar do, or with 1973, as the Children's Defense Fund does. Real incomes fell sharply during the runaway inflations of 1974–75 and 1979–80. Median real income among black families, for example, fell 15 per cent from 1973 to 1980, then rose 16 per cent from 1982 to 1990.

The table shows the actual real income of households by fifths of the income distribution, for the most commonly cited years. There is no question that *all* in-come groups experienced significant income gains from 1980 to 1989, despite the

Average Household Income
(In 1990 Dollars)

	Lowest Fifth	Second Fifth	Third Fifth	Fourth Fifth	Highest Fifth	Top 5%
1990	7,195	18,030	29,781	44,901	87,137	138,756
1989	7,372	18,341	30,488	46,177	90,150	145,651
1980	6,836	17,015	28,077	41,364	73,752	110,213
1977	7,193	17,715	29,287	42,911	76,522	117,023

Bureau of the Census, *Money Income of Households, Families & Persons: 1990*, p. 202.

1981–82 recession, and were still well ahead of 1980 even in the 1990 slump. For all U.S. households, the mean average of real income rose by 15.2 per cent from 1980 to 1989 (from $33,409 to $38,493, in 1990 dollars), compared with a 0.8 per cent decline from 1970 to 1980.

This table (above) shows that the "income gap" did not widen merely between the bottom fifth and any "top" group, but also between the bottom fifth and the next highest fifth, the middle fifth, and so on.

A common complaint about these figures is that they exclude capital gains, and therefore understate income at the top. However, the figures also exclude taxes. Average income taxes and payroll taxes among the top fifth of households amounted to $24,322 in 1990, according to the Census Bureau, but capital gains among the top fifth were only $14,972. To add the capital gains and not subtract the taxes, as some CBO figures do, is indefensible. Indeed, all CBO estimates of income gains are useless, because they include an estimate of capital gains based on a sample of tax returns. Since lower tax rates on capital gains after 1977 induced more people to sell assets more often, the CBO wrongly records this as increased income. It also ignores all capital losses above the deductible $3,000, and fails to adjust capital gains for inflation.

The Middle-Class Boom

One thing that we know with 100 per cent certainty is that most Americans—far more than half—did very well during the long and strong economic expansion from 1982 to 1989. In those fat years, real after-tax income per person rose by 15.5 per cent, and real *median* income of families, before taxes, went up 12.5 per cent. That means half of all families had gains *larger* than 12.5 per cent, while many below the median also had income gains, though not as large. Many families had to have gained even more than 12.5 per cent, since the more familiar *mean* average rose 16.8 per cent from 1982 to 1989. Even if we begin with 1980, rather than 1982, median income was up 8 per cent by 1989, and mean income by 14.9 per cent. And even if we end this comparison with the slump of 1990, median family income was still up 5.9 per cent from 1980, and mean income was up 12 per cent.

In *U.S. News & World Report* (March 23, 1992), Paul Krugman claimed that "the income of a few very well-off families soared. This raised average family income—but *most* families didn't share in the good time" (emphasis added). Mr. Krugman apparently does not understand what a rising median income means.

The whole idea of dividing people into arbitrary fifths by income ignores the enormous mobility of people in and out of these categories. What was most unusual about the Eighties, though, was that the number moving *up* far exceeded the number moving *down*. A Treasury Department study of 14,351 taxpayers shows that 86 per cent of those in the lowest fifth in 1979, and 60 per cent in the second fifth, had moved up into a higher income category by 1988. Among those in the middle income group, 47 per cent moved up, while fewer than 20 per cent moved down. Indeed, many more families moved up than down in every income group except the top 1 per cent, where 53 per cent fell into a lower category. Similar research by Isabel Sawhill and Mark Condon of the Urban Institute found that real incomes of those who started out in the bottom fifth in 1977 had risen 77 per cent by 1986—more than 15 times as fast as those who started in the top fifth. Miss Sawhill and Mr. Condon concluded that "the rich got a little richer and the poor got much richer."

This remarkable upward mobility is the sole cause of "The Incredible Shrinking Middle Class," featured in the May 1992 issue of *American Demographics*. Measured in constant 1990 dollars, the percentage of families earning between $15,000 and $50,000 fell by 5 points, from about 58 per cent to 53 per cent. This is what is meant by a "shrinking" middle class. We know they didn't disappear into poverty, because the percentage of families earning less than $15,000 (in 1990 dollars), dropped a bit, from 17.5 per cent in 1980 to 16.9 per cent in 1990. What instead happened is that the percentage earning more than $50,000, in constant dollars, *rose* by 5 points—from less than 25 per cent to nearly 31 per cent. Several million families "vanished" from the middle class by earning much more money!

It is not possible to reconcile the increase in median incomes with the often-repeated claim that low-wage service jobs ("McJobs") expanded at the expense of high-wage manufacturing jobs. Actually, there were millions more jobs in sectors where wages were rising most briskly, which meant competitive export industries but also services. From 1980 to 1991, average hourly earnings rose by 6.8 per cent a year in services, compared with only 4.8 per cent in manufacturing. The percentage of working-age Americans with jobs, which had never before the 1980s been nearly as high as 60 per cent, rose to 63 per cent by 1989.

The Myth of Low-Wage Jobs

An editorial in *Business Week* (May 25, 1992) claimed that, "according to a just-released Census Bureau study, the number of working poor rose dramatically from 1979 to 1990." This is completely false. In fact, the report shows that the percentage of low-income workers who are in poverty *fell* dramatically. Among husbands with such low-income jobs, for example, 35.7 per cent were members of poor families in 1979, but only 21.4 per cent in 1990.

Low incomes, in this report, were defined as "less than the poverty level for a four-person family" ($12,195 a year in 1990). Yet very few people with entry-level or part-time jobs are trying to support a family of four. Husbands now account for only a fifth of such low-income jobs, which are instead increasingly held by young singles and by dependent children living with their parents. Wives had 34 per cent of such jobs in 1979, but fewer than 28 per cent in 1990. That reflects the impressive fact that the median income of women rose by 31 per cent in real terms from 1979 to 1990.

It is true that the absolute *number* of low-income jobs increased in all categories, but that increase was not nearly as large as the increase in medium- and high-

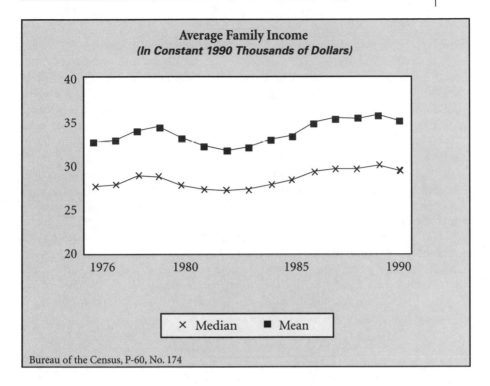

Average Family Income
(In Constant 1990 Thousands of Dollars)

× Median   ■ Mean

Bureau of the Census, P-60, No. 174

income jobs. All that the rise in low-income jobs really shows is that students living with their parents and young singles found it much easier to find acceptable work. The only reason fewer young people had low-income jobs back in the glorious Seventies is a large percentage of them had no jobs at all! Only 51.4 per cent of single males had full-time jobs in 1974, but 61.8 per cent did by 1989. Young people always start out with low earnings, if they get a chance to start out at all.

In his new book, *Head to Head*, Lester Thurow writes that "between 1973 and 1990, real hourly wages for non-supervisory workers . . . fell 12 per cent, and real weekly wages fell 18 per cent." Yet these averages include part-time workers, which is why *average* wages appeared to be only $355 a week in 1991, even though half of all full-time workers (the *median*) earned more than $430 a week. Because many more students and young mothers were able to find part-time jobs in the Eighties, that diluted both the weekly and the hourly "average" wage. It most definitely did not mean that the wages of the "average worker" went down, but rather that otherwise unemployed part-time and entry-level workers were able to raise their wages above zero. The increase in part-time jobs also does not mean that families are poorer; rather, they are richer. Out of 19.3 million part-time workers in 1991, only 1.2 million were family heads, and only 10 per cent said they were unable to find full-time work.

The Rich Work Harder

Although the vast majority clearly had large income gains in the Eighties, Mr. Krugman and Miss Nasar nonetheless assert that those at the top had even larger gains, and that this is something that ought to provoke resentment or envy. Yet the figures they offer to make this point are grossly misleading. Moreover, the whole static routine of slicing up income into fifths is bound to show the highest percentage increases in average (mean) incomes among the "top" 20 per cent or 1 per cent. *That is because for top groups alone, any and all increases in income are included in the average, rather than in movement to a higher group.*

In his *U.S. News* article, Krugman first claimed that CBO figures show that "Ronald Reagan's tax cuts" boosted after-tax income of the top 1 per cent "by a whopping 102 per cent." That figure, though, is based on a "tax simulation model" which estimates "adjusted" incomes as a multiple of the poverty level. The top 1 per cent supposedly earned less than 22 times the poverty level in 1980, but 44 times the poverty level in 1989—hence the gain of 102 per cent. Yet this is a purely relative measure of affluence, not an absolute gain in real income. As more and more families rose further and further above the unchanged "poverty line" in the Eighties, thus lifting the income needed to be in the "top 1 per cent," the CBO technique had to show a "widening gap."

Furthermore, the share of federal income tax paid by the top 1 per cent soared from 18.2 per cent in 1981 to 28 per cent in 1988, though is slipped to 25.4 per cent in 1990. Indeed, this unexpected revenue from the rich was used to double personal exemptions and triple the earned-income tax credit, which was of enormous benefit to the working poor.

By the time Mr. Krugman's alleged 102 per cent gain at the top had reached the *New York Times*, it had shrunk to 60 per cent. However, the CBO wrote a memo disowning this estimate too, noting that "of the total rise in aggregate income . . . about one-fourth went to families in the top 1 per cent." By fiddling with "adjusted" data, the CBO managed to get that share of the top 1 per cent up to one-third. Whether a fourth or a third, these estimates still begin with 1977, not 1980. Between 1977 and 1980, the CBO shows real incomes falling by 6.6 per cent for the poorest fifth. The top 5 per cent fared relatively well before 1980, because everybody else suffered an outright drop in real income.

Even if the Krugman-Nasar figures had been remotely accurate, the whole exercise is conceptually flawed. In every income group except the top, many families can move up from one group to another with little or no effect on the average income of those remaining in the lower group. Above-average increases in income among those in the lower groups simply move them into a higher fifth, rather than raising the average income of the fifth they used to be in. Only the top income groups have no ceiling, as those in such a group cannot possibly move into any higher group. A rap star's first hit record may lift his income from the lowest fifth to the top one per cent, with no perceptible effect on the average income of the lowest fifth. But two hit records in the next year would raise the total amount of income counted in the top one per cent, and thus raise the average for that category.

Nobody knows exactly how much income is needed to be counted among the top one per cent, because the Census Bureau keeps track only of the top five per cent. Census officials argue that apparent changes in the small sample used to estimate a "top one per cent" may largely reflect differences in the degree of dishonest reporting. When marginal tax rates fell from 70 per cent to 28 per cent, for example, more people told the truth about what they earned, so "the rich" *appeared* to earn much more.

One thing we do know, though, is that the minimum amount of income needed to be included among the top 1 per cent has to have risen quite sharply since 1980, because of the huge increase in the percentage of families earning more than $50,000, or $100,000. This increased proportion of families with higher incomes pushed up the income ceilings on all middle and higher income groups, and thus raised the floor defining the highest income groups.

While $200,000 may have been enough to make the top 1 per cent in 1980, a family might need over $300,000 to be in that category a decade later. Clearly, any average of all the income above $300,000 is going to yield a much bigger number than an average of income above $200,000. The CBO thus estimates that average pre-tax income among the top one per cent rose from $343,610 in 1980 to $566,674 in 1992. But this 65 per cent increase in the average does *not* mean that those specific families that were in the top 1 per cent in 1980 typically experienced a 65 per cent increase in real income. It simply means that the standards for belonging to this exclusive club have gone way up. That is because millions more couples are earning higher incomes today than in 1980, not because only a tiny fraction are earning 65 per cent more.

Sylvia Nasar totally misreported the CBO's complaints with her first article, and audaciously quoted her own discredited assertions in a later *New York Times* piece (April 21). This front-page editorial changed the subject—from income to wealth. It claimed a "Federal Reserve" study had found that the wealthiest 1 per cent had 37 per cent of all net worth in 1989, up from 31 per cent in 1983. Paul Krugman, writing in the *Wall Street Journal*, likewise cited this "careful study by the Federal Reserve." Yet the cited figures are from a mere *footnote* in a rough "working paper" produced by one of hundreds of Fed economists Arthur Kennickell, along with a statistician from the IRS, Louise Woodburn. It comes with a clear warning that "opinions in this paper . . . in no way reflect the views of . . . the Federal Reserve System."

At that, all of the gain of the top one per cent was supposedly at the expense of others within the top 10 per cent, not the middle class or poor. In any case, the figures are little more than a guess. The authors acknowledge that they "cannot offer a formal statistical test of the significance of the change."

"The 1983 and 1989 sample designs and the weights developed are quite different," they write. "The effect of this difference is unknown." Their estimated range of error does not account for "error attributable to imputation or to other data problems." Yet it is nonetheless within that range of error for the share of net worth held by the top one per cent to have risen imperceptibly, from 34.5 to 34.6 per cent.

This is why Kennickell and Woodburn say their estimates merely "suggest that there may have been an increase in the share of wealth held by this top group in 1989." Or maybe not.

The actual, official Federal Reserve study tells a quite different story. It shows that real net worth rose by 28 per cent among 40 per cent of families earning between $20,000 and $50,000, but by only 6.6 per cent for the top 20 per cent, earning more than $50,000. Since this huge increase in net worth among those with modest incomes means their assets grew much faster than their debts, this also puts to rest the myth that the Eighties was build upon "a mountain of debt." It was, instead, built upon a mountain of assets, particularly small businesses.

Children without Fathers

What about the poor? There is no question that there has been a stubbornly large increase of people with very low incomes. However, annual "money income" turns out to be a surprisingly bad measure of ability to buy goods and services. In 1988, average consumer spending among the lowest fifth of the population was $10,893 a year—more than double their apparent income of $4,942. That huge gap occurs

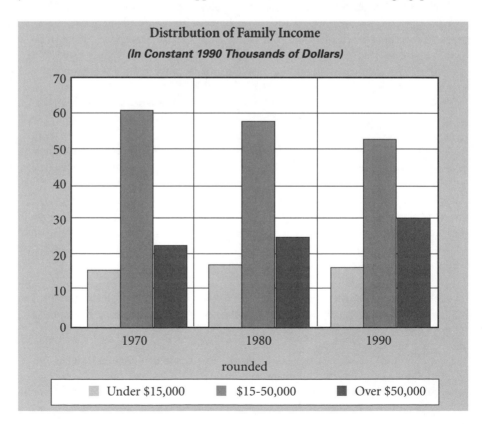

Distribution of Family Income
(In Constant 1990 Thousands of Dollars)

rounded

■ Under $15,000   ■ $15-50,000   ■ Over $50,000

partly because annual incomes are highly variable in many occupations, and many people have temporary spells of low income, due to illness or job loss. People can and do draw upon savings during periods when their income dips below normal.

Another reason why those in the bottom fifth are able to spend twice their earnings is that many in-kind government transfers (such as food stamps) are not counted as "money income." Census surveys also acknowledge that a fourth of the case income from welfare and pensions is unreported. And, of course, very little income from illegal activities is reported. In CBO figures, incomes of low-income families are further understated by counting singles as separate families, as though young people stopped getting checks from home the minute they get their first apartment.

Despite such flaws in measured income, nearly all of the income differences between the bottom fifth and the top fifth can nonetheless be explained by the number of people per family with full-time jobs, their age, and their schooling. Among household heads in the lowest fifth, for example, only 21 per cent worked full-time all year in 1990, and half had no job all year. In the top fifth, by contrast, the average number of full-time workers was more than two.

The May 25 *Business Week* editorial noted that "the percentage of Americans below the poverty line rose from 11.7 per cent in 1979 to 13.5 per cent in 1990." Yet this poverty rate is exaggerated, because it is based on an obsolete consumer price index that mismeasured housing inflation before 1983. Using the corrected inflation measure, the poverty rate was 11.5 per cent in 1980 and 11.4 in 1989, before rising to 12.1 per cent in 1990. That 12.1 per cent figure, though, is only one of 14 different Census Bureau measures of poverty, and not the most credible. Like income for the "bottom fifth," the usual measure of poverty excludes many in-kind transfer payments, as well as cash from the earned-income tax credit. By instead including such benefits, and also subtracting taxes, the Census Bureau brings the actual poverty rate down to 9.5 per cent for 1990, or to 8.5 per cent if homeownership is considered (those who own homes need less cash because they don't pay rent).

Even by the conventional measure, the poverty rate among married-couple families dropped slightly, from 5.2 per cent in 1980 to 4.9 per cent in 1990, and poverty rates among those above age 65 have fallen quite substantially. On the other hand, among female household heads with children under the age of 18 and "no husband present," poverty rose from 37.1 per cent in 1979 to 39.9 per cent in 1980, and then to 41.6 per cent by 1990.

The poverty rate among fatherless families, then, is slightly higher now than it was in the previous decade, and is lower if these young women work. (Among female householders with children under the age of 6, the poverty rate among those with jobs dropped from 20.2 per cent in 1979 to 17.9 per cent in 1989, and the percentage of such mothers who worked full-time rose from 24.9 to 30.6 per cent.) But there are so many more female-headed households, and so few of these women work, that the net effect is nonetheless to keep the overall poverty rate from falling. The number of female-headed households with children under age 18 rose from 5.8

million in 1979 to 7.2 million in 1989. In too many cases, these mothers are so young that child-labor laws would not allow them to work in any case.

In March 1991, the average money income of female-headed families with children was only $17,500, and most of that money (plus food stamps, housing allowance, and Medicaid) came from taxpayers. For married couples who both worked full-time, average income was $55,700 before taxes—about enough to put the *average* two-earner family in the top fifth. Taxing hardworking two-earner families to subsidize broken, no-earner families can only discourage the former, encourage the latter, and thus exacerbate the problems it pretends to solve.

To summarize what actually happened in the 1980s, the "middle class," and the vast majority by any measure, unquestionably experienced substantial gains in real income and wealth. With millions more families earning much higher incomes, it required much higher incomes to make it into the top 5 per cent or top one per cent, which largely accounts for the illusion that such "top" groups experienced disproportionate gains. The rising tide lifted at least 90 per cent of all boats. About 9 to 12 per cent continued to be poor, but this group increasingly consisted of female-headed households with young children. More and better jobs cannot help those who do not work, improved investment opportunities cannot help those who do not save, and increased incomes cannot help families whose fathers refuse to support their own children.

A Lie about Reagan: Anti-Gay Gipper

By Deroy Murdoch

> EDITOR'S NOTE: *This article was published on December 3, 2002, on* National Review Online.

"You're president of the United States," Nancy Reagan, reminded Ronald Reagan as he sat up in bed in 1983. She begged him to do something about the growing scourge of AIDS. "If you don't talk about it, nobody will talk about it. Nobody will do anything, and all these people—these children, these young boys—they're all going to die. And the blame will be on our heads, Ronnie."

President Reagan quietly kept reading through his half glasses. He seemed very cozy, clad in his bathrobe, beneath his blankets.

"Ronnie, say something," Nancy pleaded. The president coolly maintained his silence. He never even looked at his beloved First Lady.

That's how Showtime Sunday night depicted a scene from the White House residence in *The Reagans*, the controversial TV movie about the conservative chief executive and his devoted wife. Reagan's alleged homophobia and indifference to AIDS patients are among the reasons Reaganites attacked the program, leading CBS to cancel its broadcast premiere and shift it instead to Showtime, the network's sister pay-cable channel.

The original script was far worse.

"Those who live in sin will die in sin," says President Reagan, as portrayed by actor James Brolin. Teleplaywright Elizabeth Egloff eventually admitted she had no evidence on which to base this scandalous comment. "We know he ducked the issue over and over again," she told the *New York Times* in self-defense.

Ronald Reagan's supposed malign neglect on AIDS and hostility to gays are twin pillars of the Left's anti-Reaganism. He still is scorned for supposedly avoiding the topic in his public pronouncements. Throughout the 1980s, protests by ACT-UP and other AIDS–advocacy groups routinely featured vicious effigies of Reagan. In one vulgar manifestation of this viewpoint, a 1994 cover illustration for Benetton's *Colors* magazine featured photographer Oliviero Toscani's computer-generated image of President Reagan covered with AIDS-related skin lesions. Toscani denounced Reagan and former British Prime Minister Margaret Thatcher in *La Stampa*, a newspaper based in Turin, Italy. "They didn't understand anything about AIDS, they did everything wrong," Toscani said that June 24. "They never realized the emergency."

Is any of this fair?

Few men have known Ronald Reagan longer or better than Edwin Meese III. He began working in 1967 with then-governor Reagan in Sacramento, California. He became a president adviser on January 20, 1981, and was appointed Reagan's attorney general in February 1985.

Meese described to me the TV movie's take on Reagan, AIDS, and gays as "totally unfair, and totally unrepresentative of his views or anything he ever said." Meese, who now chairs the Heritage Foundation's Center for Legal and Judicial Studies, recalls AIDS as a key issue with which Reagan's senior staff grappled.

"I can remember numerous sessions of the domestic-policy council where the surgeon general provided information to us, and the questions were not whether the federal government would get involved, but what would be the best way. There was support for research through the NIH. There also were questions about the extent to which public warnings should be sent out. It was a question of how the public would respond to fairly explicit warnings about fairly explicit things. Ultimately, warnings were sent out."

"As I recall, from 1984 onward—and bear in mind that the AIDS virus was not identified until 1982—every Reagan budget contained a large sum of money specifically earmarked for AIDS," says Peter Robinson, a former Reagan speechwriter and author of *How Ronald Reagan Changed My Life*. "Now, people will argue that it wasn't enough," Robinson adds. "But, of course, that's the kind of argument that takes place over every item in the federal budget. Nevertheless, the notion that he was somehow callous or had a cruel or cynical attitude toward homosexuals or AIDS victims is just ridiculous."

In February 1986, President Reagan's blueprint for the next fiscal year stated: "[T]his budget provides funds for maintaining—and in some cases expanding—high priority programs in crucial areas of national interest . . . including drug enforcement, AIDS research, the space program, nonmilitary research and national security." Reagan's budget message added that AIDS "remains the highest public health priority of the Department of Health and Human Services."

Precise budget requests are difficult to calculate, as online records from the 1980s are spotty. Nevertheless, New York University's archived, hard copies of budget documents from fiscal year 1984 through FY 1989 show that Reagan proposed at least $2.79 billion for AIDS research, education, and treatment. In a Congressional Research Service study titled *AIDS Funding for Federal Government Programs: FY1981–FY1999*, author Judith Johnson found that overall, the federal government spent $5.727 billion on AIDS under Ronald Reagan. This higher number reflects President Reagan's proposals as well as additional expenditures approved by Congress that he later signed.

Government Spending on HIV/AIDS

Fiscal Year	($ Millions)	per cent growth over previous year
1982	8	
1983	44	450.00
1984	103	134.09
1985	205	99.03
1986	508	147.80
1987	922	81.50
1988	1,615	75.16
1989	2,322	43.78
Total	5,727	

Source: Congressional Research Service

Free-marketeers may argue that the federal government should have left AIDS research and care to the private sector. Whether or not one embraces that perspective, no one justifiably can regard Reagan's requested and actual AIDS spending as a gleefully applied death sentence for AIDS sufferers.

Besides, could much have been done with an even larger cash infusion during the infancy of AIDS?

"You could have poured half the national budget into AIDS in 1983, and it would have gone down a rat hole," says Michael Fumento, author of *BioEvolution: How Biotechnology Is Changing Our World*. "There were no anti-virals back then. The first anti-viral was AZT which came along in 1987, and that was for AIDS." As an example of how blindly scientists and policymakers flew as the virus took wing, Fumento recalls that "in 1984, Health and Human Services Secretary Margaret Heckler predicted that there would be an AIDS vaccine by 1986. There is no AIDS vaccine to date."

Reagan also is accused of staying mum about AIDS. According to *The Encyclopedia of AIDS: A Social, Political, Cultural, and Scientific Record of the HIV Epidemic* edited by Raymond A. Smith, "Reagan never even mentioned the word 'AIDS' publicly until 1987."

Actually, as official White House papers cited by Steven Hayward, author of the multivolume *Age of Reagan* show, the 40th president spoke of AIDS no later than September 17, 1985. Responding to a question on AIDS research, the president said:

> [I]ncluding what we have in the budget for '86, it will amount to over a half a billion dollars that we have provided for research on AIDS in addition to what I'm sure other medical groups are doing. And we have $100 million in the budget this year; it'll be 126 million next year. So, this is a top priority with us. Yes, there's no question about the seriousness of this and the need to find an answer.

President Reagan's February 6, 1986, State of the Union address included this specific passage where he says the word "AIDS" five times:

> We will continue, as a high priority, the fight against Acquired Immune Deficiency Syndrome (AIDS). An unprecedented research effort is underway to deal with this major epidemic public health threat. The number of AIDS cases is expected to increase. While there are hopes for drugs and vaccines against AIDS, none is immediately at hand. Consequently, efforts should focus on prevention, to inform and to lower risks of further transmission of the AIDS virus. To this end, I am asking the Surgeon General to prepare a report to the American people on AIDS.

So, AIDS policy aside, was Ronald Reagan a homophobe? Here again, those who know him best just say, "No."

"According to the screenplay . . . my father is a homophobic Bible-thumper who loudly insisted that his son wasn't gay when Ron took up ballet, and who in a particularly scathing scene told my mother that AIDS patients deserved their fate," wrote Ronald and Nancy Reagan's daughter, Patti Davis, on *Time* magazine's Web site. "Not only did my father never say such a thing, he never would have."

In fact, she recalls "the clear, smooth, non-judgmental way" in which her dad discussed the topic of homosexuality with her when she was age eight or nine.

> My father and I were watching an old Rock Hudson and Doris Day movie. At the moment when Hudson and Doris Day kissed, I said to my father, "That looks weird." . . . All I knew was that something about this particular man and woman was, to me, strange. My father gently explained that Mr. Hudson didn't really have a lot of experience kissing women; in fact, he would much prefer to be kissing a man. This was said in the same tone that would be used if he had been telling me about people with different colored eyes, and I accepted without question that this whole kissing thing wasn't reserved just for men and women.

"I remember Reagan telling us that in Hollywood he knew a lot of gays, and he never had any problem with them," says Martin Anderson, a high-level Reagan adviser since 1975, coeditor of *Reagan: A Life in Letters*, the latest collection of material that Ronald Reagan wrote in his own hand. "I think a number of people who were gay worked for the Reagans," Anderson told me. "We never kept track. But he never said anything even remotely like that comment in the movie. His basic attitude was 'Leave them alone.'"

Reagan publicly demonstrated this outlook when he opposed Proposition 6, a 1978 ballot measure that called for the dismissal of California teachers who "advocated" homosexuality, even outside of schools. Reagan used both a September 24, 1978, statement and a syndicated newspaper column to campaign against the initiative.

"Whatever else it is," Reagan wrote, "homosexuality is not a contagious disease like the measles. Prevailing scientific opinion is that an individual's sexuality is determined at a very early age and that a child's teachers do not really influence this." He also argued: "Since the measure does not restrict itself to the classroom, every aspect of a teacher's personal life could presumably come under suspicion. What constitutes 'advocacy' of homosexuality? Would public opposition to Proposition 6 by a teacher—should it pass—be considered advocacy?"

That November 7, Proposition 6 lost, 41.6 per cent in favor to 58.4 per cent against. Reagan's opposition is considered instrumental to its defeat.

"Despite the urging of some of his conservative supporters, he never made fighting homosexuality a cause," wrote Kenneth T. Walsh, former *U.S. News and World Report* White House correspondent, in his 1997 biography, *Ronald Reagan*. "In the final analysis, Reagan felt that what people do in private is their own business, not the government's."

But what about the comment in *Dutch*, Edmund Morris's authorized biography of President Reagan? Morris claimed that Reagan once said about AIDS: "Maybe the Lord brought down this plague," because "illicit sex is against the Ten Commandments." Morris's book is suspect insofar as he deliberately transformed himself into a character, a buddy of sorts, who follows Reagan throughout his career. Did Reagan actually say this, or did Morris also invent that passage in service to a higher "truth?" And even if Reagan said such a thing, there is a huge difference between expressing Biblical beliefs about AIDS's genesis and, as *The Reagans* originally claimed, condemning AIDS victims to die from their disease and speeding their demise through official negligence.

As much as Reagan evidently has exhibited tolerance of homosexuality in his private life, when it comes to public policy, he opposed the persecution of gays and devoted considerable taxpayer resources to AIDS research and treatment.

Could Reagan have said more about AIDS? Surely, and he might have done so were he less focused on reviving America's moribund economy and peacefully defeating Soviet Communism. Could he have done more? Of course. Who could not have? But the ideas that Ronald Reagan did nothing, or worse, about AIDS and hated gays, to boot, are both tired, left-wing lies about an American legend.

What Women Wanted

By Elaine Donnelly

> EDITOR'S NOTE: *This article was published on June 7, 2004, on* National Review Online.

Every year in February, in observance of Valentine's Day as well as the birthday of Ronald Reagan, I display in my home a framed memento of the great former president. The small white presidential campaign placard, inscribed with the words "Women for Reagan" on a large red heart, bears a treasured autograph of Reagan himself.

Feminists will never credit him for this, but President Reagan motivated an entire generation of women to enter public life. Most Women for Reagan became involved in the political process not in spite of his conservative views, but because of them, and went on to become accomplished leaders in four Republican administrations, the Congress, media, and in every major field of public policy.

No one predicted this in the mid-1970s, when the charismatic California governor first sought the Republican presidential nomination. That goal, and his subsequent election, would not have been possible without the army of conservative and pro-life women nationwide who mobilized their families and friends in support of Ronald Reagan.

At the time, pollsters warned that candidate Reagan would lose because of a perceived "gender gap" among female voters. It was conventional wisdom among "moderate" Republicans that Reagan could not win without the support of "pro-choice" women, epitomized by Betty Ford. Her husband, President Gerald Ford, tried to win women's votes by signing a 1975 Executive Order establishing a National Commission on the Observance of International Women's Year (IWY).

Ford's gesture paid no political dividends in 1976, when Jimmy Carter won the White House. President Carter, an overtly religious man, shocked Christians who had voted for him by appointing ultra-liberal New York congresswoman Bella Abzug to chair a series of public conferences to "observe" International Women's Year in 1977. Funded with $5 million in tax dollars, the controversial IWY conferences became a significant turning point in national politics that is worth reviewing today.

Abzug, who was known for wearing large hats and pushing radical causes, presided over 56 state and territorial conferences in 1977, leading up to a spectacular three-day National IWY Conference in Houston. Women who opposed abortion and the still-unratified Equal Rights Amendment (ERA) tried to be heard at the state IWY conferences, but they were intimidated and repeatedly railroaded with strong-arm tactics, turned-off microphones, and manipulated elections.

Only a token few conservative and pro-life women were among the 2,000 elected delegates at the conference, which quickly escalated into a feminist Woodstock. The extravaganza received days of uncritical coverage from bedazzled television correspondents, newsweeklies, women's magazines, and almost every female newspaper reporter in America. Barbara Walters and other network-media mavens lavished attention on then-First Lady Roslyn Carter, her predecessors Betty Ford and Lady Bird Johnson, Gloria Steinem, NOW President Eleanor Smeal, actress Jean Stapleton, and tennis star Billie Jean King.

All joined hands to approve the 25-point IWY Plan of Action, an undiluted "womanifesto" for big-government and feminist liberalism taken to extremes. On the wish list were several "hot button" demands: Ratification of the ERA, universal child-care subsidies, "comparable worth" wage-control schemes, taxes on full-time homemakers in exchange for Social Security benefits, tax-funded abortions on demand without parental consent, and a full array of rights for lesbian women.

In addition to parades and fist-waving speeches, the IWY festival featured an exhibition area promoting other leftist causes, including legalized prostitution. Somehow the media failed to notice the array of lesbian pornography in plain view, despite posted signs warning visitors that "some materials and displays might not be appropriate for persons of all ages."

Meanwhile, across town at the Houston Astro Arena, a new and formidable women's movement became visible on the national scene for the first time. ERA opponent Phyllis Schlafly had organized a Pro-Family Coalition with a host of pro-life leaders. Together they planned and mobilized a massive "Pro-Life, Pro-Family" counter-rally that became a stunning success unlike anything seen before or since.

According to news reports, more than 15,000 grassroots women and families, many of whom had traveled for miles in cars or church or school buses bound for Houston, crowded the aisles and balconies of the Astro Arena. Local safety officials kept another 2,000 listening outside. Stacked high above the stage behind the podium were large boxes containing thousands of petitions, individually signed over a period of months and marked with the name of every state. The petitions called on officials at all levels of government to reject the IWY 25-point Plan of Action for radical social change.

I happened to find James J. Kilpatrick, a conservative syndicated columnist, writing notes and looking out at the huge, enthusiastic crowd from his perch behind a stack of petition boxes. Kilpatrick marveled at the resolve and energy of the women and families in the arena, and predicted that the impressive event was only the beginning of something really big.

Indeed it was. Attendees at the IWY Pro-Family rally went home to learn the basics of grassroots politics, which they saw as the key to stopping Bella Abzug and her radical agenda. In subsequent years many conservative women became precinct delegates, worked hard as county and state Republican-party officials, and became voting delegates to the Republican National Convention. In 1980, they provided a comfortable margin of victory for presidential nominee Ronald Reagan.

Coverage of that convention focused on liberal Republican women who opposed Reagan's positions on abortion and the ERA. But while feminists were marching in the streets, pro-family women delegates were quietly writing and counting the votes for platform language reflecting Reagan's views. In 1980, 1984, and 1988, the powerful grassroots pro-family movement worked tirelessly for the election of Ronald Reagan and his successor, President George H. W. Bush.

But the influence of Women for Reagan did not end there. Many of the original activists and a younger generation of women were appointed to high-level positions in the administrations of Ronald Reagan and both Presidents Bush. Others were elected to state legislatures, Congress, and the Senate, and are still in office today. Some became respected scholars at think tanks such as the Heritage Foundation, or continue to influence public policy as articulate spokeswomen for large women's organizations such as Eagle Forum and Concerned Women for America.

Every week *National Review*'s Washington editor, Kate O'Beirne, cheerfully demolishes the illogic of Margaret Carlson and other liberals on CNN's *Capital Gang.* And when the Clinton–impeachment struggle ensued, a team of "brainy blond barristers"—Kellyanne Conway, Ann Coulter, and the late Barbara Olson—appeared on television night after night to fearlessly defend the Constitution against the likes of Susan Estrich, Ellen Ratner, and Eleanor Clift.

Women for Reagan have made distinctive marks in other fields of public policy. In education, for example, Reagan women have successfully promoted school-choice and abstinence-based sex-education programs, which are now being espoused by Miss America 2003, Erika Harold.

Women who revere Reagan are writing best-selling books, editing influential Web sites such as *National Review Online,* and producing publications such as the *Women's Quarterly,* the signature publication of Independent Women's Forum. And much to the dismay of feminists, they are advising President George W. Bush on a long list of public-policy matters, including the environment, law, personnel management, labor policy, defense, and national security during the war on terrorism.

Feminists in 1977 thought that their historic IWY conferences would inspire women to take over the world. The irony is that the conferences did have that effect, but those who were motivated the most were admirers of Ronald Reagan. This chapter of political history is yet another legacy of a great president, whose match we may never see. Because of the countless women he inspired, the principles and beliefs of Ronald Reagan will live on for decades to come.

Foreign Affairs

Selections from the Debate: Yes or No on the Panama Treaties

Ronald Reagan and William F. Buckley Jr.

EDITOR'S NOTE: *The following are selections of the statements and rebuttals made by Ronald Reagan and William F. Buckley Jr. during a debate, televised over PBS in January 1979, concerning the Panama Canal treaties, the ratification of which Mr. Reagan opposed, and Mr. Buckley supported. These selections were published in the February 17, 1979, issue of* National Review.

"The Senate would do well to skip the debate on the Panama Canal and simply replay the encounter between Ronald Reagan and William F. Buckley Jr. which was staged at the University of South Carolina and aired over the Public Broadcasting System in most American cities on Superbowl Sunday."
    —*Mary McGrory, syndicated column, January 21, 1979*

Mr. Buckley's Opening Remarks

Mr. Chairman; ladies and gentlemen: If Lloyds of London had been asked to give odds that I would be disagreeing with Ronald Reagan on a matter of public policy, I doubt they could have flogged a quotation out of their swingingest betting-man. Because, judging from Governor Reagan's impeccable record, the statisticians would have reasoned that it was inconceivable that he should make a mistake. But of course it happens to everyone. I fully expect that, some day, *I'll* be wrong about something. Ronald Reagan told me over the telephone last Sunday that he would treat me very kindly tonight, as he would any friend of his suffering temporarily from a minor aberration. He does not, in other words, plan to send the Marines after me. Perhaps he is saving them to dispatch to Panama.

I find myself, Mr. Chairman, in your company, and in the present company, disarmingly comfortable. I have sat in Saigon with Ellsworth Bunker and heard him confide to me that in his opinion we should militarily cut off the Ho Chi Minh Trail. I have sat in Hawaii with Admiral McCain when, as commanding officer of CINCPAC, he fretted privately over our failure vigorously to work our will on the Vietnamese. Admiral Bud Zurnwalt, on *Firing Line*, deplored *three years ago* the progressive deterioration in American military strength. Patrick Buchanan is probably the author of every truculent anti–Communist statement uttered by Richard Nixon—the old Nixon—over a period of ten years. Roger Fontaine is that anomaly in the academic world, a scholar wholeheartedly devoted to the anti–Communist enterprise. George Will is probably the most consistent journalistic critic of the SALT treaties, insisting that they play into the hands of the Soviet Union. And my colleague James Burnham is, after all, author of *The Struggle for the World*, and has been the leading anti–Communist strategic prophet in the United States, whose books and articles have illuminated the international understanding of the global threat of the Communist world beyond those of any other scholar . . . And yet here we are, disagreed on a matter of public policy impinging on our common concerns.

We should, I think, make this dispute as easy on ourselves as possible. We are here to ask the question: Should the treaty submitted by the President to the Senate be signed? If I were in the Senate of the United States I *would* sign that treaty. So would Will. So would Burnham. So would Zumwalt. So would Bunker.

Now this does not commit us to saying anything more about that treaty—or, more properly, those treaties, because as you know there are two of them, one governing the role of the United States in Panama until the year 2000, one governing the role of the United States after that time—than that we would vote *for* them, rather than against them. To vote for them is not to endorse the foreign policy of President Carter. To vote for them is not to renounce the foreign policy of Theodore Roosevelt. To vote for them is not to say that we are frightened by any threat directed at us by Omar Torrijos. To vote for them is not to say that we are in the least influenced by the desires of the Security Council of the United Nations, which is dedicated to the decolonization of any part of the world not under Communist control.

I think I speak for my associates when I concede that the means by which we achieved our present position in Panama were a part of what one might call pre–Watergate international morality. But then, if we look about us at the activity during that period of our sister states, we do not—those of us who do not suffer from the sin of scrupulosity—think ourselves historically unique. Indeed—here I should perhaps excuse my colleagues from any identification with my own views on the subject—*I* happen to believe that there is a great deal to be said historically for the achievements of colonialism. Even so rigorous a critic of Western practices as Professor John Kenneth Galbraith manages to change the subject when you ask him whether he believes it was a good thing that Great Britain entered India in the nineteenth century. If anybody wanted to raise the banner of colonialism at this moment in Cambodia or in Uganda, I would salute him and start sounding like a bagpipe. So that what I am saying is that I for one am singularly unmoved by lachrymose appeals to pull out of Panama on the grounds that our presence there is "the last vestige of colonialism." My instinctive response to assertions put to me in those accents is: Maybe we should have a little *more* colonialism, not less of it.

Nor does our belief that it is wise to sign these treaties suggest that we harbor any illusions about the character of the head of government of Panama, or the stability of his regime; or that we find that the 32 governments that have ruled over Panama since it became an independent state are tending toward creeping stability because the current government has lasted almost ten years. And, finally, we are not unaware of the friendship struck up by General Torrijos with Fidel Castro, the premier barbarian of this hemisphere. What we are maintaining is that the United States, by signing these treaties, is better off militarily, is better off economically, and is better off spiritually.

Why militarily? The question needs to be examined in two parts. If there is a full-scale atomic war, the Panama Canal will revert to a land-mass, and the first survivor who makes his way across the Isthmus will relive a historical experience, "like stout Cortez when with eagle eyes he stared at the Pacific—and all his men looked at each other with a wild surmise—silent, upon a peak in Darien."

In a situation of hostility short of the exchange of missiles, we would desire mobility through the Canal. That mobility is more easily effected if we have the cooperation of the local population. As matters now stand, 75 per cent of the work force in the Canal is Panamanian. It is frequently asserted that the natural economic interest of Panama is sufficient to keep the Panama Canal open and operating. Those who come too readily to that kind of economic reductionism fail to take into account great passions that stir not only in the breasts of members of the Third World, but also in our own. The same man who built the Panama Canal once spoke, in the spirit of Robert Harper, of millions for defense, but not one cent for tribute. Theodore Roosevelt would not have been surprised by the closing of the Suez Canal in 1967 even though the loss of revenues to Egypt was roughly comparable to such a loss to Panama. The Panama Canal is responsible for 12 per cent of the gross national product of the Republic of Panama. Subtract 12 per cent and you have 88 per cent left over—in addition to your pride. I hope that Governor Reagan will not tell us tonight that Panamanian pride is not involved in the matter of the treaties. He may tell us that Panamanian pride must in this case be subordinated to the national interest: And if he persuades me that the national interest requires subordination of Panamanian pride, I shall side with him. But he must not tell us that pride does not count. He must not tell us that the Panamanians should not be expected to share those passions which moved Egyptians a decade ago to make huge sacrifices, closing their canal. And he ought not to suggest that American pride is one thing, Panamanian pride quite something else.

I take it, then, that the cooperation of the two million people in whose territory the Canal lies, whose personnel already do three-quarters of the work required to keep the Canal open, is, to put the matter unobtrusively—desirable. At the same time, I deem it essential, along with Admiral McCain, that the United States should continue to exercise responsibility for maintaining access to the Canal, and I note therefore with satisfaction that the first treaty reaffirms the absolute right of the United States to defend access to the Canal and to continue to garrison our troops in Panama until the year 2000; and I note with satisfaction that the second treaty reaffirms the right of the United States to defend the Canal and to guarantee access to it even after the Canal itself shall have become the physical property of the Republic of Panama. It is appropriate to reflect at this moment on the words of William Howard Taft, reiterated by Theodore Roosevelt in another context. Taft said: We do not want to own anything in Panama. What we want is a canal that goes through Panama.

I should add, before leaving the military point, that if we cannot secure access to the Canal after the year 2000 from bases outside Panama—i.e., if our power is so reduced that we cannot control the waters at either end of the little Isthmus of Panama—it is altogether unlikely that the situation would change in virtue of our having the right to bivouac a few thousand Marines within the territory of Panama.

Why would we be better off economically? Because under the first treaty, the revenues from the use of the Canal flow to the United States. The royalty retained by Panama is, at 30 cents per ton, approximately 25 per cent of the tolls, plus a share in the profits not to exceed $10 million. Ancillary economic commitments do not spring directly from the treaty, by which I mean our extra-treaty commitment to help Panama achieve credits from the Export-Import Bank, from AID and OPIC; and our commitment to give it, over the term of the treaty, $50 million of military equipment for the purpose of relieving us of expenses we currently shoulder. Those who have made a huge production over the financial price of these treaties—which figure approaches $60 million per year, the whole of it derived from Canal revenues—are perhaps most easily sedated by comparisons that come readily to mind. One billion, 290 million dollars to Spain during the last twenty years—I know, I know: we are paying Spain for the privilege of protecting Spain, such are the burdens of great nations. Or there is Turkey. For the privilege of protecting Turkey from the Soviet Union, we have spent two billion, $878 million; and are now committed to spending an extra one billion over the next four years. Dear Turkey. Lovely people.

And unlike the Canal, Turkey provides us with no off-setting revenues. Perhaps we should send Mr. Bunker to Ankara to argue that we should receive a royalty on every pound of heroin sent out from Turkey for sale in the streets of the United States? And there is Greece—one billion, 800 million, with 700 million committed over the next four years—plus reversion to Greece of U.S. military installations. Or the Philippines, which is asking for a cool billion. I do hope and pray that Mr. Reagan, whose propensity to frugality with the public purse is one of his most endearing characteristics, will not devote an extravagant amount of our time tonight to telling us how ignominious it is, under the circumstances, to cede forty or fifty million dollars a year—out of revenues—to the Republic of Panama.

I said we would be better off spiritually. Perhaps—I fear it is so—this is the most provocative point I have made, particularly in this company. That is so, Mr.

Chairman, because we are most of us agreed that the people who have been responsible for United States foreign policy during the postwar years—Republicans and Democrats—have tended to suffer from grievous misconceptions concerning what it is that makes a country popular, or prestigious. The conventional wisdom is that we earn the respect of the world by prostrating ourselves before the nearest Cherokee Indian, and promising to elect Marlon Brando as President. The factual situation suggests that the world works very differently. General Torrijos has criticized the United States far more than he has criticized Fidel Castro. American liberals accept solemnly plebiscites conducted in Panama when they see validated something they want validated, while scorning plebiscites conducted in Chile when they see validated something they don't want validated. I happen to believe that the surest road to international prestige is to pay absolutely no heed whatever to foreign opinion. However, in order to do this successfully, it helps—though it is not required—that you be a gentleman. Nikita Khrushchev had no problems whatever in getting himself admired by Nehru, the great ethical heartthrob of the century; not even when Khrushchev took to expressing his crotchets by sending Russian tanks to run over Hungarian students who wanted a little liberty. In the corridors of the United Nations, the representatives of the anticolonialist world don't rise and walk out in indignation when the Soviet overlords walk into the room, or the Chinese; they don't pass resolutions calling for the freedom of Tibet or of Lithuania, let alone Poland—which, we were advised last week by our pleasantly befuddled President, shares American principles and ideals.

No, we do not believe, those of us who favor this treaty, that it is to be favored because it will cause the president of Libya to smile upon us as he lubricates his megaphones with expropriated American oil, happily joining a consortium of extortionists whose respect for the United States—interestingly enough—diminishes as we agree to pay the price they exact from us as a reward for our defective diplomacy.

No, it is another kind of satisfaction we seek—I mean the approval given by reflective men and women to nations that disdain a false pride. Nothing should stand in the way of our resolution to maintain United States sovereignty and freedom. And nothing should distract us from the irrelevance of prideful exercises, suitable rather to the peacock than to the lion, to assert our national masculinity. We have great tests ahead of us: Are we going to disarm unilaterally? Is our word to our allies a reliable covenant? Do we really believe in human rights? Do we really believe in sovereignty? Even in sovereignty for little countries, whose natural resources, where and when necessary, we are entitled to use; but not to abuse? The kind of satisfaction a nation truly consistent in the practice of its ideals seeks for itself is the kind of satisfaction, at this moment in history, we can have—by ratifying treaties that, at once, enhance our security, and our self-esteem.

Governor Reagan's Opening Remarks

Mr. Chairman. The gentlemen who are here to help in this evening's program. Ladies and gentlemen in the audience. I, too, would recognize, but not by name, not to take the time, all those who are present. But now that I have become a journalist and a commentator myself, I can say there is no one participating here tonight that I have not quoted, sometimes without credit.

Mr. Buckley, if you don't mind, I feel compassion, also, for all those other peoples in the world that we've been hearing about here tonight. But let's get back to the Canal.

In the rhetoric surrounding the discussion of the proposed Canal treaties, there's been a tendency to make the issue one of either these treaties or the status quo. Perhaps tonight we can make it plain that rejection of these treaties does not mean an end to further negotiations, or to the effort to better our plans for the people of Panama. We're debating these specific treaties, and whether they are in our best interest and the best interest of the people of Panama.

In my opinion, they are not. They are ambiguous in their wording; they are fatally flawed.

One treaty is, you've been told, to cover the transfer of the total ownership, control, and operation of the Canal to Panama, effective December 31, 1999. The other is to guarantee the permanent neutrality of the Canal, beginning in the year 2000. The fatal flaw I mentioned is that the transfer would not be gradual, as it might seem when we look down the road to 1999.

Under the present treaty, the Hay–Bunau–Varilla Treaty of 1903, the United States has "all the rights, power, and authority which the United States would possess and exercise if it were sovereign in the territory, to the exclusion of the exercise by the Republic of Panama of any such sovereign rights, power, or authority." Ratification of the new treaty would immediately cancel that treaty of 1903. The Canal Zone would cease to exist. We would simply be a foreign power with property in Panama. There would be nothing to prevent the government of Panama from expropriating our property and nationalizing the Canal, as they have already nationalized the transit company and the power system. International law permits expropriation by governments of foreign-owned property within their borders. And the United Nations Charter, which supersedes all other treaties, prohibits a member nation from using armed force to prevent such expropriation. This rules out the practice of *force majeure*—the idea that because we have the size and strength, why, we could just move.

In 1956 Nasser broke Egypt's treaty with Britain and seized the Suez Canal. He also broke the treaty which guaranteed the right of all nations to the use of that canal. When Britain, France, and Israel moved armed forces against Egypt, the United States took the lead in declaring that they must not violate the UN Charter; and they backed away. Suez became Egypt's, and the neutrality of the canal was no more. No traffic was allowed by ships going to and from Israeli ports. If we were to become victims of expropriation, as the English were in 1956, would we take the action we refused to let them take? I don't think so.

The second treaty, which comes into effect in the year 2000 when Panama has become the sole owner and operator of the Canal, promises complete neutrality for all users. This treaty is so ambiguous in its wording as to be virtually meaningless.

Nowhere in this second treaty, or the accompanying protocol, is the word "guarantee" used. "Guarantee" is a word of art. It carries the assurance that there is a *guarantor*. Our negotiators had capable lawyers advising them. The omission could not have been an oversight. "Guarantee" must have been left out at Panama's insistence, with full knowledge of the consequences. What is there for us to cheer about when what is being granted, in word only—neutrality of the canal we built—is something which presently we have in reality?

The new treaty for neutrality makes it very clear that, in the event of war, our enemies have the same right of access to the Canal that we have. The protocol does more. It permits all other nations—like, say, the Soviet Union or Cuba—to become parties to the protocol. That's brought forth in the first "whereas."

"Permanent neutrality" is meaningless unless some nation has the right to enforce it. Our treaty advocates tell us that we can claim that right, and therefore we're safe. But if so, then any of the other parties to the protocol have the same right.

The wording of the second treaty and its protocol is so ambiguous that already the people of the United States are being told by our government that we have rights which the government of Panama is telling its people we don't have. We're told that from the year 2000 on, in perpetuity, the United States can unilaterally declare that neutrality of the Canal has been violated, and we can intervene to restore it. We're told that in time of war our naval vessels can go to the head of the line and have privileged passage through the Canal.

We are *not* told that Dr. Romulo Escobar Bethancourt, chief negotiator for Panama and the chief advisor to the dictator of Panama, has assured his people we don't have any such rights. We cannot unilaterally find that neutrality has been violated, nor can we even deny the use of the Canal to our enemies in the event of war. Here are his words: "We did not want that, with the excuse of neutrality, the United States would maintain a guarantee over the State of Panama. This was another cause for discussion that kept the negotiations detained until the United States gave up on the idea of having a guarantee of neutrality over the Canal." The Doctor doesn't seem to have any problem using the word "guarantee" himself; he just doesn't want to see it in the treaty.

As for our vessels going to the head of the line in time of emergency, he had a few words about that which have been overlooked by the treaty advocates. He says that our negotiators wanted privileged passage of American warships, but Panama refused to allow it. He said they did allow us a phrase, "expeditious passage," but it has no meaning. They gave us that, he said, because the American negotiators had to have something in order to sell the treaty to the Pentagon.

The first treaty provides for defense under a joint board composed of equal numbers of Panamanian and United States officers. Now, that has a friendly sound, even though the treaty requires us to close down ten of our 14 military bases, and to fly the Panamanian flag at the entrance of the other four and in the place of honor on each base. And, of course, since Panama will have sovereignty, Panama will also have the absolute power of decision.

Joint defense . . . now, that brings to mind a picture of friendly allies going forward, shoulder to shoulder, in friendly camaraderie, the Americans voicing, probably, their customary marching chants, such as the well-known "Sound off. One, two." The Panamanian Guardia Nacional will be chanting the words that they use in their present training. They march to these words: "*¡Muerte al gringo! ¡Gringo abajo! ¡Gringo al paredón!*" Translation: "Death to the gringo! Down with the gringo! Gringo to the wall!"

Now, that should reassure us gringos about the kind of cooperation we might have under the new treaties.

In the days just ahead, we're going to be treated to fireside chats from the Oval Office. Members of the Cabinet will barnstorm across the country, playing one-night stands on the mashed potato circuit. There'll be a Madison Avenue advertising blitz, with billboards and television spot ads in support of the Canal treaties. We might even possibly hear from some who just happen to have an interest in banking.

I don't challenge their sincerity. But, based on some of the arguments that we've already heard, we will hear history rewritten by the State Department: The Canal is fast becoming obsolete. It no longer is important to us commercially. None of the giant supertankers can use it.

Well now, that last item is true. But if that's a reason for giving away the Canal, we ought to ask General Torrijos how much he wants to take New York Harbor and San Francisco Bay off our hands, because the supertankers were not built to use either the Suez or the Panama Canal, and none of them can use a single port in the United States.

But the Panama Canal *can* handle 97 per cent of all the world's shipping and 99 per cent of all United States Navy ships, everything but 13 of our largest carriers. More than a thousand ships a month go through the Canal, and it's estimated that this will be approaching 1,500 a year by the year 2000. That hardly sounds like the Canal is obsolete and going out of business. About 75 per cent of the imports and exports for several South American countries goes through the Canal. Farm produce from our own Midwest is accounting for about $9 billion of foreign trade that passes through the Canal.

It's false to say, also, that the Canal is not vital to national defense. In the Vietnam War, substantial cargo destined for the war zone went through that canal. There are present contingency plans that call for the movement of sixty Pacific Fleet vessels to the Atlantic in the event of a NATO crisis. Among top-ranking military officers who are retired, and thus free to speak their minds, I have seen a figure that 324 are opposed to the treaties, three are in favor. The Joint Chiefs of Staff have stated that we cannot protect the Canal against terrorist sabotage. They are absolutely right. But if they'd been a little more candid, they would have admitted we can't protect the Capitol Building in Washington or the Metro subway system against that kind of attack. As a matter of fact, the Capitol Building's already been bombed. But for more than sixty years, through four wars, the Canal has never once been subjected to sabotage.

It is time, I think, to offer a rebuttal to the rewriting of history that I referred to earlier. The Panama Canal Zone is not a last vestige of colonialism wrested from the Republic of Panama by force and coercion. Our Navy did not intervene to bring about the secession of Panama from Colombia, nor did it then intimidate Panama into granting the United States the Canal Zone in perpetuity. Without the Canal, there wouldn't be a Panama. Panama tried more than fifty times to free itself from Colombia. Separated by jungle, swamp, and impassable mountains, it had no common bond with the rest of the nation, and felt neglected by the government in Bogota.

When the French failed in their effort to build a canal across the Panamanian Isthmus, our Congress authorized the President to negotiate a treaty to build a canal, in either Colombia or Nicaragua. Indeed, Nicaragua was first choice with a majority in Congress until an untimely volcanic eruption tipped the balance to Panama. Congress approved $40 million to purchase the French company's equipment, excavation, and geological research, providing, of course, that Colombia agreed to the treaty. The French agreement with Colombia had only a few months to go. The Colombian government saw a chance to maybe get that $40 million themselves if they stalled for a few months. So they rejected the treaty. Panama saw its chance for freedom, declared its independence, and informed us it would sign a treaty.

Much has been made of the fact that there were American warships standing off Panama. There was nothing unusual in this. The railroad across Panama was American-built and owned, and our 1846 treaty with Colombia pledged us to protect the right-of-way and guarantee that there would be no interruption of traffic across the Isthmus. When the revolution in Panama was announced, the captain of the *U.S.S. Nashville* received these secret orders: "Maintain free and uninterrupted transit across the Isthmus, and prevent the landing of any armed force with hostile intent, government or insurgent." I submit that has a neutral sound.

The uprising began at 6 P.M. on November 3, 1903. No shots were fired, the revolution was bloodless, and it came about because Panama wanted us to build a canal.

In the current discussions, our President, the dictator of Panama, and Ambassador Linowitz have made much of the fact that no Panamanian signed the 1903 treaty. The inference is that this indicates some kind of skulduggery on our part. That is pure, unadulterated nonsense.

On November 8, the provisional government of the new Republic of Panama named a Frenchman, Bunau-Varilla, as minister plenipotentiary to negotiate the canal treaty with the United States. They knew what they were doing. He was a representative for the bankrupt French company, as avid to get that $40 million for his clients as the Panamanians were to get the canal. Bunau–Varilla negotiated the treaty with our Secretary of State, Hay. It was immediately and unanimously ratified by the provisional government of Panama, and subsequently by the permanent government. Our own Senate spent three months fighting over it, and then the vote was 66 to 14. The United States paid Panama $10 million in gold. Later, in 1922, we paid Colombia $25 million, because the land was actually theirs. We also gave Panama $250,000 a year in railroad royalties which had previously gone to Colombia. We've since raised that to about $2.3 million.

Now, let this put an end to any talk that we pay rent, and that thus our claim to the Canal Zone is a kind of a lease-hold. It's nothing of the kind. We not only bought the Zone from Panama, we did something I believe was unique in the history of great nations in their dealings with smaller countries. We went into the Zone and we bought, in fee simple, all the privately owned land from the owners, including even homestead claims and squatters' rights. I've seen the figure of those purchases set at $163 million. This should answer the charges of some treaty advocates that we have no claim to ownership of anything in Panama.

We built a sanitation system for their cities. We built bridges and highways and a water and power system. Our greatest contribution, of course, was the elimination of disease—mainly yellow fever, which had killed more than 20,000 of the French workers on the Canal. We took a country which was a disease-infested, swampy jungle and we gave it a death rate that was actually lower than the one we have in the United States. The first president of Panama, at his inauguration, announced that he would preside over an economic boom and the end to centuries of plague. The new nation began free of debt with a $10 million endowment. They set three-quarters of a million aside for working capital, two million for public works, and invested six million in New York real-estate mortgages—which shows they were inexperienced. But the interest from this provided the revenue for running their country. They had no fear of aggressive neighbors or of retaliation from Colombia because, at their request, the United States guaranteed their independence.

Then we proceeded to build the eighth wonder of the world.

We have operated the Canal for more than sixty years on a non-profit basis, open to all the world's shipping. Panama—and forgive my correction—Panama derives one-fourth of its gross national product from the Canal and has the highest per capita income of any country in Central America, the fourth highest in all of Latin America. The citizens of Panama make up 70 per cent of the Canal workforce, with a payroll of $110 million.

Somehow, it boggles the mind to think that we're being asked to turn over a $10-billion investment, including hospitals, schools, and even homes that the workers live in, and to place American people and the American military under the jurisdiction of a government that was not elected by the Panamanian people, that holds power at the point of a gun, and is an authoritarian dictatorship. In return for that, there's no talk of purchase or a purchase price. We will, instead, pay that government what will total about a billion and a half dollars over twenty-odd years to take this thing off our hands, and also for them not to engage in bloody riots and disturbances. And we also promise not to build another canal anywhere else without their consent.

Of course, we have agreed to continue our foreign aid to them, which is now the highest per capita of any country in the world that we help.

Ah, but we're told this will make us loved in all Latin America. But will it? He himself, General Torrijos, has told journalists that only four countries in Latin America support his demand. I have had personal contact with representatives of governments who tell us: No, we don't.

I think there are alternatives. The alternatives could involve a governing or policy-making board made up of Panamanians, Americans, and representatives of the other Latin American neighbor states. I think that we could make vast tracts of the Zone available for commercial development for the nearly bankrupt economy of Panama. Even now the Panama Canal Zone is not a barrier which the Panamanians are not free to cross as they will to get to the other parts of their country.

We could proceed with the third-lock plan, which would contribute about a billion and half dollars over a few years into their economy. There are other alternatives I could name. But we cannot abdicate our responsibility for the operation of the Canal and the security of the Western Hemisphere. Let us reject these treaties and negotiate as a great nation should, and have no more yielding to threats or blackmail.

Governor Reagan's Rebuttal

Mr. Chairman and ladies and gentlemen, we come back again to my original premise. And I would start, I think, with the question that I didn't have time to answer: the defensibility of the Canal. If we're talking nuclear defense of the Panama Canal: No—if a missile is aimed to come in on it. But you have to ask yourself: In the event of a nuclear war, who's going to waste a missile on the Canal? They'll be dropping missiles on New York, Chicago, San Francisco, Los Angeles, and so forth, and it would be a waste of time to use one there. So we come down to conventional warfare, and we come down to sabotage.

I claim that with the United States's military force—trained on the ground, which has defended the Canal against any attempt at sabotage through four wars— it's going to take more than a single saboteur slipping in in the night with a hand grenade or an explosive charge. It's going to take a trained demolition team, with plenty of time to work and no interruption, to do something to disable the gates, the locks, and so forth. Or the alternative would be to assault the dams that hold back the lakes—a two-hundred-square-mile lake, for one; there are three lakes— that provide the water that, through gravity, floods these locks. Now I submit that with an American armed force on hand guarding those vulnerable points, they are far safer than if the Panamanians were in charge and the Americans were not there. And the sabotage we could expect would come from people within the ranks of the Panamanians. I don't know who else it could be.

We also know that there are elements in Panama who have said that these treaties are unsatisfactory because they would take twenty years, and that they're going to riot and cause trouble unless they're given the Canal now.

And so we come back to the point that is at issue. Yes, there is a problem: sensitivity to the Panamanian people, to what they want, to their pride. I agree with that. But also, on our side, is the responsibility we cannot abdicate: to protect the Canal and make sure that it remains open to all shipping, and that it is there for the defense of this hemisphere and of our own nation.

Now we have to face the Panamanians again in negotiations—but *not* because we've been threatened that they'll cause trouble. Because I say that this is one of the first things that should have caused us to call off the negotiations. When they threatened violence, I believe the United States should have said to them, "We don't negotiate with anyone under threats. If you want to sit down and talk in a spirit of good will, we'll do it." But we should go back now and say, "If we can find a way that ensures our right to provide the security the Canal must have, we'll do everything we can to find a way to erase the friction points"—some of which I pointed out there in my previous remarks. The Canal is not a natural resource of Panama that has been exploited by the United States. We haven't taken minerals out of the Canal Zone. We haven't lumbered it. We've gone in for one purpose and one only, the one the Treaty called for: to build and operate a canal. And I don't know of anyone who has benefited more than the people of Panama. Their ships even have an advantage in the tolls they must pay, as do the ships of Colombia.

We're dealing with a government that, as I've said repeatedly here, has not been elected. A dictatorship that in nine years has accumulated the highest per capita debt of any nation in the world. Thirty-nine per cent of the Panamanian budget goes to service that debt. If our debt were comparable, per capita, it would be five times as big as it is right now, and it's already seven hundred billion dollars.

I don't believe that we would do anything to strengthen our position in Latin America by, again, yielding to this unpleasantness. I think, if anything, we would become a laughingstock by surrendering to unreasonable demands. And by doing so, I think we would cloak weakness in the suit of virtue.

This has to be treated in the context of the international situation; the Panama Canal treaty is just one facet of our foreign policy. What are we doing to ourselves in the eyes of the world, and to our allies? Will they, as Mr. Buckley says, see it as the magnanimous gesture of a great and powerful nation? I don't think so, not in view of our recent history, not in view of our bugout in Vietnam, not in view of an Administration that is hinting that we're going to throw aside an ally named Taiwan. Not in view of our policy in Africa. I think that the world would see it as, once again, a case where Uncle Sam put his tail between his legs and crept away rather than face trouble.

I think Professor Fontaine was right to question the ability of the Panamanians to run the Canal. This particular administration of Panama has started three sugar mills, a hydroelectric project, an airport, a public transportation system, a resort island, an agricultural development program, and a program of exploration for natural resources, and it has failed in every one of them. They're all failures and back on the shelf. So again I say that there are alternatives by which we could benefit the people of Panama. But I believe this treaty is aimed at benefiting the *dictator* of

Panama. Until someone can suggest a way that we can meet our responsibility other than by retaining our right of sovereignty, then I say that we have to retain it.

I would suggest, as I said before, the third-lock plan, which would make it possible for the Canal to take our carriers. The benefits accruing to Panama, the increase in industry, would do much to rescue what is virtually a bankrupt economy now. But, again, I come down to the basic argument of whether it is to be these treaties or whether we, as a great nation, are to say to Panama, "We cannot forsake this one responsibility. Now, here are the things that we are prepared to do, and if you have any other suggestions, raise them in negotiations."

But I submit, with all due respect to those who negotiated, I think they were put in an untenable position. I think our negotiators did the best they could in circumstances where they were sent not to negotiate, but literally to concede as little as they had to in order to pacify a dictator and to avoid violence.

Mr. Buckley's Rebuttal

Mr. Chairman, Governor Reagan. James Thurber once said, "You know, women are ruling the world. And the reason they're ruling the world is that they have so insecure a knowledge of history. I found myself sitting next to a lady on an airplane the other day who all of a sudden turned to me and said, 'Why did we have to pay for Louisiana when we got all the other states free?' So I explained it to her. I said, 'Louisiana was owned by two sisters called Louisa and Anne Wilmot. And they offered to give it to the United States, provided it was named after them. That was the Wilmot Proviso. But President Winfield Scott refused to do that. That was the Dred Scott Decision.' So the lady said, 'That's all very well. But I still don't understand why we had to pay for the Louisiana Purchase.'"

Now, intending no slur on my friend Ronald Reagan, the politician in America I admire most, his rendition of recent history and his generalities remind me a little bit of Thurber's explanation. He says we don't negotiate under threats. And everybody here *bursts* out in applause. The trouble with that is that it's not true. We *do* negotiate under threats. Ninety-nine per cent of all the negotiations that have gone on from the beginning of this world have gone on as a result of threats. When somebody says to his boss, "If you don't give me a raise. I'm quitting," that's a threat, isn't it? What do you call what we did to George III? It was a most convincing threat.

Secondly, the fact of the matter is that there are people in Panama who don't accept Governor Reagan's notion that the United States exercises undisputed, unambiguous sovereignty over that territory.

In 1928, in the *Luckenback Steamship Company Case*, the Supreme Court of the United States referred to the Canal Zone as a place in which there were "foreign ports." William Howard Taft said to Panama that we had "not the slightest interest in colonizing." In 1936 we reaffirmed the titular sovereignty of Panama. Children born of foreign parents in Panama don't become Americans. Dulles said to the United Nations in 1946: "Panama is sovereign." In 1948, the Supreme Court, in its decision in *Vermilya-Brown Co. v. Connell,* made the following reference: "Admittedly, Panama is territory over which we do not have sovereignty."

We do have there the absolute right, which I do not deny and which my colleagues do not deny, to stay as long as we want. But to say that we have *sovereignty,* as Governor Reagan has said, is to belie the intention of the people who supervised our diplomacy in the early part of the century. And it is also to urge people to believe that we harbor an appetite for colonialism, which we shrink from, having ourselves set forth in the Declaration of Independence principles that are applicable not only to people fortunate enough to be born in Massachusetts or in New York or in Virginia, but to people born everywhere.

And all of a sudden we find that we resent it when people say they're willing to fight for their freedom. There was fighting done within hundreds of yards of where we're standing because the people of the South wanted their freedom from the Union. We fought back, and it continues to be an open question whether there was successful diplomacy in the course of resisting that insurrection. But is there anyone who believes that we should feel contempt for the people who backed up their demands for freedom by being willing to die for them? I don't feel that contempt, Mr. Chairman, and I don't think the American people feel it either.

I think Governor Reagan put his finger on it when he said the reason this treaty is unpopular is that we're tired of being pushed around. We were pushed out of Vietnam because, just as Admiral McCain told us, we didn't have the guts to go in there and do it right. We're now prepared, it's been said, to desert Taiwan because three and a half Harvard professors think that we ought to "normalize" our relations with Red China. We are prepared to allow 16 semi-savage countries to cartelize the oil that is indispensable to the entire industrial might of the West because we don't have a diplomacy that's firm enough to do something about it. And, therefore, how do we get our kicks? By saying no to the people of Panama.

When I am in a mood to say no, representing the United States, I want to be looking the Soviet Union in the face; I want to say no to the Soviet Union the next time it starts to send its tanks running over students in Czechoslovakia who want a little freedom. I want to say no to China when it subsidizes genocide in Cambodia on a scale that has not been known in this century, rather than simply forget that it exists. I don't feel that the United States has to affirm its independence by saying we must not distinguish between the intrinsic merits of rewriting the treaty with Panama and of pulling out of Taiwan because it is all a part of the same syndrome.

Who in this room doubts that if the President of the United States weren't Jimmy Carter but, let us say, Douglas MacArthur, and if the Chairman of the Joint Chiefs of Staff were Curtis LeMay, and if the Secretary of State were Theodore Roosevelt, and if this instrument were then recommended to the Senate—who doubts that the conservative community of America would endorse it?

We are being convinced not by our minds, not by hard analytical arguments, certainly not by those ideals to which we profess allegiance every time we meditate on the Declaration of Independence. We are allowing ourselves to be beguiled by a quite understandable bitterness at the way we have been kicked around. We should not be mad at the Panamanian students, who are asking for nothing more than what our great-great-grandparents asked for; we should be mad at our own leaders for screwing up the peace during the last 25 years. Do we want to go down and take it out on people who simply want to recover the Canal Zone? What we have done to Panama is the equivalent of taking the falls away from Niagara. Is it the kind of satisfaction that we feel we are entitled to, to assert a sovereignty which is, in any case, not a part of the historical tradition?

No. Let's listen to reason. Let's recognize, as Admiral Zumwalt has said, that we are so impoverished militarily as a result of so many lamentable decisions that we need the Panama Canal; and we need the Panama Canal run by a people who can understand themselves as joined with us in a common enterprise because, when they look at the leaders of the United States, they can recognize that, not as a result of an attempt to curry favor with anybody, but as a result of our concern for our own self-esteem, we are big enough to grant little people what we ourselves fought for two hundred years ago.

Reagan's Leadership, America's Recovery

By Margaret Thatcher

EDITOR'S NOTE: *The former Prime Minister of Britain wrote this essay for the December 30, 1988, issue of* National Review.

There have not been many times when a British Prime Minister has been Prime Minister through two consecutive terms of office of the same President of the United States. Indeed there have been only three such cases so far. One was Pitt the Younger, who was in Number 10 Downing Street while George Washington was President. Another was Lord Liverpool, who held the prime ministership throughout the whole period in office of President James Monroe. And I am the third. It gives me a vantage point which, if not unique, is nonetheless historically privileged from which to survey the remarkable Presidency of Ronald Reagan.

I cannot pretend, however, to be an entirely unbiased observer. I still remember vividly the feelings with which I learned of the President's election in 1980. We had met and discussed our political views some years before, when he was still Governor of California, and I knew that we believed in so many of the same things. I felt then that together we could tackle the formidable tasks before us: to get our countries on their feet, to restore their pride and their values, and to help create a safer and better world.

On entering office, the President faced high interest rates, high inflation, sluggish growth, and a growing demand for self-destructive protectionism. These problems had created—and in turn were reinforced by—a feeling that not much could be done about them, that America faced inevitable decline in a new era of limits to growth, that the American dream was over. We in Britain had been in the grip of a similar pessimism during the Seventies, when political debate revolved around the concept of the "British disease." Indeed, during this entire period, the Western world seemed to be taking its temperature with every set of economic indices.

President Reagan saw instinctively that pessimism itself was the disease and that the cure for pessimism is optimism. He set about restoring faith in the prospects of the American dream—a dream of boundless opportunity built on enterprise, individual effort, and personal generosity. He infused his own belief in America's economic future in the American people. That was farsighted. It carried America through the difficult early days of the 1981–82 recession, because people are prepared to put up with sacrifices if they know that those sacrifices are the foundations of future prosperity.

Having restored the faith of the American people in themselves, the President set about liberating their energies and enterprise. He reduced the excessive burden of regulation, halted inflation, and first cut and, later, radically reformed taxation. When barriers to enterprise are removed and taxes cut to sensible levels (as we have found in Britain in recent years), people have the incentive to work harder and earn more. They thereby benefit themselves, their families, and the whole community. Hence the buoyant economy of the Reagan years. It has expanded by a full 25 per cent over 72 months of continuous economic growth—the longest period of peacetime economic growth in U.S. history—it has spread prosperity widely; and it has cut unemployment to the lowest level in over a decade.

The international impact of these successes has been enormous. At a succession of Western economic summits, the President's leadership encouraged the West to cooperate on policies of low inflation, steady growth, and open markets. These policies have kept protectionism in check and the world economy growing. They are policies which offer not just an economic message, but a political one: Freedom works. It brings growth, opportunity, and prosperity in its train. Other countries, seeing its success in the United States and Britain, have rushed to adopt the policies of freedom.

President Reagan decided what he believed in, stuck to it through thick and thin, and finally, through its success, persuaded others. But I still recall those dark early days of this decade when both our countries were grappling with the twin disasters of inflation and recession and when some people, even in our own parties, wanted to abandon our policies before they had had a proper chance to take effect. They were times for cool courage and a steady nerve. That is what they got from the President. I remember his telling me, at a meeting at the British Embassy in 1981, that for all the difficulties we then faced, we would be "home safe and soon enough."

The economic recovery was, however, but part of a wider recovery of America's confidence and role in the world, for the malaise of the 1970s went beyond economics. The experience of Vietnam had bred an understandable but dangerous lack of national self-confidence on the U.S. side of the Atlantic, or so it seemed to outsiders. There was a marked reluctance in American public opinion to advance American power abroad even in defense of clear American and Western interests. And politicians struggled against this national mood at their electoral peril.

President Reagan took office at a time when the Soviet Union was invading Afghanistan, placing missiles in Eastern Europe aimed at West European capitals, and assisting Communist groups in the Third World to install themselves in power against the popular will, and when America's response was hobbled by the so-called Vietnam syndrome. And not just America's response. The entire West, locked in a battle of wills with the Soviets, seemed to be losing confidence.

President Reagan's first step was to change the military imbalance which underlay this loss of confidence. He built up American power in a series of defense budgets. There have been criticisms of this build-up as too expensive. Well, a sure defense is expensive, but not nearly so expensive as weakness could turn out to be.

By this military build-up, President Reagan strengthened not only American defenses, but also the will of America's allies. It led directly to NATO's installation of Cruise and Pershing missiles in Western Europe. This took place in the teeth of Moscow's biggest "peace offensive" since the Berlin crises of the early Sixties. That offensive included a Soviet walkout from the Geneva talks on nuclear disarmament and mass demonstrations and lobbies by "peace groups" in Western Europe. Yet these tactics failed, the missiles were installed, and the Soviets returned to the bargaining table to negotiate about withdrawing their own missiles.

President Reagan has also demonstrated that he is not afraid to put to good use the military strength he had built up. And it is noteworthy—though not often noted—that many of the decisions he has taken in the face of strong criticism have been justified by events. It was President Reagan who, amid cries that his policy lacked any rationale, stationed U.S. ships alongside European navies in the Persian Gulf to protect international shipping. Not only did this policy secure its stated purpose, it also protected the Gulf states against aggression and thus hastened the end of the conflict by foreclosing any option of widening the war.

The President enjoyed a similar success in the continuing battle against terrorism. He took action against one of the states most active in giving aid and comfort to terrorist organizations: Colonel Qaddafi's Libya. We in Britain had experienced Qaddafi's murderous methods at first hand when a member of the Libyan Embassy shot down a young policewoman in cold blood in a London square. We had no doubts about the reality of Libyan involvement. I therefore had no hesitation in supporting the American air strike, which has resulted in a marked reduction of Libyan-sponsored terrorism.

And thirdly, President Reagan has given America's support to nations which are still struggling to keep their independence in the face of Soviet-backed aggression. The policy has had major successes:

- The withdrawal of Soviet forces from Afghanistan, due to be completed next February
- The real prospect of Cuban withdrawal from Angola, encouraged by patient and constructive American diplomacy
- And even the prospect of Vietnamese withdrawal from Cambodia

These are all remarkable achievements, which very few observers predicted even three years ago.

Indeed, when we compare the mood of confidence and optimism in the West today with the mood when President Reagan took office eight years ago, we know that a greater change has taken place than could ever have been imagined. America has regained its confidence and is no longer afraid of the legitimate uses of its power. It has discussed those uses with its allies in the NATO alliance at all stages and with great frankness. Today our joint resolve is stronger than ever. And, finally, the recovery of American strength and confidence has led, as President Reagan always argued it would, to more peaceful and stable relations with the Soviet Union.

For strength, not weakness, leads to peace. It was only after the Soviet threat of SS-20s had been faced down and cruise and Pershing missiles installed that the Soviets were prepared to embark on genuine arms-control negotiations and wider peace negotiations. It therefore fell to the President, less than four years after the Soviet walkout at Geneva, to negotiate the first arms-control agreement that actually reduced the nuclear stockpiles. And when he visited Moscow for the third Summit of his Presidency, he took the first for human rights into the very heart of Moscow, where his words shone like a beacon of hope for all those who are denied their basic freedoms. Indeed the very recovery of American strength during his Presidency has been a major factor prompting and evoking the reform program under Mr. Gorbachev in the Soviet Union. The Soviet authorities would have had much less incentive for reform if they had been faced by a weak and declining United States.

The legacy of President Reagan in East–West relations is the realistic appreciation that maintaining sure defenses, bridging the East–West divide, and reducing weapons and forces on both sides are not contradictory but policies that go comfortably together. Nothing could be more short-sighted for the West today than to run down its defenses unilaterally at the first sign of more peaceful and stable relations between East and West. Nothing would be more likely to persuade those with whom we negotiate that they would *not* need to make any concessions, because we would cut our defenses anyway. Britain will not do that. We will maintain and update our defenses. And our example is one which I hope our partners and allies will follow, because Europe must show that she is willing to bear a reasonable share of the burden of defending herself. That would be the best way for the NATO allies to repay America's farsighted foreign and defense policies of the Reagan years.

When we attempt an overall survey of President Reagan's term of office, covering events both foreign and domestic, one thing stands out. It is that he has achieved the most difficult of all political tasks: changing attitudes and perceptions about what is possible. From the strong fortress of his convictions, he set out to enlarge freedom the world over at a time when freedom was in retreat—and he succeeded. It is not merely that freedom now advances while collectivism is in retreat—important though that is. It is that freedom is the idea that everywhere captures men's minds while collectivism can do no more than enslave their bodies. That is the measure of the change that President Reagan has wrought.

How is it that some political leaders make the world a different place while others, equally able, equally public-spirited, leave things much as they found them? Some years ago, Professor Hayek pointed out that the social sciences often neglected the most important aspects of their subjects because they were not capable of being examined and explained in quantitative terms. One such quality which resists quantitative analysis is political leadership. Which also happens to be the occupational requirement of a statesman.

No one can doubt that President Reagan possesses the ability to lead to an unusual degree. Some of the constituent qualities of that leadership I have referred to in passing—his firm convictions, his steadfastness in difficult times, his capacity to infuse his own optimism into the American people so that he restored their belief in America's destiny. But I would add three more qualities that, together with those above, enabled him to transform the political landscape.

The first is courage. The whole world remembers the wit and grave which the President displayed at the time of the attempt on his life. It was one of those occasions when people saw the real character of a man when he had none of the assistances which power and office provide. And they admired what they saw—cheerful bravery in the face of personal danger, no thought for himself but instead a desire to reassure his family and the nation by jokes and good humor.

The second is that he holds opinions which strike a chord in the heart of the average American. The great English journalist Walter Bagehot once defined a constitutional statesman as a man of common opinion and uncommon abilities. That is true of President Reagan and one of his greatest political strengths. He can appeal for support to the American people because they sense rightly that he shares their dreams, hopes, and aspirations; and he pursues them by the same route of plain American horse-sense.

Finally, President Reagan speaks with the authority of a man who knows what he believes and who has shown that he will stand by his beliefs in good times and bad. He is no summer soldier of conservatism, but one who fought in the ranks when the going wasn't good. Again, that reassured even those who do not share those beliefs. For authority is the respect won from others by the calm exercise of deep conviction.

The results of that leadership are all around us. President Reagan departs the political scene leaving America stronger and more confident, and the West more united than ever before. I believe that President-elect Bush, a man of unrivaled experience in government and international affairs, will be a worthy successor, providing the forthright leadership which the world has come to expect from the U.S. President. We wish him well.

How Reagan Won the Cold War

By Dinesh D'Souza

EDITOR'S NOTE: *This article appeared in the November 24, 1997, issue of* National Review. *It was adapted from Mr.* D'Souza's book, Ronald Reagan: How an Ordinary Man Became an Extraordinary Leader.

Ten years ago Ronald Reagan stood at the Brandenburg Gate and said, "General Secretary Gorbachev, if you seek peace, if you seek prosperity for the Soviet Union and Eastern Europe, if you seek liberalization: Come here to this gate! Mr. Gorbachev, open this gate! Mr. Gorbachev, tear down this wall!" Not long afterward, the wall came tumbling down and the most formidable empire in world history collapsed so fast that, in Vaclav Havel's words, "we had no time even to be astonished."

With the disintegration of the Soviet Union, the most ambitious political and social experiment of the modern era ended in failure, and the supreme political drama of the twentieth century—the conflict between the free West and the totalitarian East—came to an end. What will probably prove to be the most important historical event of our lifetimes has already occurred.

Given these remarkable developments, it is natural to wonder what caused the destruction of Soviet Communism. Yet, oddly, this is a subject that no one seems to want to discuss. The reluctance is especially acute among intellectuals. Consider what happened on June 4, 1990, when Mikhail Gorbachev addressed the students and faculty at Stanford University. The Cold War was over, he said, and people clapped with evident relief. Then Gorbachev added, "And let us not wrangle over who won it." At this point the crowd leapt to its feet and applauded thunderously.

Gorbachev's desire to avoid this topic was understandable. But why were the apparent winners of the Cold War equally resolved not to celebrate their victory or analyze how it came about? Perhaps the reason is simply this: virtually everyone was wrong about the Soviet Union. The doves or appeasers were totally and spectacularly wrong on every point. For example, when Reagan in 1983 called the Soviet Union an "evil empire," Anthony Lewis of the *New York Times* was so indignant that he searched his repertoire for the appropriate adjective: "simplistic," "sectarian," "dangerous," "outrageous." Finally Lewis settled on "primitive—the only word for it."

In the mid 1980s, Strobe Talbott, then a journalist at *Time* and later an official in the Clinton State Department, wrote: "Reagan is counting on American technological and economic predominance to prevail in the end," whereas, if the Soviet economy was in a crisis of any kind, "it is a permanent, institutionalized crisis with which the USSR has learned to live."

Historian Barbara Tuchman argued that instead of employing a policy of confrontation, the West should ingratiate itself with the Soviet Union by pursuing "the stuffed-goose option—that is, providing them with all the grain and consumer goods they need." If Reagan had taken this advice when it was offered in 1982, the Soviet empire would probably be around today.

The hawks or anti–Communists had a much better understanding of totalitarianism, and they understood the necessity of an arms build-up to deter Soviet aggression. But they too believed that Soviet Communism was a permanent and virtually indestructible adversary. This Spenglerian gloom is conveyed by Whittaker Chambers's famous remark to the House Un-American Activities Committee in 1948 that in abandoning Communism he was "leaving the winning side for the losing side."

The hawks were also mistaken about what steps were needed to bring about the final dismantling of the Soviet empire. During Reagan's second term, when he supported Gorbachev's reform efforts and pursued arms-reduction agreements with him, many conservatives denounced his apparent change of heart: "ignorant and pathetic" was the way Charles Krauthammer viewed Reagan's behavior. William F. Buckley Jr. urged Reagan to reconsider his positive assessment of the Gorbachev regime: "To greet it as if it were no longer evil is on the order of changing our entire position toward Adolf Hitler." George Will mourned that "Reagan has accelerated the moral disarmament of the West by elevating wishful thinking to the status of political philosophy."

No one likes to have his expertise called into question, but the doves are especially averse to admitting that they were wrong and Reagan was right. Consequently this group has in the last few years made a determined effort to rewrite history. There is no mystery about the end of the Soviet Union, the revisionists say: it suffered from chronic economic problems and collapsed of its own weight. "The Soviet system has gone into meltdown because of inadequacies and defects at its core," Strobe Talbott writes, "not because of anything the outside world has done or not done."

In Talbott's view, "the Soviet threat is not what it used to be. The real point, however, is that it never was. The doves in the great debate of the past forty years were right all along." Meanwhile, the "extreme militarization" pursued by Reagan and the hard-liners in the Pentagon, George Kennan insists, "consistently strengthened comparable hard-liners in the Soviet Union." Far from accelerating the end of the Cold War, it may have actually postponed it.

This analysis is impressive, if only for its audacity. The Soviet Union did indeed suffer from debilitating economic problems. But why would this by itself bring about the end of the political regime? Historically it is common for nations to experience poor economic performance, but never have food shortages or technological backwardness been sufficient causes for the destruction of a large empire. The Roman empire survived internal corrosion for centuries before it was destroyed by the invasion of the barbarian hordes. The Ottoman empire persisted as the "sick man of Europe" for generations and ended only with catastrophic defeat in World War I.

Nor can the economic argument explain why the empire collapsed at the particular time that it did. The revisionists say in effect: It happened, therefore it was inevitable. But if Soviet collapse was so certain, why wasn't it foreseen by the revisionists, who were unanimous in proclaiming—in the words of a 1983 column by Anthony Lewis—that the Soviet regime "is not going to disappear"?

It is no less problematic to assert that Gorbachev was the architect of the collapse of the Soviet Union. He was undoubtedly a reformer and a new kind of Soviet leader. But Gorbachev did not wish to lead the party, and the regime, over the precipice. Consequently, when the Soviet Union collapsed, no one was more surprised than Gorbachev. He was incredulous when he was swept out of power, and he is still openly indignant and bewildered about the fact that he got less than 1 per cent of the vote in the Russian election in 1996.

The man who got things right from the start was, at first glance, an unlikely statesman. When he became the leader of the free world he had no experience in foreign policy. Some people thought he was a dangerous warmonger; others considered him a nice fellow, but a bit of a bungler. Nevertheless, this California lightweight turned out to have as deep an understanding of Communism as Aleksandr Solzhenitsyn. This rank amateur developed a complex, often counter-intuitive strategy for dealing with the Soviet Union which hardly anyone on his staff fully endorsed or even understood. Through a combination of vision, tenacity, patience, and improvisational skill, he produced what Henry Kissinger terms "the most stunning diplomatic feat of the modern era." Or as Margaret Thatcher put it, "Ronald Reagan won the Cold War without firing a shot."

Reagan had a much more skeptical view of the power of Soviet Communism than either the hawks or the doves. In 1981 he told an audience at the University of Notre Dame, "The West won't contain Communism. It will transcend Communism. It will dismiss it as some bizarre chapter in human history whose last pages are even now being written." The next year, speaking to the British Parliament, Reagan predicted that if the Western alliance remained strong it would produce a "march of freedom and democracy which will leave Marxism-Leninism on the ashheap of history."

These prophetic assertions—dismissed as wishful rhetoric at the time—raise the question: How did Reagan know that Soviet Communism faced impending collapse when the most perceptive minds of his time had no inkling of what was to come? To answer this question, the best approach is to begin with Reagan's jokes. Over the years he had developed an extensive collection of stories which he attributed to the Soviet people themselves. One of these involves a man who goes up to a store clerk in Moscow and asks for a kilogram of beef, half a kilogram of butter, and a quarter kilogram of coffee. "We're all out," the clerk says, and the man leaves. Another man, observing this incident, says to the clerk, "That old man must be crazy." The clerk replies, "Yeah, but what a memory!"

Another favorite anecdote concerns a man who goes to the Soviet bureau of transportation to order an automobile. He is informed that he will have to put down his money now, but there is a ten-year wait. So he fills out all the various forms, has them processed through the various agencies, and finally gets to the last agency. He pays them his money and they say, "Come back in ten years and get your car." He asks, "Morning or afternoon?" The man in the agency says, "We're talking about ten years from now. What difference does it make?" He replies, "The plumber is coming in the morning."

Reagan could go on in this vein for hours. What is striking, however, is that Reagan's jokes are not about the evil of Communism but about its incompetence. Reagan agreed with the hawks that the Soviet experiment which sought to create a "new man" was immoral. At the same time, he saw that it was also basically stupid. Reagan did not need a Ph.D. in economics to recognize that any economy based upon centralized planners' dictating how much factories should produce, how much people should consume, and how social rewards should be distributed was doomed to disastrous failure. For Reagan the Soviet Union was a "sick bear," and the question was not whether it would collapse, but when.

Yet while the Soviet Union had a faltering economy, it had a highly advanced military. No one doubted that Soviet missiles, if fired at American targets, would cause enormous destruction. But Reagan also knew that the evil empire was spending at least 20 per cent of its gross national product on defense. (The actual proportion turned out to be even higher.) Thus Reagan formulated the notion that the West could use the superior economic resources of a free society to outspend Moscow in the arms race, placing intolerable strains on the Soviet regime.

Reagan outlined his "sick bear" theory as early as May 1982 in a commencement address at his alma mater, Eureka College. He said, "The Soviet empire is faltering because rigid centralized control has destroyed incentives for innovation, efficiency, and individual achievement. But in the midst of social and economic problems, the Soviet dictatorship has forged the largest armed force in the world. It has done so by pre-empting the human needs of its people and, in the end, this course will undermine the foundations of the Soviet system."

Sick bears, however, can be very dangerous—they tend to lash out. Moreover, since in fact we are discussing not animals but people, there is the question of pride. The leaders of an internally weak empire are not likely to acquiesce in an erosion of their power. They typically turn to their primary source of strength: the military.

Appeasement, Reagan was convinced, would only increase the bear's appetite and invite further aggression. Thus he agreed with the anti–Communist strategy of dealing firmly with the Soviets. But he was more confident than most hawks that Americans were up to the challenge. "We must realize," he said in his first inaugural address, "that no weapon in the arsenals of the world is so formidable as the will and moral courage of free men and women." What was most visionary about Reagan's view was that it rejected the assumption of Soviet immutability. At a time when no one else could, Reagan dared to imagine a world in which the Communist regime in the Soviet Union did not exist.

It was one thing to envision this happy state, and quite another to bring it about. The Soviet bear was in a blustery and ravenous mood when Reagan entered the White House. Between 1974 and 1980, it had, through outright invasion or the triumph of its surrogates, brought ten countries into the Communist orbit: South Vietnam, Cambodia, Laos, South Yemen, Angola, Ethiopia, Mozambique, Grenada,

Nicaragua, and Afghanistan. Moreover, it had built the most formidable nuclear arsenal in the world, with thousands of multiple-warhead missiles aimed at the United States. The Warsaw Pact had overwhelming superiority over NATO in its conventional forces. Finally, Moscow had recently deployed a new generation of intermediate-range missiles, the giant SS-20s, targeted on European cities.

Reagan did not merely react to these alarming events; he developed a broad counteroffensive strategy. He initiated a $1.5 trillion military buildup, the largest in American peacetime history, which was aimed at drawing the Soviets into an arms race he was convinced they could not win. He was also determined to lead the Western alliance in deploying 108 Pershing II and 464 Tomahawk cruise missiles in Europe to counter the SS-20s. At the same time, he did not eschew arms-control negotiations. Indeed he suggested that for the first time ever the two superpowers should drastically reduce their nuclear stockpiles. If the Soviets would withdraw their SS-20s, he said, the U.S. would not proceed with the Pershing and cruise deployments. This was called the "zero option."

Then there was the Reagan Doctrine, which involved military and material support for indigenous movements struggling to overthrow Soviet-sponsored tyrannies. The Administration supported such guerrillas in Afghanistan, Cambodia, Angola, and Nicaragua. In addition, it worked with the Vatican and the international wing of the AFL-CIO to keep the Polish trade union Solidarity going, despite a ruthless crackdown by General Jaruzelski's regime. In 1983, U.S. troops invaded and liberated Grenada, ousting the Marxist government and sponsoring free elections. Finally, in March 1983, Reagan announced the Strategic Defense Initiative (SDI), a new program to research and eventually deploy missile defenses which offered the promise, in Reagan's words, of "making nuclear weapons obsolete."

At every stage, Reagan's counteroffensive strategy was denounced by the doves, who exploited public fears that Reagan's military buildup was leading the world closer to nuclear war. Reagan's zero option was dismissed by Strobe Talbott as "highly unrealistic" and as having been offered "more to score propaganda points than to win concessions from the Soviets." With the exception of support for the Afghan mujahedin, every effort to aid anti–Communist rebels was resisted by doves in Congress and the media. SDI was denounced as, in the *New York Times*'s words, "a projection of fantasy into policy."

The Soviet Union was equally hostile to the Reagan counteroffensive, but its view of Reagan's objectives was far more perceptive than that of the doves. *Izvestiya* protested, "They want to impose on us an even more ruinous arms race." General Secretary Yuri Andropov alleged that Reagan's SDI program was "a bid to disarm the Soviet Union." The seasoned diplomat Andrei Gromyko charged that "behind all this lies the clear calculation that the USSR will exhaust its material resources and therefore will be forced to surrender."

These reactions are important because they establish the context for Mikhail Gorbachev's ascent to power in early 1985. Gorbachev was indeed a new breed of Soviet general secretary, but few have asked why he was appointed by the Old

Guard. The main reason was that the Politburo had come to recognize the failure of past Soviet strategies.

Reagan, in other words, seems to have been largely responsible for inducing a loss of nerve that caused Moscow to seek a new approach. Gorbachev's assignment was not merely to find a new way to deal with the country's economic problems but also to figure out how to cope with the empire's reversals abroad. For this reason, Ilya Zaslavsky, who served in the Soviet Congress of People's Deputies, said later that the true originator of perestroika (restructuring) and glasnost (openness) was not Mikhail Gorbachev but Ronald Reagan.

Gorbachev inspired wild enthusiasm on the political Left and in the Western media. Mary McGrory of the *Washington Post* was convinced he had a "blueprint for saving the planet." Gail Sheehy was dazzled by his "luminous presence." In 1990 *Time* proclaimed him its "Man of the Decade" and compared him to Franklin Roosevelt. Just as Roosevelt had to transform capitalism in order to save it, so Gorbachev was credited with reinventing socialism in order to save it.

The reason for these embarrassing "Gorbasms" was that Gorbachev was precisely the kind of leader that Western intellectuals admire: a top-down reformer who portrayed himself as a progressive; a technocrat who gave three-hour speeches on how the agriculture program was coming along. Most of all, the new Soviet leader was attempting to achieve the great twentieth-century hope of the Western intelligentsia: Communism with a human face! A socialism that works!

Yet as Gorbachev discovered, and as the rest of us now know, it cannot be done. The vices that Gorbachev sought to eradicate from the system turned out to be the essential features of the system. If Reagan was the Great Communicator, then Gorbachev turned out to be, as Zbigniew Brzezinski puts it, the Grand Miscalculator. To the degree he had a Western counterpart, it was not FDR but Jimmy Carter. The hard-liners in the Kremlin who warned Gorbachev that his reforms would cause the entire system to blow up turned out to be right. Indeed, hawks in the West were also vindicated: Communism was immutable and irreversible, in the sense that the system could only be reformed by destroying it.

Gorbachev, like Jimmy Carter, had one redeeming quality: he was a decent and relatively open-minded fellow. Gorbachev was the first Soviet leader who came from the post-Stalin generation, the first to admit openly that the promises of Lenin were not being fulfilled.

Reagan, like Margaret Thatcher, was quick to recognize that Gorbachev was different. What changed his mind about Gorbachev was the little things. He discovered that Gorbachev was intensely curious about the West and showed a particular interest in anything Reagan could tell him about Hollywood. Also Gorbachev had a sense of humor and could laugh at himself. Moreover, he was troubled by Reagan's earlier reference to the Soviet Union as an "evil empire." To Reagan, it was significant that the concept of presiding over an evil regime bothered Gorbachev. In addition, Reagan was struck by the fact that Gorbachev routinely referred to God and Christ in his public statements and interviews. When asked how his reforms were likely to turn out, Gorbachev would say, "Only Jesus Christ knows the answer to that." This could be dismissed as merely a rhetorical device, but Reagan didn't think so.

As they sat across the table in Geneva in 1985, however, Reagan saw that Gorbachev was a tough negotiator, and he responded in a manner that may be described as "cordial toughness." While State Department communiques warned of U.S. concerns about the "destabilizing" influence of the Soviet occupation in Afghanistan, Reagan confronted Gorbachev directly. "What you are doing in Afghanistan is burning villages and killing children," he said. "It's genocide, Mike, and you are the one who has to stop it." At this point, according to aide Kenneth Adelman, who was present, Gorbachev looked at Reagan with a stunned expression; Adelman gathered that no one had ever talked to him this way before.

Reagan also threatened Gorbachev. "We won't stand by and let you maintain weapon superiority over us," he told him. "We can agree to reduce arms, or we can continue the arms race, which I think you know you can't win." The extent to which Gorbachev took Reagan's remarks to heart became obvious at the October 1986 summit in Reykjavik. There Gorbachev astounded the arms-control establishment in the West by accepting Reagan's zero option. Gorbachev embraced the very terms that Strobe Talbott and other doves had earlier dismissed as absurdly unrealistic.

Yet Gorbachev had one condition: The U.S. must agree not to deploy missile defenses. Reagan refused. The press immediately went on the attack. "Reagan-Gorbachev Summit Talks Collapse as Deadlock on SDI Wipes Out Other Gains," read the banner headline in the *Washington Post*. "Sunk by Star Wars," *Time*'s cover declared.

To Reagan, however, SDI was more than a bargaining chip; it was a moral issue. In a televised statement from Reykjavik he said, "There was no way I could tell our people that their government would not protect them against nuclear destruction." Polls showed that most Americans supported him.

Reykjavik, Margaret Thatcher says, was the turning point in the Cold War. Finally Gorbachev realized that he had a choice: continue a no-win arms race, which would utterly cripple the Soviet economy, or give up the struggle for global hegemony, establish peaceful relations with the West, and work to enable the Soviet economy to become prosperous like the Western economies. After Reykjavik, Gorbachev seems to have resolved on this latter course.

In December 1987, he abandoned his "non-negotiable" demand that Reagan give up SDI and visited Washington, D.C., to sign the Intermediate-Range Nuclear Forces (INF) treaty. For the first time ever the two superpowers agreed to eliminate an entire class of nuclear weapons. Moscow even agreed to on-site verification, a condition that it had resisted in the past.

The hawks, however, were suspicious from the outset. Gorbachev is a masterly chess player, they said; he might sacrifice a pawn, but only to gain an overall advantage. "Reagan is walking into a trap," Tom Bethell warned in *The American Spectator* as early as 1985. "The only way he can get success in negotiation is by doing what the Soviets want." Republican senators like Steven Symms and Jesse Helms planned "killer amendments" to sink the INF Treaty. Howard Phillips of the Conservative Caucus even charged Reagan with "fronting as a useful idiot for Soviet propaganda."

Yet, as at least some hawks like Bethell now admit, these criticisms missed the larger current of events. Gorbachev wasn't sacrificing a pawn, he was giving up his bishops and his queen. The INF treaty was in fact the first stage of Gorbachev's surrender in the Cold War.

Reagan knew that the Cold War was over when Gorbachev came to Washington. Gorbachev was a media celebrity in the United States, and the crowds cheered when he jumped out of his limousine and shook hands with people on the street. Out of the limelight, Reagan had dinner with a group of conservative friends, including Ben Wattenberg, Georgie Anne Geyer, and R. Emmett Tyrrell Jr. As Wattenberg recounted the incident to me, the group complained that Gorbachev was getting all the media credit for reaching an agreement essentially on Reagan's terms. Reagan smiled. Wattenberg asked, "Have we won the Cold War?" Reagan hedged. Wattenberg persisted. "Well, have we?" Reagan finally said yes. Then his dinner companions understood: he wanted Gorbachev to have his day in the sun. Asked by the press if he felt overshadowed by Gorbachev, Reagan replied, "I don't resent his popularity. Good Lord, I co-starred with Errol Flynn once."

To appreciate Reagan's diplomatic acumen, it is important to recall that he was pursuing his own distinctive course, rejecting the recommendations of both the hawks and the doves. Reagan knew that the movement for reform was fragile, and that hard-liners in the Kremlin were looking for U.S. actions that they could use to undermine Gorbachev's initiatives. Reagan recognized the importance of permitting Gorbachev a zone of comfort in which to pursue his program of reform.

At the same time, when doves in the State Department implored Reagan to "reward" Gorbachev with economic concessions and trade benefits for announcing that Soviet troops would pull out of Afghanistan, Reagan recognized that this ran the risk of restoring the health of the sick bear. Reagan's goal was—as Gorbachev himself once joked—to lead the Soviet Union to the edge of the abyss and then induce it to take "one step forward."

Thus Reagan simultaneously supported Gorbachev's reform efforts and applied constant pressure on him to move faster and further. This was the significance of Reagan's trip to the Brandenburg Gate on June 12, 1987, in which he demanded that Gorbachev prove that he was serious about openness by pulling down the Berlin Wall. The State Department kept taking that line out of Reagan's speech, and Reagan kept putting it back in. And in May 1988 Reagan stood beneath a giant white bust of Lenin at Moscow State University and gave the most ringing defense of a free society ever offered in the Soviet Union. On that trip he visited the ancient Danilov Monastery and preached about the importance of religious freedom and a spiritual revival. At the U.S. ambassador's residence, he assured a group of dissidents and "refuseniks" that the day of freedom was at hand. All of these measures were calculated to force Gorbachev's hand.

First Gorbachev agreed to deep unilateral cuts in Soviet armed forces in Europe. Starting in May 1988, Soviet troops pulled out of Afghanistan, the first time the Soviets had voluntarily withdrawn from a puppet regime. Before long, Soviet and satellite troops were pulling out of Angola, Ethiopia, and Cambodia. The race toward freedom began in Eastern Europe, and the Berlin Wall was indeed torn down.

During this period of ferment, Gorbachev's great achievement, for which he will be credited by history, was to abstain from the use of force—the response of his predecessors to popular uprisings in Hungary in 1956 and Czechoslovakia in 1968. By now not only were Gorbachev and his team permiting the empire to disintegrate, as Reagan had foreseen and intended, but they even adopted Reagan's way of talking. In October 1989 Soviet Foreign Ministry spokesman Gennadi Gerasimov announced that the Soviet Union would not intervene in the internal affairs of Eastern Bloc nations. "The Brezhnev Doctrine is dead," Gerasimov said. Reporters asked him what would take its place, and he replied, "You know the Frank Sinatra song 'My Way'? Hungary and Poland are doing it their way. We now have the Sinatra Doctrine." The Gipper could not have said it better himself.

Finally the revolution made its way into the Soviet Union. Gorbachev, who had completely lost control of events, found himself ousted from power. The Soviet Union voted to abolish itself. Serious problems of adjustment to new conditions would remain, but emancipated people know that such problems are infinitely preferable to living under slavery.

Even some who were previously skeptical of Reagan were forced to admit that his policies had been thoroughly vindicated. Reagan's old nemesis Henry Kissinger observed that while it was Bush who presided over the final disintegration of the Soviet empire, "it was Ronald Reagan's Presidency which marked the turning point." Cardinal Casaroli, the Vatican secretary of state, remarked publicly that the Reagan military buildup, which he had opposed at the time, had led to the collapse of Communism.

These conclusions are widely accepted in the former Soviet Union and in Eastern Europe. When Czech president Vaclav Havel visited Washington, D.C., in May 1997 I asked him whether Reagan's defense strategy and his diplomacy were vital factors in ending the Cold War. Of course, Havel said, adding that "both Reagan and Gorbachev deserve credit" because while Soviet Communism might have imploded eventually, without them "it would have taken a lot longer."

Havel's point is incontestable. Yet Reagan won and Gorbachev lost. If Gorbachev was the trigger, it was Reagan who pulled it. For the third time in this century, the United States has fought and prevailed in a world war. In the Cold War, Reagan turned out to be our Churchill: it was his vision and leadership that led us to victory.

Legacy and Remembrance

Head of the (Middle) Class

By Tom Wolfe

EDITOR'S NOTE: *This article appeared in the August 5, 1988, issue of* National Review *as part of a symposium on "The Reagan Legacy."*

Remember the "little old ladies in tennis shoes"? That was the term dreamed up in the 1960s to characterize the constituency of Barry Goldwater's version of the conservative movement. After Goldwater's rout in the 1964 election it seemed accurate enough.

It was used again two years later when another avowed conservative, Ronald Reagan, ran for governor in California. But Reagan won, a result so astounding that for the next ten years columnists spoke of the California electorate as "volatile." Reagan's popularity in California increased steadily, however. So the voter surveys began in earnest—with another astounding result. At the heart of Reagan's support were California's new, young, and very numerous working-class families.

In the 1940s, when a war economy finally hoisted the United States out of the Depression, the boom occurred earliest in California, with its aircraft plants and other key military industries. Wages climbed rapidly. It was in California that the term "worker" first ceased to mean someone who is defined (or enslaved) by his job. The California worker became an owner: first, of an automobile; then, soon enough, of a house (and then of a second automobile). He began to think of civic life in the same way as any new property owner. He wanted stability, including one of its major props: moral decency. He wanted freedom from government intrusion, particularly high taxes. He wanted public policy to favor people like himself, people who had earned what they possessed. He wanted to take pride in what he had accomplished; and two of pride's most popular forms were official optimism and patriotism.

How much of this had Reagan figured out analytically? Perhaps none of it, although it seems to me he has always been much more of an issue-oriented (shall I try out the adjective *intellectual?*) politician than those who call him "the great communicator" are willing to admit. In any case, his views resonated perfectly with those of the new California working class. (It might even be worth mentioning that Reagan is the only labor-union member who ever became President.)

Since the 1960s the prosperity and ethos of the California working class have spread to workers all over America—so much so that the terms *working-class* and *workers* have become archaic. Today electricians, air-conditioning mechanics, burglar-alarm installers, cablevision linemen are routinely spoken of as middle-class. Many journeyman mechanics live on a scale that would have made the Sun King blink. They are a new class that has seriously altered the political make-up of this country over the past 25 years. And Ronald Reagan was their first spokesman, their first leader, their first philosopher. The existence of this class continues to baffle Democratic Party leaders. Their biggest problem in the presidential election this fall is what to do about these people whose goals they still do not understand.

Only the Start

By Robert Bork

EDITOR'S NOTE: *This article appeared in the August 5, 1988, issue of* National Review *as part of a symposium on "The Reagan Legacy."*

An unjustified loss of morale afflicts conservatives as Ronald Reagan's Administration winds down, its last two years largely devoid of accomplishments and so much of the conservative agenda unaccomplished. Reagan's legacy is mixed, of course, as are the legacies of all major politicians, but a realistic assessment would stress how much the nation's condition has improved since 1980 and how much Reagan has done.

Domestically, Reagan achieved large cuts in marginal tax rates, with enormous benefits for the economy. He leaves voters with an aversion to substantial tax increases that even a Democratic President and Congress will find difficult to overcome.

A major achievement, due in large measure to the much-maligned Ed Meese, has been the re-orientation of the federal judiciary. Care was taken to select judges who understand that judging is not politics. The constitutional philosophy of original understanding, and the judicial restraint it begets, have become a public issue. A time may even come when the liberal policy-making of modern courts will be as discredited as the conservative policy-making of the courts before 1937 now is.

In national security and foreign affairs a bright beginning has darkened as the Administration abandons some of what had seemed its major premises. The Soviet Union is certainly changing, but the ultimate extent and durability of the change is unknown. Since the Soviets remain a Communist Party dictatorship, whose expansionist ideology remains intact, now is hardly the time for the President to signal that the danger is past. Americans spend too little on military preparedness as it is and are too eager to believe that the world has become safe. This can lead, has already led, to a kind of arms control that is a net loss for Western security, and to virtual abandonment of the Contras, whom we encouraged to fight a Marxist dictatorship sponsored by the Soviet Union in our hemisphere. But U.S. aid may have achieved its aims in Afghanistan, so that the symbol, and some of the substance, of the Reagan Doctrine remains and can be built upon by a future conservative Administration.

Finally, Reagan leaves a larger and more self-confident conservative movement, many of whose members now have invaluable experience in government. One of the President's unintended legacies, however, is a reinvigorated ultra-liberalism. We had thought that the political culture had shifted with the 1980 and 1984 elections. We were quite wrong. The American Left, infuriated by a world turned upside down, has simultaneously adopted irresponsible tactics and learned to cloak its radical intentions in "mainstream" rhetoric.

If Reagan's is a mixed legacy, it is on the whole a good one, and certainly better than most. Whether its assets are to be squandered or reinvested depends on the heir chosen this fall.

Socialism's Death Rattle

By George Gilder

EDITOR'S NOTE: *This article appeared in the August 5, 1988, issue of* National Review *as part of a symposium on "The Reagan Legacy."*

Ronald Reagan's legacy is a new epoch of American leadership in liberty and strength. Through his economic policies, Reagan brought the United States to world leadership among major industrial nations in all the key dimensions of economic growth: investment (51 per cent growth), industrial production (30 per cent growth), manufacturing productivity (26 per cent growth), job creation (15 million new jobs), real per-capita income (18 per cent increase), and technological innovation (a rising U.S. market share in information technologies).

Defying a worldwide siege of economic stagnation, the Reagan boom was unique in the postwar era. By contrast, the U.S. economic recoveries of the 1950s, 1960s, and 1970s all fed on faster growth abroad. During all these prior upturns, the U.S. lagged behind Europe and Japan in all the key indices of expansion. During the Reagan era, the U.S. surpassed Europe by a wide margin and caught up with Japan in rates of economic growth, and led the world in growth of investment and employment. Since Reagan assumed office, the U.S. has been the only major industrial nation to increase investment as a share of GNP or to reduce unemployment.

Unlike the last U.S. surge in job creation, in the 1970s, when productivity and real incomes declined, Reagan's world-beating employment boom was accompanied by a record six-year surge in manufacturing-productivity growth, a steady rise in per-capita income, and a striking increase in the quality of jobs.

Reagan fostered an entrepreneurial resurgence that has restored the U.S. edge in innovation. Over the last several years U.S. firms have been expanding their global lead in the key technologies of the information age. Contrary to many false claims, U.S. firms still produce half the world's microchips. The U.S. share of global computer-software production has been increasing since 1982. At a time when value-added information technology is moving toward software, microcomputers, and networks, U.S. production of computer software, telecom products, and personal computers is between four and five times Japan's. With scores of new firms in microchips, bioengineering, superconductivity, and supercomputing, Reagan is leaving a legacy of the largest and most rapidly growing generation of high-technology business start-ups in history.

Under Reagan, leading investors around the globe renewed their commitment to the U.S. economy. U.S. investors happily ended their feckless role as "net lenders" to the world, stopped pouring their money into Third World and Communist ratholes, and repatriated funds to the United States. Foreign investors also spurned their own economies and focused investment on America.

This capital flight from abroad and capital repatriation by Americans allowed the U.S. to become the world's leading importer of advanced goods and equipment. Much decried by misinformed mercantilists and xenophobes, this influx of imports and investments was a thoroughly positive reflection of U.S. success in integrating the world economy in the interests of Americans. More than a decade ago, supply-side pioneer Robert Mundell predicted that one necessary and benign effect of tax cuts would be a trade gap. With the U.S. market growing twice as fast as foreign markets, exporters to the U.S. naturally outperformed U.S. exporters to the rest of the world.

On the government side, the Reagan Administration decisively improved the federal debt position. In one of the least-reported transformations of the century, a restructuring of Social Security under Reagan reduced the actual burden of national debt (the real net liabilities of the government) by some $2 trillion. Under Reagan the governmental budget deficit remained lower than the average in other industrial countries; in 1988 it was projected by the OECD to be smaller even than West Germany's as a share of GNP.

Under Reagan's tax-cutting regime, real federal revenues in 1982 dollars followed the Laffer curve, growing nearly twice as fast during the 1980s as during the 1970s, and far faster than the revenues of tax-hiking and bracket-creeping European nations. The overall balance sheet of the U.S. economy improved decisively; with the stock market doubling in real terms, bond values increasing by about $2 trillion, and a general rise in real-estate values all dwarfing the deficit, national assets climbed faster than liabilities after declining during the 1970s.

Through his inspiring speeches and cogent example, Reagan has launched a global revival of capitalism. From Margaret Thatcher in Britain to Edward Seaga in Jamaica, a long list of political leaders have cited low U.S. tax rates as a key reason for their own tax reductions. After long delay, Mrs. Thatcher has now unleashed a surge of investment, job growth, and trade deficits that soon may prove comparable to Reagan's.

Taking the argument to the USSR in his historic address to the students at Moscow University, Reagan has carried his global crusade for freedom into the teeth of the Kremlin. Supply-side arguments now resound at the Politburo. All over the Third World, from Ghana to the Philippines, national leaders are sloughing off the coils of socialism and emancipating their workers and entrepreneurs.

Finally, a key Reagan legacy is a defense program based on a recognition that our national peril may rise apace with our national prosperity. Reagan's economic and philosophical defeat of socialism will remain in jeopardy without the complement of new national military strength. Rattling sabers and tin cups, the mendicant militarists of the evil empire—impotent to create wealth—still can wreak havoc. Whatever happens in the Soviet Union, moreover, the United States will have to continue an arms race for the next century with international terrorists and military criminals of socialism lashing out from their caves and covens against the triumph of freedom. In hunching the strategic defense initiative, Ronald Reagan left perhaps his most indispensable legacy: a commitment to use the ongoing ten-thousandfold ascent in the efficacy of the new information technologies to bring the arms race under control at last—under American control, the only kind that matters.

Not the Authorized Biography

By John O'Sullivan

EDITOR'S NOTE: *This article appeared in the October 25, 1999, issue of* National Review.

Dutch is described very firmly on its cover as a "memoir" of Ronald Reagan. This announces an oddity from the first, because a memoir is usually a personal account of some famous person by an old friend or colleague. It supplements, but does not replace, the full-dress biography because it is a less comprehensive and more intimate portrait of its subject, painted not in the harsh primary colors of historical evaluation but in the gentler hues of reminiscence.

But Edmund Morris is not an old friend of President Reagan, nor even an old colleague. He is a professional writer, the author of an acclaimed biography of Theodore Roosevelt, who was commissioned in 1985 to write the authorized biography of Ronald Reagan and accordingly given unparalleled access to the White House as a kind of historian in residence. The idea was that he should combine the skills of a practiced biographer with the privilege of a bird's-eye view.

This was a unique opportunity. As Morris accompanied the president to meetings in the Oval Office, summits with Mikhail Gorbachev, and political events around America, he must have realized that his experience would give unusual depth and richness to his overall portrait of Reagan. And this is, in part, so. The passages in which he accompanies "Dutch" on a post-retirement visit to the town where he was born, or watches from the wings as the president strides out to take control of Gorbachev and the Geneva summit, are among the liveliest and most revealing in the book.

Unfortunately, he also realized that he would not enjoy the same advantage when he came to deal with events that had occurred before he himself arrived on the scene. And since that period covered Reagan's life from his birth to the end of his first presidential term, Morris must have feared that the greater part of his book would lack the immediacy of its final chapters. So the biographer decided to grant himself privileged access to the whole of Reagan's life by writing himself into it as an acquaintance who hovered on the fringe of Reagan's circle.

Morris has therefore written not one book, but three books that jostle uneasily together between the same hard covers. The first book is an authorized presidential biography that, because of the space devoted to the other two, falls short in certain respects, notably in assessing Reagan's full historical achievement; the second is notes and jottings for a memoir of Reagan drawn from his real experiences as Reagan's literary shadow; and the third is a postmodern novel, *The Man Who Knew Ronald Reagan*, in which a fictional character called Edmund Morris describes how his own life has intertwined with Ronald Reagan's in the course of writing a memoir about him.

Does this literary device of a fictional author actually work? Arguments can certainly be advanced for it. The author in a biography always has elements of a fictional character, because he possesses an apparently godlike knowledge that enables him to make the most sweeping judgments of his subject's life. Thus do professors who can scarcely keep order in the classroom correct Bismarck's statecraft. At least Morris's fiction is clearly and candidly a device; no one is deceived. It gives the entire book a uniformity of tone and style—that of the aforementioned memoir—while also allowing Reagan's career to be seen and judged from several different perspectives, not just "Edmund Morris's," and not all of them friendly. Both Morris's "son," Gavin, and his "friend," Paul Rae, are witnesses for the prosecution, Gavin a student revolutionary who sees the Gipper as the smiling face of a corrupt corporate "power elite," Paul Rae a bitchy homosexual writer (and early AIDS victim) who regards him as the vacant repository of narrow small-town virtues. And the fictions are closely tethered to the facts of Reagan's life, confirmed in detailed footnotes that give the real sources for accounts that appear here in the mouths of Morris, Rae, Gavin, and others.

Set against these arguments is the large and unavoidable fact that the final product is a mixture of fact and fiction, and we cannot be sure which is which on any one page. George Will, for instance, has cited one passage in which the later (and thus presumably more factual) Edmund Morris seems to be present at a medical examination where Reagan is diagnosed as harboring a dangerous cancer. In fact, the scene is an invented one, based to be sure on the doctor's subsequent notes, but supplemented by what W. S. Gilbert sardonically called "merely corroborative detail, intended to give artistic verisimilitude to an otherwise bald and unconvincing narrative." Such a mixture of fact and fiction is ultimately fiction, and its presence disables a biography that by definition claims to be the nearest approximation to documentary truth that the biographer can achieve. Whatever the reason, however, I found the fictional characters and their accounts an irritant and had to conquer an urge to skip them as I went along.

At times Morris justifies this unusual technique as necessary to explore the mystery of Ronald Reagan's personality. Just how mysterious, however, is the Gipper? Reagan himself, in his own post-presidential autobiography, has conceded one surprising trait—namely, that he is essentially a private person, convivial in a crowd but remote and even aloof in private, who uses jokes and anecdotes to keep others at bay (and, incidentally, who can fire and forget formerly close colleagues at will). Unembarrassed by any mystery here, Reagan advances the commonsense speculation that this remoteness is the result of his short-sightedness, which, unrecognized until his early teens, placed a curtain between himself and the world in his formative years. It is, of course, Nancy Reagan who pierced this curtain and has since been his indispensable ambassadress to the world.

Morris agonizes over a slightly different point of psychology—namely, the mystery of what complex private reality lies behind Reagan's public personality, with its firm opinions and genial demeanor. Maybe, though, the mystery of Reagan is that he is not mysterious. An English Tory friend once explained wistfully to me that the only place he could express his true opinions was on a public platform: "If I were to say at a dinner party that England is a great country and that we have shaped the modern world for the better, from ending the international slave trade to holding the line against Hitler, people would mock me unmercifully. I can say such things in a public speech because the same people assume I am playing to the gallery. In fact, those are the things I really believe; it is my cynical remarks over the dinner table that are insincere." What distinguishes Reagan from the platform patriot is that he was not afraid to be patriotic in private. The virtues he admired in the small-town America in which he grew up, the decisive contribution America made to saving the world from two totalitarianisms—these he was prepared to celebrate equally at a dinner party or in a public speech. As he himself said, he is "an open book," all of a piece. It is such simple, uncomplicated honesty that strikes the modern mind, especially the mind of a postmodern literary intellectual, as requiring explanation.

And here Morris has been seriously misjudged by his critics. Several of his dismissive remarks—in particular his question to himself as to whether President Reagan was "an airhead"—have been quoted as if they were his final and considered judgment. In fact, he threw out the "airhead" speculation when, as he admits, he was undergoing a biographical crisis: The more he tried to grasp Reagan's personality, the more it eluded him. And as he goes along, he tests out various other explanations of the Gipper.

This juggling of judgments, as well as inviting charges of inconsistency, has the effect of making Morris a much more central figure than he should be in someone else's biography. Indeed, it occasionally produces some almost comic egocentricities, as my *National Review* colleague, Michael Potemra, observed in an otherwise largely favorable account: "On page 327, the author recounts the reaction of a fictional character named Edmund Morris to the assassination of President Kennedy. Consigned to an endnote on page 761 is the following: 'For the less-than-anguished reaction of the Reagans to JFK's death, see [Reagan daughter Patti] Davis, *The Way I See It*, 81–83.' In other words, if you want to know about a fictional character based on me, read this text; if you're curious about some Reagan facts, read Patti's book."

Yet there is at least some method in this madness. For the fictional Morris means something beyond himself projected backward in time. He is a not-quite-representative member of what Professor Whittle Johnson calls "the academic-media complex," disliking its "vituperative" hostility to Reagan, but sharing many of its prejudices all the same. As the book proceeds, however, both the fictional and real Edmund Morris gradually overcome these prejudices and struggle toward a discovery of the Reagan in plain sight. They abandon their initial condescension and grow to appreciate both his decency as a private man and his far-sighted statesmanship as a public one. And though the president's fictional critics, Gavin and Paul Rae, retain their hostility to him until they both depart—Paul Rae to the next world, Gavin into the leftist underground—nonetheless they shrink into dogmatic and insignificant critics before our gaze. Paul Rae in particular is bound to resent a man who has remained true to the early American verities he himself has rejected—and not merely remained true to them, but made them sing and fostered their victory.

By the end of the book, therefore, Morris has rendered a judgment on President Reagan that, though not without qualifications, is massively favorable. A few points of character at random: He is a brave man who, as a lifeguard, saved 77 lives. He is without bigotry and, in the early '40s, when such acts were still risky, resigned from a country club that excluded Jews. He has a high sense of public duty and, when asked to present a prize to the top student at West Point, insisted on staying for several hours to hand diplomas to the entire class, on the grounds that one day he might have to send them into action. He has a crisp sense of priorities and was always on top of what he judged, usually rightly, to be important. As a hostile critic, Arthur Liman, chief counsel to the Iran-contra committee, said on reading Reagan's private journal: "I'm amazed at the clarity of his executive thinking, his modesty and lack of emotion. Not at all what I expected." And he had the moral courage to tell the simple truths that brought down an evil empire.

Not that Morris's final judgments are entirely satisfactory. He gets the Big Picture triumphantly right—Reagan is, before all else, the man who "won the Cold

War without firing a shot," in Margaret Thatcher's words. But there are curiously few references to Reagan's historic partnerships with both the Pope and Lady Thatcher—even François Mitterrand gets more ink (perhaps because he has the wittier lines). And there is a lack of balance and perspective in other respects. While making the obligatory mention of "deficits as far as the eye can see," for instance, Morris acknowledges that "Reaganomics" led to the longest peacetime expansion in history. But there is less about economics than there should be in a Reagan biography. After all, the longest peacetime expansion in history has now lasted, with only the briefest interruption, for 17 years, and Reagan's reshaping of U.S. industry in the 1980s plainly created the world-beating modern information economy whose cascading revenues have transformed the predicted deficits into large surpluses. Mrs. Reagan is given full credit for both giving and inspiring great love, but she is otherwise treated shabbily as a rich Republican with a blinkered view of life— evidence, surely, that Morris is simply wearing a different set of blinkers. And it is both snobbish and wrong to criticize Reagan for lack of interest in poetry when you have quoted him as reciting Robert (*Songs of a Sourdough*) Service after only one reading; a difference in taste is not the same thing as a lack of interest. (Besides which, I happen to like Service myself.)

In a final moving "Epilogue," Morris attends an academic conference at which, amid some criticism, the dominant note is one of growing recognition that Reagan was one of our greatest presidents and that his greatest achievement was the toppling of the Soviet Union. The biographer writes a report to the president, describing this heartening debate in which the Russian speakers had been among his strongest partisans. But we know that already Alzheimer's had begun to wreak its havoc on the Old Man, and that therefore any reevaluation of his achievements will have to depend on others. With all its faults, this book contributes to that reevaluation. Hence the desperate relief with which liberal critics have seized upon postmodern techniques they might otherwise have praised to discredit conclusions that utterly undermine the picture they have painted of a genial half-wit presiding half-asleep over a Decade of Greed and the self-generated implosion of the Soviet Union. The *Saturday Night Live* sketch, showing a dynamic Reagan barking commands in various languages to Swiss banks and Mideast weapons brokers, is actually nearer the mark.

And there is the sadness of it. If Morris had written a conventional biography and followed it up a few years later with this book, describing it as a novel that drew upon real historical facts and his own meetings with Ronald Reagan, we might all now be acclaiming his genius. Indeed, we would probably be arguing that the book conveyed far more deeply than any conventional biography two elusive truths: first, the manly straightforwardness of Reagan, and, second, the agonizing difficulty that modern self-conscious intellectuals have in comprehending simplicity of character. (Remove their skepticism, indeed, and one would have to ask, "Where's the rest of them?") Once the immediate controversy over Morris's postmodern literary methods has receded, therefore, *Dutch* may have a long afterlife as Reagan's historical reputation inevitably rises and as people want to learn more about America's lifeguard.

For the moment, however, it remains a companion volume to the authorized biography of Ronald Reagan that remains to be written, that needs to be written, and that Morris had an unparalleled opportunity to write. And in the end that makes *Dutch* a failure—but a failure more fascinating and moving than many a pedestrian success.

A Book Unglued

By John Podhoretz

EDITOR'S NOTE: *This article appeared in the October 25, 1999, issue of* National Review.

Edmund Morris had writer's block and suffered a breakdown while trying to commit his biography of Ronald Reagan to paper. And a close reading of his *Dutch* suggests that Morris never emerged from either condition. The book has been misunderstood by those who accuse Morris of succumbing to postmodern solipsism when he cast it as a novel featuring a fictionalized version of Morris observing and interacting with Reagan for 70 years.

This is no postmodernist jape of a biography. If it were, *Dutch* would be a text worth engaging with and arguing with in an effort to preserve the traditions of biography and history. But engaging with and arguing with *Dutch* is a little like getting into a quarrel with a high-functioning schizophrenic. Every time you think the schizophrenic is saying something interesting, the madness begins to emerge, and you find yourself trapped by the glittering eye of the Ancient Mariner.

Dutch is a work of lunacy—a horrifying display of personality disintegration spread across 674 tightly printed pages and 150 pages more of the most bizarre footnotes since Vladimir Nabokov used annotations to depict an academic's descent into madness in his novel *Pale Fire*. The book may be long, but it is not a coherent or complete text. It is, rather, a patchwork quilt made up of desperate writing exercises that Morris must have engaged in over the space of the 14 years he worked on the book to find some way, any way, to get from the beginning of Ronald Reagan's life to his senescence.

The book is chockablock with incidents from Reagan's life written in the form of film scripts. It relays important information about Reagan's career in dozens of fictional letters sent to the fictional Morris by imaginary people. It depicts the last two years of the Reagan presidency largely through excerpts from Morris's contemporaneous notebooks. The book even concludes with three pointless poems by Morris—two about Reagan and one about the Bergen-Belsen concentration camp, presumably because he went there with Reagan in 1985.

All of these devices are the outgrowth of Morris's writer's block, which he publicly admitted to in 1990. Imagine a bricklayer who suddenly finds himself unable one morning to lay one brick on top of the next for no apparent reason other than a crippling fear. Or imagine that the bricklayer in question is suddenly convinced that he no longer knows how to place a brick next to another. Or imagine that he convinces himself he has placed the brick in the wrong spot, even though he hasn't.

That's what writer's block is—a form of depressive paralysis unique to those who take up the pen for a living. Writers will often try to trick themselves out of a block by trying to put words on paper in any way they can. Thus, the film scripts, the letters, the diary entries, the poems—these were all ways for Morris to put something down until Clio, the Muse of history, returned to his side.

But Clio never reappeared. And Morris was into Random House for almost $2 million by this time (his $3 million advance was paid off in yearly installments). And so, in 1993, Morris hit upon the device of aging himself into Reagan's contemporary.

This was a terrible idea, but you can see how Morris might think he had found salvation in it. The book he couldn't write was a biography of Reagan. But a fictionalized autobiography? That was different. That raised all kinds of fun issues that he could explore, like, who would the new Edmund Morris be? Who would his parents be? What would "I" do for a living? And how could "I" be brought into proximity with the real Ronald Reagan, early on?

Reagan appears on every page of this book, but until he becomes president on page 411 he shares equal time with "Edmund Morris," Morris's son "Gavin," and Morris's friend "Paul Rae." So intent is Morris on exploring this fictional setup that he excludes discussion of several key events in Reagan's political career. Of the nationally televised speech Reagan gave in 1964 for Barry Goldwater that made him overnight the hottest political figure in America, Morris writes only: "Nothing is more dated than old campaign rhetoric, so I won't belabor 'The Speech' except to say it was (for all of Reagan's innocent protestations) clearly a proclamation of himself as Goldwater's successor."

Later, there isn't a word about how Reagan became the foremost opponent of Jimmy Carter's surrender of the Panama Canal—when he both spoke on a matter of principle and kept himself in the public eye during the late 1970s, in preparation for his successful presidential run in 1980.

These are all part of history, and Morris found himself incapable of writing Reagan's history. Instead, we get eight endless pages in which he converts the fluffy plot of Reagan's first movie, *Love Is on the Air*, into a grandiloquent epic that parallels his bewildering comparison of Reagan's life journey with the quest for the Holy Grail. Or four pages on how he, Morris, couldn't get aboard Air Force One on the way to the 1985 summit in Geneva and had to sit next to a researcher in the speechwriting office.

Or we get the saga of that phony son, Gavin—whom another character in the book calls "Gawain" in yet another nutso parallel with the Holy Grail saga. Gavin becomes a radical at Berkeley in the 1960s. His "dad," "Morris," goes up to find him during the riots around Sproul Hall and gets a dose of tear gas: "Some cop, seeing me limp, took pity on me and helped me through. 'C'mon, old fella, you don't want to be messed up in this.'"

Gavin ends up going underground, which embitters Morris. "Hundreds of other old men," he writes, "nurture querulous hopes that one day their graying sons will come back home from Sweden or Vancouver. But Gavin won't. Child of the south, beach boy, desert lover, he never took to northern light. Going underground, where there was no light at all, meant the same to him as to any ancient Greek. And it was you, Dutch, who sent him there."

This entire storyline, which I suppose is intended to show the dark side of Reagan's tenure as governor of California, is detailed and vividly described as no single act of governance by Reagan ever is. Whatever symbolic purpose it may have is swallowed up in the sense you get as a reader that Morris is sitting at his desk, weeping as he writes of the disappearance forever of his beloved son—a person who never existed.

This isn't even the craziest thing about *Dutch*. Describing the mood of Los Angeles after World War II, Morris says, "Those of us who had to make do on less than six figures were conscious only of vague loss and gloom." (Oh, really? Only a month after V-J Day?) He claims that "the social equipoise" of the years before the war—those notorious days of social equipoise known as the Great Depression—were now "disintegrating."

And then he unleashes this as evidence: "Black GIs, returning stateside from French whorehouses, furtively ogled your wife."

Let me repeat that. "Black GIs, returning stateside from French whorehouses, furtively ogled your wife."

Did his editor actually read that sentence? Or had he, by page 219, simply given up, lost as he must have become in the thickets of the author's prosodic madness?

Don't let it happen to you.

The Reagan Presidency: A Turning Point in History

By Paul Johnson

EDITOR'S NOTE: *This article first appeared in the June 28, 2004, issue of* National Review.

President Reagan is likely to occupy a significant place in history. His eight-year presidency was a turning point both in the fortunes of his own country and in the history of the world—and the two were closely connected. It is not easy, now, to cast one's mind back to the year in which Reagan won office, because everything has changed so radically. Nineteen eighty found an America wearied by what was perhaps the worst decade in its history—-worse even than the '30s, because there was no anticipation of recovery. The 1970s had seen a president forced to retire in disgrace, and an unelected president with no mandate, beaten in turn by a feeble Democrat from the South who had no obvious policy or coherent view of the world. In Washington, a triumphant but leaderless Congress usurped executive authority, allowing a triumphant Soviet Union, and its surrogates in Cuba and Vietnam, to do what they willed in Africa and Asia. America's apparent decline as a great power was symbolized, in a terrible moment early in 1980, by a shocking military fiasco in Iran.

Reagan reversed all these trends decisively. He was not exactly a scholarly man, but he had the four characteristics required of any great leader. First, he had a few simple, strongly held, and tenaciously pursued convictions, which also happened to be right and popular. Second, he knew how to present them in plain terms that all could grasp. Third, on the issues he cared about most, he exercised a formidable will, which, though courteous, brooked no opposition till what he wanted was done. Fourth, he had style.

The style came to the front first. Reagan, upon taking office, was appalled by the decline in presidential ceremony, which he rightly connected with the collapse of presidential authority. He found a young man with a passion for restrained grandeur, made him chief of protocol at the White House, and soon all the smartness, precision, timing, and democratic swagger of presidential authority were restored. Against this backdrop, Reagan played the Big Role—with high seriousness and gravity, with deep respect for traditions going back to George Washington, but also with a huge, all-pervading sense of humor. To a great extent, he communicated in jokes, which themselves hid half-conscious political convictions—as when he said, "I'm not too worried about the deficit. It's big enough to take care of itself." (It did!)

Thus the American people, after a dismal decade, learned to laugh again, and to laugh at the invitation of their cheerful First Magistrate. And they laughed conscious of the fact that there was a good deal of steel behind the grin. Reagan almost effortlessly recovered the presidential powers usurped by Congress, which, to be fair, was only too willing to relinquish them. He stood up to the unions, making it clear that, where vital public interests are at risk, the presidential will must prevail. He made it plain to Latin American dictators that the rule of law applied to them no less than to others. Then he turned to the Soviet Union.

Here his few, simple convictions yielded real, flesh-and-blood results. Like Truman in his day, Reagan said, "Thus far and no further." Encroachments by the Communists would no longer be permitted. This was expressed in plain terms, and to back them the U.S. military was rearmed on a prodigious scale, and the go-ahead was given to advanced weapons systems that no other nation could match. For the first time since the Second World War, America's lead in high technology was exploited for all it was worth—both to demonstrate to the Soviet leaders its actuality as well as its potential, and so break their will, and to reestablish America's position as the world's most advanced economic power. The reassertion of American productive and spending vigor was aimed just as much at Japan—and her imitators and admirers—as at the men in the Kremlin.

Yet Reagan was also prepared to negotiate for peace, and he did so in a most energetic manner, offering to scrap arms provided that reciprocal reduction could be verified. This combination of rearmament and search for a settlement had a catalyzing effect on the Soviet leadership, persuading them, or enough of them, to embark on a critical reexamination of Communist fundamentals. And this, in turn, led to the shattering discovery that the command economy could not be reformed—it could only be abandoned.

Thus, in an astonishing paradox that will continue to intrigue historians for generations to come, Reagan's successful attempt to restore American self-confidence provoked the collapse of Soviet self-confidence, producing in rapid succession the demise of the Communist state, the dismantlement of the Russian empire, and the dissolution of the Soviet Union itself. The end of the Cold War came after Reagan retired, but he had clearly set in motion the chain of events that made the West's victory inevitable.

Reagan's efforts to reassert the paramountcy of American military power, and his accompanying restoration of the nation's belief in itself—not unaided, incidentally, by tax cuts and other measures improving economic freedom—led to a reinvigoration of America's spirit of enterprise on a scale no one had anticipated or dared to hope for. This too continued long after Reagan retired—it continues still—and it ended all loose academic and media talk of the inevitable decline of a once-great power.

The Reagan presidency was a turning point in U.S. and world history. The world began to move more rapidly than ever toward a global society under the informal leadership of a United States that had recovered its morale and its sense that the future held limitless potential. All this was brought about not by one man, but by a society led by a man whose time for greatness had come—and who knew it.

The details were highly technological, but the essence was traditional: Reagan was a wagon-train leader, conducting his followers over the mountains, without an accurate map or a precise idea of their destination, or what exactly they would do when they got there, but confident in a happy ending.

Of course, there are no final happy endings in history, because history does not end. But Reagan offered Americans an opportunity to open a fresh chapter, to reinvent themselves in new guises but on traditional lines, and they eagerly grasped it. Then the star said goodbye and the epiphany ended. But it was a good thing to have seen.

Reagan and the American Psyche

By Victor Davis Hanson

EDITOR'S NOTE: *This article first appeared in the June 28, 2004, issue of* National Review.

Ronald Reagan's legacy is not one of ideological purity. He raised taxes and signed liberal abortion legislation in California. Despite his "evil empire" speech, he was not the preeminent Cold Warrior: Truman and Eisenhower had both fashioned the policy of containment and deterrence. It was Barry Goldwater who laid the foundation of sagebrush conservatism. In contrast, federal spending went up during Reagan's two presidential terms. It was Reagan, not George W. Bush, who set the precedent of a Republican piling up larger federal deficits than do many Democrats.

And we forget now the various resignations, palace coups, and job switches that occurred during Reagan's terms in office. Iran-Contra and the withdrawal from Lebanon weakened America's reputation abroad. Astrology, the sometimes embarrassing confessions of the presidential children, and occasional misstatements about the past did not always reflect bedrock values.

Instead, Reagan's greatest contributions were more psychological, amounting to nothing less than a reawakening of the American faith in common sense and blunt speech. True, his one-liners sometimes reflected intellectual laziness, but far more often they were insightful ways of cutting through obfuscation to separate truth from lies.

Remember Reagan's debates against more experienced and conventional politicians that he was supposed to lose? He won them precisely because he showed that his opponents' purported greater grasp of detail and nuance did not result in real wisdom. In 1980, Jimmy Carter thought that he could rattle the older and supposedly less experienced Reagan by scaring the nation silly over Social Security and nuclear warfare—until Reagan scoffed, "There you go again." And if that was not enough to crush the sitting president, his closing line—"Are you better off than you were four years ago?"—surely was. With those two sentences he revealed to the nation a different sort of Jimmy Carter, whose orneriness in fact hid his own incompetence.

Reagan's uncommon good sense extended to sound judgments about controversial people who were similarly outspoken and principled. He was an early supporter of Pat Moynihan's courageous efforts to end decades of hypocrisy at the United Nations at a time when even many Republicans still viewed the institution as a sacred cow. Jeane Kirkpatrick's insightful distinctions between Communists and right-wing dictators won over an unabashedly supportive Reagan. He praised Soviet dissidents—even as a cautious Gerald Ford refused to meet Aleksandr Solzhenitsyn.

In some cases, Reagan's blunt words and decisive actions changed the course of both national and global history. In August 1981 the air-traffic controllers' union assumed it could not only ignore its sworn pledge not to strike, but could shut down the entire American aviation grid if it did not obtain a 100 per cent raise. Reagan ignored the conventional wisdom that the union was essential to the American economy, and instead gave the 13,000 federal employees 48 hours to return to work—or else. When 11,400 forfeited their jobs, he sent a message to Americans that he was serious about fighting inflation and holding unions to their word—and showed the world that the Soviets had a tough new negotiator on their hands.

Unlike the supposedly maverick Carter, who in fact surrounded himself with liberal-establishment academics and policy insiders, Reagan not only held a deep distrust of the accepted cargo of American governance—Ivy League education, intimate and long familiarity with Washington and New York, and intellectual pretension—but also deliberately tried to avoid the usual language of diplomatic prevarication. His reduction of complex and nuanced problems into simple equations involving right and wrong infuriated the elites, not because he was necessarily wrong, but precisely because he was so often right and thus called into question the prerequisites of political sagacity. Reagan's habit was to reduce a dilemma to an easy choice between principle and expediency. His rhetoric was memorable precisely because it flew in the face of conventional wisdom and drew responses like, "He can't say that." But of course he could—and did—because "that" was so often true.

We often think that democratic societies are by nature wholly populist, and so distrust snooty experts and vapid intellectuals. In fact, historically speaking, democracies often are vulnerable precisely because the People sometimes feel that they lack the capacity for self-governance without an array of specialists and advisers who know better than they. Thus, in all democratic cultures we occasionally witness the strange spectacle of grandees who masquerade as common men even as they talk down to the unwashed. It is rarer still, however, to see conservative politicians who both distrust the creed of state-enforced egalitarianism and speak plainly to the masses as one of their own.

What, then, is Reagan's legacy? In some ways, George W. Bush—"the axis of evil" and "smoke 'em out"—is to Clinton as Reagan was to Carter: the supposedly less capable man displaying a far greater understanding than his predecessor in times of peril. The current idea that volumes of position papers and hordes of professors might not be just superfluous, but downright silly, is Reaganesque to the core.

In the end Reaganism encompassed the very strange ideas that a conservative who wished to cut government entitlements could be more popular with the People than their liberal benefactors; that a wealthy, self-made man could feel more at home with a ranch hand or a policeman than would a Marxist Harvard professor; that an "aw shucks" naif could out-debate the best-prepped policy wonk; and that a Hollywood actor could take the measure of a Soviet apparatchik or a Third World cutthroat far better than the brain trust of the U.S. State Department.

Only in America.

The Victory of "Reaganomics"

By Lawrence Kudlow

EDITOR'S NOTE: *This article first appeared in the June 28, 2004, issue of* National Review.

Economists were vexed during the 1970s, as unemployment and inflation rose together to stifle economic growth and all forms of investment. The Keynesian Phillips-curve paradigm, whereby employment and inflation are supposed to move in opposite directions, completely broke down. The Ivy League formula of increasing the money supply to spur growth, and high taxes to hold back inflation, had failed utterly.

Between the late 1960s and 1980, the U.S. inflation rate rose from 2 per cent to 14 per cent, while the unemployment rate gradually drifted higher, from 4 per cent to almost 10 per cent. It was a period of decline for the country. Americans were demoralized.

As stagflation became more deeply embedded in the U.S. economy, Soviet adventurism in Central and South America, Asia, and elsewhere around the world became more pronounced. The Soviets saw the U.S. cut and run from Vietnam. Our Cold War adversary saw nothing but weakness emanating from the U.S.

Ronald Reagan changed all that. From the moment of his swearing-in in January 1981, with his extraordinarily strong character and deep and abiding faith in God, Reagan acted relentlessly to revive the nation.

More than any modern president, Reagan understood the link between economic growth at home and American strength overseas. It was the Gipper's most brilliant insight. He acted swiftly to show our enemies that we would produce the necessary economic resources to do whatever it would take, for however long was necessary, to triumph over the Communist menace.

Immediately upon assuming office, he reversed the economic policy of the decline years. He brought down marginal tax rates, restoring the incentives necessary for economic growth. He gave Federal Reserve chairman Paul Volcker the strong ground to stand on, allowing him to harden the value of the dollar and slay inflation.

At bottom, what became known as Reaganomics was a new pro-growth policy mix of tax incentives at the margin and stable money. But there was more. The Californian launched a massive military buildup totaling about $1.5 trillion. He deregulated oil prices, proving the conventional wisdom wrong as energy became much cheaper. He launched U.S.-Canadian free trade. He was unyielding in his opposition to the air-traffic controllers' strike, firing thousands of these government workers and ending the anti-growth union stranglehold on private industry. He created individual retirement accounts and 401(k)s, giving birth to the investor class. He also slashed social spending by reducing domestic program levels (excluding Social Security and health care) by nearly $50 billion in 1981. That amount would come to about $90 billion today.

By 1986, Reagan's tax-reform plan left two marginal rates of 28 per cent and 15 per cent, a long stone's throw from the 70 per cent top rate he had inherited. His plan also cut about 2,000 pages from the tax code.

Ideas matter. Results quickly followed for Reagan. Between 1982 and 1989, the economy grew, adjusting for inflation, by 35 per cent: more than 4.5 per cent per year. As growth was restored, tax revenues came flowing in. Income-tax revenues grew by 50 per cent during this period even as tax rates dropped. By 1986, the inflation rate had fallen to 1 per cent. By the end of his term, unemployment had dropped to 5.5 per cent. Interest rates had plunged. The stock market had soared.

From July 1982 through the end of 1988, the S&P 500 averaged a near 21 per cent annual gain. Brand-new industries arose in computing, software, communications, and the Internet—original endeavors that completely streamlined and transformed the American economy for the decades to come. In effect, Reaganomics launched a 20-year boom, the longest prosperity period in the 20th century.

Reagan critics to this day continue to harp on deficits and debt, rather than the growth miracle produced by Reaganomics. But they are factually wrong. Reagan inherited a budget gap of roughly 2.5 per cent of the economy. By the end of his two terms, he left it exactly where he found it. In between, he restored our economic health and revitalized our standing around the world.

By the time of his summit meetings with Soviet chairman Gorbachev, Reagan was able to say calmly and diplomatically that the U.S. could produce the goods and the Soviets could not. In the next few years, the Berlin Wall came down and the Soviet Union collapsed.

Reagan's visionary linkage of domestic economic recovery, military preparedness, and worldwide peace had worked with a stunning swiftness that literally no one but the former Hollywood actor had ever visualized.

The greatness of Ronald Reagan was his optimistic vision. His unequivocal belief in freedom and democracy, in America as a city on the hill, never faltered. His free-market prescription for economic growth relied on the creativity of ordinary people working in free enterprise rather than under government planning. He believed in entrepreneurship, not welfarism. He understood how to use military power. And his optimistic faith in America gave a moribund country a new life.

Reagan saved America. His passing is a sad occasion. But as his soul gazes down from the heavens, he will see that his ideas will live forever.

Two Accusations, Rebutted

By Mark Helprin

EDITOR'S NOTE: *This article first appeared in the June 28, 2004, issue of* National Review.

In remembering Ronald Reagan with affection and pride, recounting his achievements, and recalling the rare qualities of the man himself, conservatives have been, in my view, inadequately defensive. Reagan's detractors are perfectly happy to concede that he had wit and warmth. They do not dispute his popularity. Some will even admit that Reagan had some involvement in ending the Cold War. They will allow all this because they do not give way on two essential points—the "Reagan Deficits" and "Star Wars"—that, if not checked, they will continue to press in the hope that history will condemn him.

First, his critics believe that even if the military buildup did cause or accelerate the fall of the Soviet Union it was an immoral risk that punished and pauperized the nation, filling its cities with the homeless as in Hogarth's London (though they miraculously disappeared on the first day of the Clinton presidency), and contributing to the enormous deficit that threatened to ruin the economy and the fiscal underpinnings of the state. Coupled with Reagan's inhumane opposition to proactive government it was a double disaster. Cutting taxes while at the same time allowing military spending to soar was the act not merely of a conservative, but of a Nero.

For the intelligentsia this is a postulate of faith. That is why, in my daughter's American history textbook, the eminent authors write, "The combination of tax reduction and huge increases in military spending opened a vast 'revenue hole' of $200 billion annual deficits. . . . The staggering deficits of the Reagan years assuredly constituted a great economic failure." That is why, in the lead story of his death, the AP wrote, "Reagan . . . tripled the national debt to $3 trillion in his singleminded competition with the other superpower." It is why, in analyzing his legacy, it wrote that because "Reagan powered up the military . . . his shining city was built on a mountain of debt," and why many learned articles treat of the "Reagan deficit(s)" and the phrase brings 1,200 Google hits.

Its only flaw is that it isn't true. For preserved in the tranquil and everlasting record are the figures that show that something almost everyone has come to believe is not so and never was so, no matter how many times it is repeated. If the deficits are to be attributed to tax cuts and military spending, the combined shortfall in revenues and increase in military outlays must reflect this. In the "Federal Budget Summary" of the 1991 Statistical Abstract of the United States, one can see what would have been spent if in the years 1982–1989 (the Reagan budget years) military spending had remained at 1981 levels, which is $1.26 trillion. Actual spending in the period was $2.024 trillion, a net increase of $764 billion.

Had revenues remained at 1981 levels, the government would have collected in the period 1982–1989 $4.7944 trillion. With the tax cuts that are generally believed to have choked off receipts, the government actually collected $6.1419 trillion, an increase (rather than a shortfall) of $1.3475 trillion.

Therefore, the net change attributable to the combined Reagan revenue and defense-spending policies was an increase of $583.5 billion, or just short of $73 billion/yr. It doesn't matter how much smarter than Ronald Reagan you think you are, or that you write for *The New York Review of Books* and he was an actor, or that you were a Rhodes Scholar and he a graduate of Eureka College—an increase of more than half a trillion dollars does not and cannot a deficit make. Despite the extra half a trillion dollars available during those years for funding growth in entitlement and discretionary spending, this growth, far above and beyond such a gargantuan sum, is what produced the deficit—not military spending, not tax cuts, and not the reasonable Reagan budgets that were dead on arrival in Democratic Congresses.

Given that Mr. Reagan's critics are those for whom a "cut" can mean a rate of growth slower than the one they propose, they may protest that the increase in funds available as a result of the two Reagan policies they condemn was actually a decrease because it might have been greater. By this logic they would run the government, and by this logic often they do.

Second, in regard to what they derisively call "Star Wars" (something as piggish and uncivil as if conservatives persistently referred not to "welfare" but to "Welfare Cadillac"), they believe that Reagan understood nothing but false simplicities and was incapable of grasping their authoritative refutations. These refutations, however, an instant academic orthodoxy, were forged with only one side speaking, and as such became a perpetual spring of untenable arguments the chief virtue of which has been repetition.

They believed that though a strategic defense was not workable the Soviets would react as if it were, and thus that theirs was the task of curing benighted world leaders of inflammatory delusions. As mechanical challenges were met and kinetic intercepts accomplished, SDI opponents took refuge in their conviction that the computational power of the middle '80s was insufficient for guidance and battle management. Given the simple alternative of dividing the watched sky into as many sectors as were necessary to reduce the load on appropriately duplicated systems, it was not insufficient then, and it certainly is not now, after computational power has advanced by orders of magnitude. Retrenching, they assert that countermeasures will always foil an anti-missile system, that the offense is always superior to the defense. Military history, however, consists of the alternating successes of the one over the other, and as nothing less than survival may be at stake, it is the responsibility of statesmen to remain in the competition of move and countermove.

But the heart of their case, still seldom refuted, was their claim that a missile shield would allow the U.S. a first strike, therefore destabilizing the strategic balance and pushing the Soviets toward preemption. What they missed, however, and still miss, is that though the shield could never be impervious enough to tempt whoever wielded it to begin a nuclear war, it could be impervious enough nonetheless to protect the bulk of American missiles and thus ensure that no first strike against the United States could succeed—thus not threatening but increasing nuclear force stability. At the same time, such a full-scale system would offer a high degree of protection in case of a general nuclear exchange, and a near-perfect defense against accidental launches or nuclear-armed missiles flying from the rogue nations that eventually would possess them.

These two accusations, unless they are forced into the light, are the sharp rock upon which Ronald Reagan's historical reputation will founder even as it floats on a sea of encomiums. Their tremendous power arises from the fact that those who trade in them and those who credulously receive them have neither the ability nor the inclination to delve into the arcana of national accounts or nuclear strategy. Their existence means that it is not enough to remember the fortieth president with pride and affection, for he is still under assault, and still must be defended, even in the hour of his death.

Reagan's Gift of Humor

By William A. Rusher

EDITOR'S NOTE: *This article first appeared in the June 28, 2004, issue of* National Review.

Ronald Reagan's famously relaxed personality was, of course, one of his biggest assets. He had a wonderful gift for making people feel at ease in his presence. And one of his favorite means of doing so was to tell a joke.

Jokes, of course, can take many forms. Some people build them right into their conversational style—the biting remark, the sarcastic aside, etc. Reagan's conversations, and even his speeches, were never biting, let alone sarcastic, though he enjoyed poking gentle fun at his opponents.

There was, for example, his story of the fellow who was invited to a costume party, but didn't know what costume to wear. "Finally he just slapped some egg on his face and went as a liberal economist." And then there was the Russian who bought a car, and was told it would be delivered ten years from the purchase date. "Morning or afternoon?" he inquired. "What does it matter?" asked the salesman.

"The plumber is coming in the morning."

He was equally capable of poking fun at himself—and sometimes the humor seemed aimed at the situation in general. In one early presidential press conference, he was confronted with evidence that the White House had contradicted itself on some point. "I will admit," he conceded, "that around the White House it sometimes seems as if the right hand doesn't know what the far right hand is doing."

Jokes were the solvent with which he laced his conversations. They didn't necessarily have to illustrate a point (though, then again, they might); often they simply afforded a moment's rest in the midst of a tense discussion. They were never sharply edged, or uncomfortably barbed. Most commonly they were anecdotes about believable situations, with an unexpected and hilarious punch line.

His public addresses almost always included touches of humor, deployed in aid of the political point he was making. His description of the federal government as a squalling infant was unforgettable: "A ravenous appetite at one end and no sense of responsibility at the other."

And then there was his description of the average hippie: "He acts like Tarzan, dresses like Jane, and smells like Cheetah."

His private conversations brimmed with wonderful jokes that, for one reason or another, were unsuitable for public use (though they were never in the least "improper"). One of the best was about the cardinal who came to the Pope.

"Some good news and some bad news," the cardinal said. "First, the good news: Christ has returned to earth. God walks again among men."

"Well!" said the Pope. "After that, what news could be bad?"

To which the cardinal replied, "The call came from Salt Lake City."

But my personal favorite was the one about the United Way canvasser who called on the very wealthy—and notoriously stingy—Mr. Jones.

"Mr. Jones," he began, "our records indicate that you have never given so much as a cent to the United Way."

"Oh?" replied Mr. Jones. "And do they also indicate that I have an elderly mother with no independent means of support?"

"Well, no," the canvasser admitted.

"Do they indicate that I have a brother who has been a quadriplegic since the Vietnam War?" "No."

"Do they indicate I have a sister whose husband deserted her and their five children after 20 years of marriage?" Again, "No."

"Well," concluded Mr. Jones with a chuckle, "if I don't do anything for them, what makes you think I'm going to do anything for you?"

And the chuckle would be right there, in the final line.

Which brings me to perhaps the most important point of all: Ronald Reagan was an actor, and told jokes superbly. His timing was flawless, and often he would act out the parts of the various characters. Once I saw him stand up, lean back against a wall, and assume the role of a stoned hippie dreamily smoking a joint in Los Angeles International Airport. As Reagan told it:

"A pilot walked by, carrying a suitcase. 'Hey, hey,' said the hippie. 'Where're ya goin'?' 'I'm flying to New York,' the pilot answered. The hippie took a long draw on the joint and said, 'Yeah? How high're ya flyin'?' 'Oh, about 35,000 feet,' the pilot replied. The hippie took another draw. Then: 'Yeah? How fast're ya goin'?' 'About 550 miles an hour,' said the pilot.

"'Yeah?' said the hippie. Then"—here Reagan drew again and offered a slow smile—"'Race ya!'"

I always admired the way Nancy bore up during these performances. She had heard and seen them all a thousand times, of course, but as Reagan launched into a story new to his audience she would assume a sort of fixed, anticipatory smile and then, at the punch line, join gently in the laughter.

Critics often assumed that Reagan's penchant for humor—and especially for humor of the good-natured, non-wounding type—was simply evidence of his essential superficiality. But this was no truer of Reagan than it was of Lincoln, another president who loved to tell a joke. Both men used humor to shape and control the emotional tone of the often tense and almost always consequential situations in which they found themselves. Sandburg, in his monumental biography of Lincoln, tells of the president's confrontation with a deputation of senators who called on him to protest vigorously against something or other. In the midst of the argument, which was getting heated, Lincoln strolled up to one of the protesters and inspected his face intently.

"My, senator," Lincoln finally said, "how close you shave!"

Anybody who thinks Lincoln simply wasn't paying attention seriously underestimates Honest Abe.

At a profound level, Reagan's inherently serene disposition and his love of humor resonated deeply with the American people. They too love a good joke, and admire a person who can tell it well. That is just one more reason they loved Ronald Reagan, and will treasure his memory forever.

At His Side

By Edwin Meese III

One day, during the height of the furor over the Iran–Contra matter, I was alone with President Reagan, and I decided to ask him about it in a way I hadn't before.

Having worked with him for nearly three decades, I felt I was as closely personally to the president as anyone besides Nancy. And I could sense some strain. It bothered him tremendously that people had used the events to impugn his credibility. It bothered him, too, that he had to dismiss those involved. Ronald Reagan hated to fire anyone. And it bothered him that all of this seemed to be holding back the country.

So I finally said to him, "I hope this isn't getting you down." "Don't be concerned, Ed," he replied. "Nancy worries enough for both of us."

This was Ronald Reagan in a nutshell. Disarming yet strong, and always concerned about the well-being of others. More importantly, it demonstrated a characteristic shared by truly great leaders—he could see over the next hill. He knew the storm would pass and things would get better. This was part of the genius of our 40th president.

From the time I joined his staff in Sacramento in 1967 to oversee legal, crime, and judicial issues, until Alzheimer's forced him from public view, I never once remember Ronald Reagan losing his temper with those who served him, even when they disappointed him.

Ronald Reagan never expressed hard feelings even toward John Hinckley, the man who shot him and three others outside the Washington Hilton in 1981. The bullet lodged an inch from his heart, and the most I heard him say about it was, "God must have spared me for a reason." His good-natured response to that crisis was vintage Reagan: He was graceful while literally under fire.

To work for Ronald Reagan, you had to know that comedy was the standard. Every morning, the president received a security briefing, attended by the national security adviser, Vice President Bush, and two or three top aides. The agenda seemed to consist of one difficult and discouraging item after another. But every day, as the meeting ended, President Reagan told a joke and everyone walked out laughing. It was his way of reassuring us that we would overcome any challenge, no matter how dire it seemed. I've often wondered what the people sitting outside those meetings thought after seeing the leader of the free world and his top assistants walk out of a meeting about the most serious business of the nation laughing—every day.

It was the same at cabinet meetings. When tension mounted, President Reagan would reach toward the middle of the table, grab his jar of jellybeans, pull out a few, and pop them in his mouth. Then he'd pass them around the table, and everyone would take a few. It was hard to stay mad at people when you were chomping on jellybeans, and he knew it.

Ronald Reagan had an endless store of tales, often about Hollywood. His less friendly biographers have used this to suggest that he wasn't a serious person. This completely misses the mark: President Reagan's wit was part of his management style, and he used it to keep up confidence and morale. His genius was that he knew precisely when to use humor, and how.

The president also had a unique feel for when to accept half a loaf from Congress, rather than, as he said, "ride off the cliff with full flags flying." He never forgot his objectives, and he mastered the art of achieving them in stages.

His lack of guile, and his sincere commitment to those objectives, enabled him to establish a rapport with people in a way few political leaders ever have—and this paid huge dividends for the country. These qualities forged, for example, the bonds of his special relationship with Margaret Thatcher. But they are best illustrated by his relationship with Mikhail Gorbachev. Reagan's sincerity seemed to remove from Gorbachev the inherent distrust Soviet politicians had of Americans, and probably shaped, at least in part, Gorbachev's reaction to the implosion of the Soviet Union.

President Reagan was genial, yet tied tightly to his convictions. Gorbachev arrived at the 1986 summit in Reykjavik prepared to offer whatever cuts in Soviet weapons it would take to convince President Reagan to drop the Strategic Defense Initiative. To Ronald Reagan, SDI—safeguarding American from nuclear attack—was a core principle. He was ready to walk away from an arms deal rather than capitulate. And walk away he did.

Above all else, Ronald Reagan believed in God and country—beliefs he shared with our nation's Founders. He believed America had a purpose, which was to promote liberty, humanity, and prosperity for people across the globe. And in the end, this was the formula for peace. This was why President Reagan sought public office, and why he was enormously successful. He revived the American spirit, which he knew was suffering under the burden and consequences of big government. He unleashed American know-how by slashing tax rates and regulations, resulting in unprecedented economic growth. He rebuilt our military after years of neglect, ensuring American security and foreign-policy objectives, including the once-unimaginable dissolution of the Soviet Union. And he did all of it with his trademark wink, and a joke, and smile from ear to ear.

Ronald Reagan was a great man, and my great friend. I will miss him.